Boredom Is in Your Mind

Josefa Ros Velasco
Editor

Boredom Is in Your Mind

A Shared Psychological-Philosophical Approach

Springer

Editor
Josefa Ros Velasco
Department of Romance
Languages & Literatures
Harvard University
Cambridge, MA, USA

ISBN 978-3-030-26397-3 ISBN 978-3-030-26395-9 (eBook)
https://doi.org/10.1007/978-3-030-26395-9

This Springer imprint is published by the registered company Springer Nature Switzerland AG
The registered company address is: Gewerbestrasse 11, 6330 Cham, Switzerland

Dedicated to Peter Toohey,
my greatest inspiration.

Preface

Coming to Terms: A Shared Understanding of Boredom from Psychology and Philosophy

Boredom has been considered the punishment of the entire humanity throughout its lengthy history. Authors like Siegfried Wenzel (1967), Reinhard Kuhn (1976), and Peter Toohey (2011) have demonstrated that boredom was part of the daily lives of the ancient and medieval peoples, and Patricia Meyer Spacks (1995) and Lars Svendsen (1999) have explained it is the son of modernity. Whatever, the ancients understood it as a shameful emotion resulting from the lack of dedication to the public affairs; in the Middle Ages, it became a sin inside the walls of the monasteries under the names of *acedia* or *demon of noontide*; and the modernity made of it the correlate of the rationalized time, the pre-planned entertainment, and the existential feeling of angst and nonsense. We have to admit we are talking about an old, even very old phenomenon. Perhaps so old that some philosophers have suggested that it was the metaphysical principle of the world—as the German thinker Hans Blumenberg did in *Beschreibung des Menschen* [Description of man] (2006)—the Gods' most common mood—Nietzsche said in *Der Antichrist* [The antichrist] (1895)—and the Gods' reason to create us—according to Kierkegaard's words in *Enten—Eller* [Either/Or] (1843). The phenomenon of boredom was commonly addressed from its sociocultural condition by philosophers, theologists, and sociologists in the past. Almost none treatise on boredom as a medical condition was launched then, except for those in which boredom was linked to another well-known affection, *melancholy*, during the Renaissance and the early modern times and, going back to previous eras, these superficial mentions that pulled together boredom and depression. From the eighteenth to the twentieth century, what proliferated were, overall, the literary works of those who found in writing the remedy for coping with 'the boredom' they used to call 'disease,' metaphorically speaking.

At the end of the nineteenth century, however, boredom became a matter of serious discussion among mental health professionals who started carrying out their researches by hundreds. Perhaps one of the first works on boredom from disciplines such as psychology and psychiatry was *De l'ennui, taedium vitae* [On boredom, tired of life] (1850), by the physician Brière de Boismont. Soon after, the first industrial psychological tests of efficiency in the workplace took place by the psychologist Hugo Münsterberg, in *Psychology and industrial efficiency* (1913). Little by little, the focus was geared toward the affective and cognitive components of boredom. One of the main representatives of this stage was Émile Tardieu, who published *L'ennui: Étude psychologique* [Boredom. Psychological study] (1903) in which he described boredom as psychological pain. Over the same period, Theodor Lipps suggested one of the first psychodynamic definitions of boredom, in his work entitled *Leitfaden der Psychologie* [Guidelines of psychology] (1909). He went a step further and stated that boredom was a psychological pain caused by a conflict between the individual need for mental activity and the lack of it *or* the individual inability to stimulate oneself.

This was a turning point in the understanding of boredom: One can experience a continuous lack of stimulation not as a result of a boring circumstance but because of some kind of mental or personality-related pathology. Moreover, Lipps introduced, in a pioneering move, that boredom may be connected with the lack of attention. Some years later, the psychoanalyst Otto Fenichel lent continuity to these ideas in his essay "Zur Psychologie der Langeweile" ["On the psychology of boredom"] (1934). According to him, boredom was experienced because of a contrast between the individuals' mental engagement and their simultaneous inhibition.

During the first half of the twentieth century, these approaches to boredom as a psychopathological personality-related issue resulted in self-help books whose aim was to orientate bored people toward the search of the release of their activity mental need and their inability for self-stimulation. Nevertheless, due to their lack of success, some psychiatrists opted for looking to the brain. For instead, psychiatrist Joseph Barmack started playing with the environmental conditions and the temperature of a room in which there was a subject bored. Additionally, he began supplying benzedrine sulfate and ephedrine hydrochloride to them to complete his studies on boredom from 1937 to 1939. In extreme cases, specialists like Edmund Bergler went as far as to say that boredom was a psychotic disorder with significant neurotic implications whose cure did need genetic intervention, as we can read in his paper "On the disease-entity boredom ("alyosis") and its psychopathology" (1945).

From the second half of the twentieth century to the end, the blossoming interest of the mental health professionals on the phenomenon of boredom increased as expected. Particularly, the psychoanalysts riddled the journals' pages with titles such as "Boredom in psychoanalytic perspective," and "Some psychoanalytic observation on boredom"—in this example, both by Martin Wangh (1975, 1979). Thus, by 1996 the understanding of boredom as a psychopathological personality trait was so extended that the concept of 'boredom' got a place in the Campbell's *Dictionary of psychiatry*. Nowadays, boredom is simply another encyclopedia entry in volumes of psychology and applied psychology and lexicons of psychology, usually really close to depression and ADHD.

Presently, the mental health disciplines keep being in charge of studying boredom. Psychologists have inherited those first approaches from the psychodynamic theory and still understand boredom as a symptom of an inability of the individual to find stimuli in the environment, what has been termed *endogenous boredom* by researchers like McWelling Todman—in papers such as "Boredom and psychotic disorders: Cognitive and motivational issues" (2003) and that ironically entitled "Psychopathology and boredom: A neglected association" (2007). Now, some disorders connected with boredom have been well-established: the pathology of chronic boredom; the disorder of a propensity toward boredom (boredom proneness), or the problem of subjective perception of boredom (see my previous work "Boredom: humanising or dehumanising treatment," 2018).

In normal circumstances, following the psychodynamic explanation and the flow theory by Csíkszentmihályi in *Beyond boredom and anxiety* (1975), people suffer from boredom when environmental stimuli are repetitive and monotonous (understimulation) or excessive (overstimulation) and do not meet their psychic needs. What happens then is a lack of correspondence, of flow or mutual adaptation that makes the subject react to the environment. The experiments of London et al.—in "Increase of autonomic arousal by boredom" (1972)—and those by Berlyne—especially in *Conflict, arousal and curiosity* (1960)—have demonstrated, by measuring individual physiological changes, that when people are bored the level of cortical excitement falls down and the reticular activating system (RAS) releases to promote an autonomic activation that pushes 'the bored' to look for something else capable of normalizing the excitement cortical levels. That is to say, following Damrad-Frye and Laird—in "The experience of boredom: The role of the self-perception of attention" (1989): When the pattern of external stimulation is very low and boredom shows up, the internal excitement increases to compensate for the environmental weakness resulting in different actions.

However, in certain cases of pathological boredom, we will see individuals in which such an autonomic activation does not take place. In other words, their RAS does not act as expected, and consequently, the subject does not go for the exploration of novelties and stimuli to put boredom aside. This kind of boredom raises from the inside of the subject, from their brain, like any other mental pathology or disorder going as far as to become a real—not metaphorical—chronic disease with serious psychosocial consequences. Such paralysis is the corollary of other pathologies, such as the inability to clarify one's own desires; the distorted perception of time; the excess or lack of self-awareness; attention deficit disorder; depression and anxiety, or many of them at the same time.

In this sense, specialists state that if such pathologic boredom and its associated disorders are not intervened but, on the contrary, prolonged over time, boredom can lead to all kinds of deviant behaviors. Boredom has been made responsible for promoting depressions, anxieties, hostile and aggressive behaviors, sleep disorders, drug, sex, and gambling addiction, reckless driving, states of despair and loneliness, criminal actions, school deviations, suicidal tendencies, low self-esteem, lack of social affiliation, and eating disorders, among many others. Consistently, the study of boredom is motivated, in most cases, by the need to learn more about the phenomenon to predict harmful or deviant behaviors. What actually matters to researchers on boredom is the consequences arising from its suffering.

This is also the reason why they attempt to conduct more research on boredom, to move toward the achievement of better elements of diagnosis and essential treatments. A large part of the extant literature on boredom is devoted to this purpose. Specialists in psychoanalysis and existential philosophy have learned to deal with boredom and teach others how to get to grips with its symptoms—as it is the case of Conrad in "It's boring: Notes on the meanings of boredom in everyday life" (1997). Some others, like psychiatrist Saša Branković—in "Boredom, dopamine, and the thrill of psychosis: Psychiatry in a new key" (2015)—explore the effects of dopamine on boredom or suggest, like Bennet and Morris—in "Drug abuse" (2007)—or Hancock and Mckim—in "Caffeine and the methylxanthines" (2013)—the methylxanthines—a group of naturally occurring agents present in caffeine, theophylline, and theobromine—as a drug capable of reversing performance decrements caused by boredom and fatigue in manuals on pharmacology. Our time, more than any other before, is witnessing a proliferation of innumerable antidotes to the *evil of boredom*, whether through the implementation of confrontation or avoidance strategies.

Now that not only have the mental health disciplines described the phenomenon of boredom under their categories but also have them raised it to the status of 'disorder,' we should start talking about boredom from the clinical approach. This is a tall order. De Chenne and Moody warned, in "Boredom: Theory and therapy" (1988), that mental health professionals are not simply phenomenologists but that they study to shift away from theory toward therapy. There are strong limitations to diagnose and treat boredom currently since almost nothing is known about its cognitive and neural implications. Many researchers are attempting to locate the neural basis of boredom and are tentatively suggesting the insula plays a key role. However, for the time being, how boredom neurologically affects people and how drugs will affect 'the bored' one—including side effects—remain unknown.

It is not surprising that bringing boredom to the clinical side arouses certain concern and criticism. Many authors, including the abovementioned Blumenberg, point out that the *Diagnostic and statistical manual of mental disorders* (DSM) promotes life medicalization and expands the number of pathologies resulting in more transitional behaviors and common moods become a disease. Alles Frances himself, the editor of the 4th edition of the DSM, still denounces, in his book *Saving normal: an insider's revolt against out-of-control psychiatric diagnosis, DSM-5, big pharma, and the medicalization of ordinary life* (2014), that mental health professionals are selfish and unable to look beyond their own perspectives, turning daily annoyances into diseases by making wrong decisions and overstating the importance of their fieldwork, even when they admit that, at the very beginning of the twenty-first century, there is a lack of agreement on what is boredom, its cognitive implications and neurological bases and acknowledge that the lack of assessment and measuring instruments makes it impossible for specialists to reach a true understanding of the matter.

If one thing is clear at present is that we know almost nothing about boredom, which makes it easier to make a mistake in the clinical setting and also awaken the criticism of those who do not trust in the mental health approach to the matter of boredom. Undoubtedly, more research is needed in this regard. The mental health researchers themselves are consistent in decrying the paucity of the existing literature on boredom and a perceived lack of interest among the scholars. Experts point out to both problems as the reasons why it still remains impossible to understand what is boredom exactly. Throughout the years I have been investigating boredom, I have realized that several academic papers on this topic alluded to a shortage of literature and the lack of research interest as being responsible for the lack of understanding of the subject. As a result, researchers agree that the study of boredom is in its infancy and has not been paid the attention deserved. Because of this, the scientific study of boredom remains a relatively obscure niche, and boredom itself is still poorly understood. Is it possible that we are, almost a century later, in the same situation that Bertrand Russell denounced in *The conquest of happiness* in 1930?

The short answer to this question is *no*. A more detailed one leads us to analyze the amount of research that examines the phenomenon of boredom. As I have previously demonstrated in my paper "Boredom: A comprehensive study of the state of affairs" (2017), the emotion of boredom has aroused the interest of the researchers for centuries, from the very beginning, and its study has been mainly carried out from the mental health field. However, against all odds, the mental health specialists working on boredom continue complaining about the scarcity of knowledge so far achieved due to a supposed literature shortage. I did state that there exists ample literature and interest on boredom, even if we focus only on that produced in the mental health field. As far as I am concerned, there is not a problem of *a lack of research* or *interest*. The reason why we cannot take a stand on boredom is that those specialists on boredom do not work in a multidisciplinary fashion yet, that is to say, they are not taking into account the precedents, the background, even the history of boredom, and the path along which it became tinted with the colors of the *disease*, as well as their mutual approaches. Also, different research methodologies to pull the specialists together and make them read and listen to each other are needed.

It is my firm belief that only by making the effort of bringing positions closer together, will we be able to overcome the lack of consensus with regard to the origin and nature of boredom, its causes, and consequences, the total confusion and the absence of an agreement with which we are conducting our researches today. Transversalism is the key and the motto of this volume. It is time to connect the points of view of all those who are the major experts on boredom in one, the same place, at one time, to force an openness of mind for us to reach a widely accepted definition of boredom with which moves the study of boredom forward.

Boredom is in your mind was born in fall 2017, when the outstanding national and international specialists in Boredom Studies from the mental health disciplines and the humanities, including myself, started discussing the importance of research in meeting a common understanding of the phenomenon of boredom, i.e., to throw light on the holistic comprehension of boredom that scholars want to reach currently by working together. I myself promoted such an approaching when after finishing my Doctoral Dissertation—focused on an interdisciplinary understanding of boredom but, especially, on how the comprehension of boredom in terms of a mental disease has gradually formed historically—I realized that even though boredom was omnipresent in our modern society, there was a lack of agreement by specialists on its definition and understanding, despite the growing literature on this complex issue at the beginning of the twenty-first century. After having spent some years working hard on this hot-button topic, taking into account the different understandings coming from those specialists who inspired me most, and looking at how all of them claimed that the study of boredom was in its infancy and had not been paid the attention deserved, I was convinced that what it was missing was the chance of listening attentively to others beyond their own proposals.

I then made the decision to contact some of those most well-known researchers on boredom worldwide whose works had been the pillars of my study on boredom for years to share with them my concerns and ask them for their feedback about what was happening concerning boredom, I mean, to ask them why we had not understood what is boredom yet, and to promote a discussion on the state of affairs of the study of boredom. Around twelve scholars responded to my call and some of them engaged in a meaningful and constructive dialogue. Some of us met in 2018 to discuss face to face some of the keys we had been exchanging during the last months. For example, I met the contributor María C. Antón in March at the University of California in Los Angeles (UCLA), as part of a Seminar I organized in the framework of the American Comparative Literature Association (ACLA) Annual Meeting, entitled "Boredom and literature: Cross-paradigmatic research and theorizing approach." Moreover, I met the contributor John D. Eastwood last April at The Helix Center (New York Psychoanalytic Institute, NYPSI) on the occasion of the celebration of a *Roundtable on boredom* organized by Dr. Edward Nersessian. Apart from that, communication was fluent with the rest of the collaborators during the academic year to tap into this connection.

This contact intended to rethink the phenomenon of boredom and the researches we all are conducting on it. We felt we had to do that, that is to say, to discuss on boredom, to try to understand it since much depends on our understanding of boredom and our response to it. Many essential ideas were put on the table during that time; some other widely accepted premises were called into question; a clear conclusion was reached: The issue of boredom is one that cannot be considered from a single standpoint but from a holistic approach. We all realized that one viewpoint came in response to the unanswered questions of another. In short, we realized that only by working together we would be able to explore boredom in depth. This is how I took the initiative of breaking the first lance for this purpose to give a strong voice to our approaches to boredom and suggest a new way of working by pulling together our efforts in one place: *Boredom is in your mind.*

This collective volume comes to pay attention to boredom as never before, i.e., by collecting in one place and at the same time the understandings and definitions of boredom of the key representatives from the mental health discipline to the philosophical perspective to see the point in which we are, right now, concerning its neural basis and causes, its experience depending on 'the bored' and the environmental conditions, its consequences and implications for individual and social well-being, and, perhaps most important, the strategies for coping with it. Authors attempt to show how their understandings of boredom can help to clarify and answer the doubts that have been stated during the past decades, from the end of the twentieth century to the present. They want to show that the study of boredom from the mental health field and philosophy is making possible for us to be closer than never before to understand this daily annoyance and to achieve an agreement among researchers. The aim is that the reader goes through the most recent understandings of boredom and their anchor points to create their own conceptual map of boredom beyond and together with the typical approaches.

We wanted to publish the book to which researchers and academics from one end to the other should come in order to be updated, to clarify their ideas, and to learn a new working methodology concerning boredom. This book provides the most updated definitions and understandings of boredom right now and, hopefully, the agreement in the approach to this phenomenon that scholars missed and demands in their papers every day. In the same vein, this book involves the most recent methodologies and assessment practices to move the study of boredom forward from its stalemate caused by the lack of agreement. Moreover, it is the baseline for future research on boredom.

This is, to my very knowledge, the first time that this famous group of specialists focused on the study of boredom gathers to promote a cross-border dialogue in order to overcome the recognized limitations of their respective viewpoints. This is a pioneering initiative in filling the knowledge gap that still exists concerning boredom. What makes this project special, in addition, is that the authors themselves are looking forward to going through the experiment of getting to the end of the book and see whether the understanding of boredom of the others was truly able to fill their own gaps. They themselves and the readers will be able to draw their own conclusions concerning boredom after finishing reading the book just by looking at how actually authors complement and reinforce each other.

The reason why all of them agreed to contribute this volume is that they themselves are convinced it is time to unite our efforts to take the study of boredom forward. We all think it is time to break with the past ways of working in solitude, without paying attention to what others are working on. This book attempts to be a precedent and also a reference point for those interested in boredom. It is a compendium of the latest proposals, after a profound reflection, from authors whose definitions of boredom are reproduced from one paper to another every day (see, e.g., those by John Eastwood or James Danckert) and whose titles have been translated into many languages (see, e.g., those by Peter Toohey—*Boredom: A lively history*, 2011—or Lars Svendsen—*Philosophy of boredom*, 1999). Some of them are young researchers devoting their careers to the study of boredom, while others are seniors and well-positioned authors in the field of Boredom Studies. Unusually, among the latter, some authors left behind the study of boredom time ago after publishing their works and were committed to reviewing their approaches just for this book.

This is a book for graduates and researchers on boredom but also for specialists in mental health and cognitive psychology. Precisely because the study of boredom involves, on the one hand, going through mental processes such as attention, memory, perception, creativity, or language use, to name a few, and, on the other, taking into account pathological conditions such as depression, stress, and anxiety, among others. In this sense, the secondary target audience may also include mental health professionals, since some authors are psychologists and their approaches to the idea of getting rid of boredom by engaging people in their 'self' and the surrounding world have a clear application in the clinical practice.

Nevertheless, as boredom is a topic that everybody loves to talk about, *Boredom is in your mind* is not directed exclusively toward a specialized audience. Anyone wants to know more about such a common, daily annoyance and, overall, to understand their boredom in order to cope with it. Furthermore, boredom is a topic that catches everyone's attention. Just telling people that one is working on boredom from a psychological and philosophical approach leads them to ask for books to read. People want to know more about this topic because we all suffer from boredom at once point. However, we should not forget that this is a specialized book which includes the most up-to-date researches on boredom by the most well-known researchers on the topic. Thus, *Boredom is in your mind* is, first of all, a meeting point for researchers and specialists in cognitive psychology and mental disorders, and philosophers. Many books on psychology–philosophy of boredom are mainly focused on how boredom affects students and how to cope with it in the student environment. None of them has been focused on what we are understanding when we are talking about boredom from a psychological, cognitive point of view, or a philosophical one, or both at the same time, which must be the starting point of further and most focalized research. Readers will enjoy this title because, according to what they claim in their papers, they all are looking forward to having a common understanding, a reference point offered by those whose definitions and methodologies are most spread in the research community. They demand to have in one place a coherent understanding of boredom proposed in agreement by the authorities in this field of study.

Following from the above, *Boredom is in your mind* consists of this Preface and nine chapters plus a special contribution. The first one, an introduction entitled "Is It a Good Thing to Be Bored?" is the presentation and the reflection on the state of affairs of the study, the understanding, and the research on boredom nowadays, just at this point before the end of the second decade of the twenty-first century. This extraordinary introduction is in charge of the Professor of Classics in the Department of Classics and Religion at the University of Calgary, Canada, Peter Toohey, renowned author of books on boredom such us *Boredom: A lively history*, and an expert in tracing the history of this emotion from ancient times as we can appreciate in papers such as "Some ancient notions of boredom" (1988) and "Acedia in Late Classical Antiquity" (1990). His books have been translated into seven languages and quoted worldwide. He is considered a leading figure in the field of boredom and the ideal researcher to explain what is happening with boredom right now, as an opening to the different approaches to the topic and the forthcoming discussion.

Chapter 2, entitled "The Unbearable Lightness of Boredom: A Pragmatic Meaning-Regulation Hypothesis," was written by a well-known couple of researchers on boredom, the Lecturer in Psychology in the Department of Psychology at King's College London, UK, Wijnand A. P. van Tilburg, and the Senior Lecturer in Psychology in the Department of Psychology at the University of Limerick, Ireland, Eric R. Igou. Focused on the research on the processes of decision-making, emotions, meaning, and motivation, using experimental methods, they have devoted a major part of their research to the study of boredom, and how this experience affects phenomena such as intergroup processes, political and religious ideology, and self-regulation. On this occasion, they will explain how boredom is easily mistaken for a minor annoyance, a nuisance preserved for those in the luxurious position of simply having too much time on their hands nowadays. They consider it is essential, however, to take into account that this ubiquitous emotion holds major correlates and consequences, ranging from depression, aggression, and discrimination, to creativity, reconnecting with our loved ones, and a willingness to help those in need. Their question is: How can boredom cause such a diverse and seemingly contradictory set of outcomes? Their chapter will show that recent experimental evidence from psychology reveals that the search for meaningful engagement plays a central role in predicting these diverse consequences of boredom. They will review and integrate findings that show that by propelling a pursuit of meaningful engagement, boredom triggers outgroup derogation, nostalgic reverie, hero adoration, prosocial tendencies, and polarization of political ideology; failing to find meaning can result in impulsiveness, unhealthy consumption, and, plausibly, mental health issues. In addition, they will discuss likely contextual and personal boundary conditions and underlying psychological processes of the effects of boredom. There is no doubt that these recent discoveries illuminate how a basic emotion such as boredom can shape both rudimentary and complex human thoughts, feelings, and behavior. By doing so, these discoveries place boredom at a pivotal position in modern society, revealing this unfairly trivialized emotion as nothing less than a reminder of the vital human quest for meaning in life.

Distinguished Professor and Head of Cognitive Neurosciences in the Department of Psychology at the University of Waterloo, Canada, James Danckert, gives shape to Chap. 3 with his work "Boredom: Managing the Delicate Balance Between Exploration and Exploitation." His research has broadly examined the cognitive and neural bases of behavior focusing on the control of attention, visuomotor control and, more recently, the cognitive and affective components of the experience of boredom. Consequently, he will be suggesting that boredom, as a cognitive-affective state, must serve some purpose. Simplistically, boredom may operate as a signal to do something, anything, other than what you are currently engaged in. But there may be more nuance to it than that. In other words, boredom may function to minimize opportunity costs. As far as Danckert is concerned, we do not all heed the message boredom has for us in optimal ways. What has been referred to as trait boredom proneness really reflects a failure to adaptively respond to the state signal. He will present evidence from self-report measures showing that a tendency to just 'get on with it' acts as a prophylactic against boredom. Turning to behavioral and genetic evidence, he will argue for a phenotype of the high boredom prone individual, one characterized by low levels of self-control and a tendency to ruminate on potential options for action. Cast in these terms, those of us who succumb to boredom more frequently could be said to be failing to launch into any activity in part due to difficulties in choosing an optimal plan of attack. This, in turn, leads to a vicious cycle: The boredom prone individual cannot choose something to effectively engage with, their current circumstance then lacks meaning and seems boring, prompting them to do something else, which then comes full circle to confront them with their difficulty in choosing just what that should be.

Chapter 4 is entitled "Boredom is a Feeling of Thinking and a Double-Edged Sword," by the prestigious researcher John D. Eastwood, registered Clinical Psychologist and Associate Professor of Clinical Psychology in the Department of Psychology at York University in Toronto, Canada, and his colleague Dana Gorelik, from the same institution. They have examined how attention is allocated to affective and socially relevant information, the influence of mood and motivation on attention, as well as the affective consequences of attention failures. As part of their current work, they seek to better understand the feeling of thinking and how such feelings are an inextricable part of cognition. In particular, they are examining the feeling of boredom associated with the unengaged mind. In their contribution, they will demonstrate that boredom is inextricably linked to attention and causes significant problems for individuals and society, acknowledging, at the same time, that we know very little about the psychological mechanisms underlying boredom. Eastwood and Gorelik propose that boredom can be usefully conceptualized as the aversive emotional concomitant of 'unused cognitive potential.' According to their point of view, understanding the cognitive-affective mechanisms that underlie moments when we are bored and struggle to engage our attention will lay the foundation for developing ways to ameliorate problems associated with the 'unengaged mind'—such as errors in medical monitoring, driving, airline piloting, and nuclear military monitoring.

Chapter 5 by María Cecilia Antón, registered Clinical Psychologist, Researcher, and Professor of Psychoanalysis at the School of Psychology at the National University of Mar del Plata, Argentina, and I myself, is entitled as simple as "Boredom and Psychoanalysis." On the basis that we prefer to talk about boredom in its plural form: *boredoms*, we will mention some characteristics of this affection that can be approached from a psychoanalytical point of view in which Freudian and Lacanian theories represent a significant contribution. First, we will talk of the kind of boredom that, being considered as an affection, comes from certain situations we can rescue from a psychoanalytical perspective stated overall by Lacan and Freud. Second, we will focus on that boredom experienced during the exercise of an activity and its relationship with the flow theory by the Italian psychologist Mihály Csíkszentmihályi (Claremont University, California). We will discuss the importance of being meaningfully engaged when doing something to avoid boredom. Third, we want to address the different possible reactions to boredom, from creative to deviant ones. Fourth, we will delve into one specific philosophical reaction related to introspection and its relationship with psychoanalysis and self-referential narration. Finally, we will quickly develop on a clinical case study to see how theory is applied into practice.

Continuing the approach, Prof. Dr. William McDonald, Chair of the Philosophy Department at the UAE University, contributed Chap. 6, "The Transformative Potential of Boredom." He will come back to the review of recent psychological literature on boredom that aims to define, categorize, and measure boredom in order to assess it, to identify correlated mental pathologies, to find the psychophysiological bases of boredom, or to apply the findings to specific settings or social groups. This literature presupposes that boredom is an aversive, individual experience, which psychology can help ameliorate, prevent or divert, as demonstrated at this point. However, he is going to focus on the potential that boredom has to create meaning by paying attention to Kierkegaard's method of 'experimenting psychology' and 'indirect communication' to *deploy* boredom in awakening his reader to the task of becoming a self. Moreover, he will introduce Heidegger's approach according to which boredom attempts to awaken the reader/listener to the possibility of attuning herself to profound boredom in a way that will enable her to become an authentic self (*Dasein*). Heidegger uses a method of historical, hermeneutic phenomenology to enable his reader to hear the call of being through attunement to profound boredom. He starts with the familiar experience of boredom, then defamiliarizes his listener to enable an original grasp of the meaning of being. On this point will build up the next chapter.

Professor Erik Ringmar, from Ibn Haldun University, Istanbul, drives Chap. 7. In his contribution, "Heidegger on Creativity: From Boredom to Re-engagement with the World," Erik Ringmar returns to Martin Heidegger's discussion of boredom in *The fundamental concepts of metaphysics*. Many people have commented on this analysis, but few have noticed the role that narratives play in Heidegger's account. It is when the stories we tell about ourselves are suspended that we get bored, when they go off on tedious digressions, or when the ability to tell a story completely breaks down. Yet if we pay closer attention to Heidegger's account, Ringmar suggests, we also notice another thing: Heidegger's body is constantly trying to help him out. That is, his body is trying to get him out of his boredom by re-engaging with the world. Heidegger is wary of following the suggestions his body comes up with, but he also acknowledges the creative potential which these suggestions contain. This teaches us something important about boredom. *Pace* the title of this collection of articles, boredom is *not* only in the mind, but it is also in the body too, and the way the body reacts to its environment is crucially important for our ability to think creatively about our lives.

The Assistant Professor and Researcher in Philosophy in the Department of Logic and Theoretical Philosophy at the Complutense University of Madrid, Spain, Ricardo Gutiérrez Aguilar, will be going deeper by claiming that boredom is *tout court* a matter of sense incorporated in meaning. In Chap. 8, "Facing Boredom: Essential Indexicals and Narratives of the Self," he states that *self-referential* narratives are crucial in referring to the pragmatic mechanisms in play within this special operation of 'giving sense.' Identity, meaning, are correlated terms. In fact, he outlines, this kind of minimal autobiographical oriented descriptions can be conceptually depicted as the general rule. Success in the process of narration seems to be dependant on the construction of an ongoing meaning that stitches together the otherwise scattered events. Meaning, sense, depends on the ascription of present and future events to oneself. Of being part of the story told. Gradual oblivion of this ability is apparently the first step in disentangling identity, personal stories and it goes hand in hand with the inviting in of weariness and boredom.

Chapter 9 is perhaps one of the most expected by the research community on boredom and is one that will break the flow of this book by making us rethink and revisit any conclusions reached until now. The reputed philosopher Lars Svendsen, known by all due to his very famous book *A philosophy of boredom*, will be reviewing and contradicting his past statements on boredom, included in the mentioned work, in a contribution entitled "Animal Boredom." He used to defend that the capacity for being bored was the essential property that separates humans from nonhuman animals and that if monkeys could be bored, we would have to recognize them as fully human. Contrary to what he claimed in *A philosophy of boredom*, there is a good reason to assume that boredom exists also outside of the human species, and this is something really important to understand human boredom. Until now, relatively little research has been done on animal boredom, and animals are virtually absent in Boredom Studies. In this regard, he will first discuss how we can justify the ascription of various mental and emotional states to non-linguistic creatures and he will argue that we can plausibly argue that boredom occurs in many other species than humans and that this is especially clear in the case of mammals, birds, and at least some species of octopus. The acknowledgment of boredom as an emotion to be found also in nonhuman animals creates problems for theories of boredom that place the concept of meaning (existential meaning, not semantic meaning) at the center of their account, and argue that boredom consists of a lack of meaning. The problem is that such meaning seems to presuppose language. He will argue that we have reason to believe, that no nonhuman animals have a capacity for proper language—and that includes even the most meticulously trained primates—but that one can nevertheless give an account of animal boredom that employs the concept of meaning.

As a grand finale, I have prepared a special contribution as Chap. 10 consisting of a half-transcription/half-summary of the ideas presented in the *Roundtable on boredom* abovementioned, which was held last April 21, 2018, and organized by The Helix Center at the NYPSI. The aim of this encounter was to pull together some specialists on boredom as a mental health issue, among whom I was fortunately included, together with John Eastwood, as well as with Professor of Neuroscience in the Kavli Institute for Brain Science and the Mortimer B. Zuckerman Institute for Mind Brain and Behavior at Columbia University, Jacqueline Gottlieb; Prof. Gerald Hurowitz, who is Assistant Professor of Clinical Psychiatry at the Columbia University Medical Center; the author and Director of the Publications Program at The Metropolitan Museum of Art, New York, Mark Polizzotti, and Dr. Edward Nersessian, Director of The Helix Center. Its motto was no other than to discuss the state of affairs of the research on boredom. This meeting and its subsequent summary consist of a brainstorming on the topic of boredom which is the benchmark of the discussion on such a phenomenon at the present time and determines future research lines.

Beyond the respective boundaries of the various disciplines studying boredom, this book demonstrates that we can still reconcile psychology and philosophy with regard to the definition of boredom. Thanks to *Boredom is in your mind*, I was able to see that our various understandings of boredom were not as far each other as it seemed at first sight. After all, we all agree that boredom is an unpleasant state that meets a function in our daily lives and concerning our individual and societal development and evolution. Whether we pay attention to the individual or environmental causes of boredom, we all acknowledge that boredom is a reactive force whatever their consequences are, those positives or negatives. This common understanding will be decisive to learn to tolerate boredom and to deal with its products while, at the same time, we are reaching a more profound comprehension of the human phenomenon.

I have to be appreciative of all those who have made possible for me to share these concerns on boredom and contribute to the discovering of such an elusive concept. First and most important, it is mandatory to say thanks to all the contributors to this volume: Without them, this project would have been impossible to carry out. Second, we all want to thank Springer, the publisher with which we wanted to work in the first place and that accepted the challenge of doing it, and my contact with the publisher, the editor Lilith Dorko. Third, we would like to thank the American Comparative Literature Asociation (ACLA) and the University of Los Angeles in California (UCLA) that held our Seminar "Boredom and literature" in 2017, and the Helix Center and Dr. Nersessian and his lovely wife Mary, who opened to me the door of their house and promotes the discussion which most inspired me to go ahead with this book project. As editor of *Boredom is in your mind*, I cannot but be grateful with the Department of Romance Languages and Literatures at Harvard University and the RCC at Harvard for granting me with the fellowship that made possible I made the time for completing this work. Finally, my personal acknowledgments are for my mentor in the field of boredom, Peter Toohey and, of course, for my family. Without all your support, I would not be writing these words.

Cambridge, USA
June 2019

Josefa Ros Velasco

Contents

Editor and Contributors

About the Editor

Dr. Josefa Ros Velasco is Associate and Teaching Assistant in the Department of Romance Languages and Literatures at Harvard University and Real Colegio Complutense at Harvard Postdoctoral Fellow. She is conducting multidisciplinary research on the evolution of the understanding of boredom as a mental pathology. As part of this approach, she is examining how the comprehension of boredom in terms of mental disease has gradually formed historically by paying attention to philosophical, theological, and literary narratives. Dr. Ros Velasco holds a Ph.D. in Philosophy with International Mention at the Excellent Program of Doctorate in Philosophy at the Complutense University of Madrid (UCM, Spain), funded by the Spanish Ministry of Culture and Education. Her Dissertation was entitled *Boredom as a selective pressure in Hans Blumenberg*, with which she got the Extraordinary Doctorate Award (2016–2017). MA in Contemporary Thinking, and MA in Teachers Training. She was visiting researcher at the *Internationales Zentrum für Kultur- und Technikforschung* at Stuttgart Universität (IZKT, Germany) as a DAAD (Deutscher Akademischer Austauschdienst) scholar, and at the Deutsches Literatur-Archiv Marbach (DLA, Germany) as a DLA fellow. She is a member of the Research Groups *Saavedra Fajardo Library for Hispanic Political Thought* at the UCM; *History and Video Games* at the University of Murcia; and *History and Philosophy of Emotions* at CCHS-CSIC. She is the editor and the author of academic papers such as "Hans Blumenberg's philosophical anthropology of boredom" (Karl Alber, 2019), "Boredom: humanising or dehumanising treatment" (Vernon, 2018); or "Boredom: A comprehensive study of the state of affairs" (*Thémata*, 2017). She is currently working on her next books: *La enfermedad del aburrimiento. El camino de la medicalización y sus alternativas* (2020), *The culture of boredom* (Brill, 2019), and *The faces of depression in literature* (Peter Lang, 2019).

Contributors

María Cecilia Antón National University of Mar del Plata, Buenos Aires, Argentina

James Danckert University of Waterloo, Waterloo, Canada

John D. Eastwood York University, Toronto, Canada

Dana Gorelik York University, Toronto, Canada

Ricardo Gutiérrez Aguilar Complutense University of Madrid, Madrid, Spain

Eric R. Igou University of Limerick, Limerick, Ireland

William McDonald United Arab Emirates University, Al Ain, United Arab Emirates

Erik Ringmar Ibn Haldun University, Istanbul, Turkey

Josefa Ros Velasco Harvard University, Cambridge, USA

Lars Svendsen University of Bergen, Bergen, Norway

Peter Toohey University of Calgary, Calgary, Canada

Wijnand A. P. van Tilburg King's College London, London, UK

Abbreviations

ACLA	American Comparative Literature Association
ADHD	Attention-deficit Hyperactivity Disorder
AI	Artificial Intelligence
APA	American Psychological Association
BPS	Boredom Proneness Scale
CAM	Cambridge Alumni Magazine
CEN	Central Executive Network
CCHS-CSIC	The Centre for Human and Social Sciences at the Spanish National Research Council
CIR	Constructive Internal Reflection
CMMC	Cognitive-Miser Model of Cognition
COMT	Catechol-O-methyltransferase
DAT1	Dopamine Active Transporter 1
DAAD	Deutscher Akademischer Austauschdienst
DLA	Deutsches Literatur-Archiv Marbach
DMN	Default Mode Network
DSM	Diagnostic and Statistical Manual of Mental Disorders
EEG	Electroencephalogram
FATS	Fifth and Tenth Street
fMRI	Functional Magnetic Resonance Imaging
IZKT	Internationales Zentrum für Kultur- und Technikforschung at Stuttgart Universität
MAC	Meaning and Attentional Components
mPFC	Medial Prefrontal Cortex
MRI	Magnetic Resonance Imaging
NYPSI	New York Psychoanalytic Institute
NYT	New York Times
NYU	New York University
OSL	Optimum Stimulation Level
OUCH	Opportunities to Understand Childhood Hurt Lab

PCC	Posterior Cingulate Cortex
PFC	Prefrontal Cortex
PRKG1	Protein Kinase CGMP-Dependent 1
RAS	Reticular Activating System
RCC	Real Colegio Complutense en Harvard
SNP	Single Nucleotide Polymorphism
SSS	Sensation Seeking Scale
STEM	Science, Technology, Engineering, and Mathematics
UAE	United Arab Emirates
UBC	University of British Columbia
UCLA	University of California in Los Angeles
UCP	Unused Cognitive Potential
UK	United Kingdom
UNED	National University of Distance Education
USA	United States of America

List of Figures

Chapter 1
Is It a Good Thing to Be Bored?

Peter Toohey

In a thoughtful opinion piece for the *New York Times* entitled "Let children get bored again" (2019) the author and *NYT* Book Review editor Pamela Paul suggested that allowing children to experience boredom is a very good thing.[1] For starters, it enables their creativity (p. SR3):

> once you've truly settled into the anesthetizing effects of boredom, you find yourself en route to discovery. [...] this is why so many useful ideas occur in the shower, when you're held captive to a mundane activity. You let your mind wander and follow it where it goes.

But boredom, Pamela Paul also argues, toughens children up: "surely teaching children to endure boredom rather than ratcheting up the entertainment will prepare them for a more realistic future, one that doesn't raise false expectations of what work or life itself actually entails" (2019, p. SR3).

It's an attractive argument on both counts, but especially on creativity. Boredom is often linked to creativity. The poet Joseph Brodsky is sometimes cited as offering strong evidence for its fertilizing qualities and maybe Pamela Paul had him in mind when she wrote her essay. Brodsky claimed, in his essay "In praise of boredom" (1995, p. 11),

> When hit by boredom, let yourself be crushed by it; submerge, hit bottom. In general, with things unpleasant, the rule is: The sooner you hit bottom, the faster you surface. The idea here is to exact a full look at the worst. The reason boredom deserves such scrutiny is that it represents pure, undiluted time in all its repetitive, redundant, monotonous splendor.

A defense of boredom's ability to encourage creativity was also made by WNYC's podcaster, Manoush Zomorodi in her *Bored and brilliant: How spacing out can*

[1]Pamela Paul's article has had a lot of readers. It was translated into Danish, for example, and published in Copenhagen's *Politiken* one week after its appearance in the *NYT*.

P. Toohey (✉)
University of Calgary, Calgary, Canada
e-mail: ptoohey@ucalgary.ca

J. Ros Velasco (ed.), *Boredom Is in Your Mind*,
https://doi.org/10.1007/978-3-030-26395-9_1

unlock your most productive and creative self (2017).[2] But do boring activities really encourage creativity as Brodsky and as Paula James and Manoush Zomorodi maintain? The devil is in the detail, rather than in the generalized formulations, yes it does, or no it does not. So, let's go to the detail even if this must relate, in the first instance, to as relaxing a topic as taking a shower.

Since when has the shower been boring? I really mean it. I love showers. The longer the better. I cannot imagine for a minute how a shower could be thought of as boring. Surely, I am not alone in thinking this way? On the other hand, I do agree that the shower may well be a good place for enabling creative ideas—it may even be true that the shower can be a good place for problem solving, if problem solving is more or less the same thing as creativity. I have read, most famously, that the Colombian Nobel Prize-winning novelist, Gabriel García Márquez was said to have taken very long showers and, under the spray, to have figured out his magically realist plots.[3] David Streitfeld explains, "his showers are said to be so lengthy that [Gabriel García Márquez] had to install a second water heater" (1994). Sometimes, continues Streitfeld, "the details [for his novels] arrive so quickly he jumps out, hair slick with shampoo, and rushes to his desk" (1994).

The novelist's inspiration is, perhaps, the sort of advantage that Pamela Paul believes will accrue to the child victim of boredom, or at least when they are in the shower. But before we jump out to that conclusion, I believe we really need to understand a little more clearly what emotional condition might actually have been brewing up within the shower. What was it that enabled Gabriel García Márquez to develop his ideas? Was it really boredom that had him streaking soapily inspired from the shower? It certainly doesn't sound that way. Could it have been some other emotion or emotional condition? What about daydreaming? I don't know about you, but I daydream a lot in the shower, provided that the water is warm enough. Many people have told me that they don't daydream so much as think of nothing at all. Their minds become quite inactive. Could it be that the great Colombian, as human as the rest of us, was daydreaming in the douche? Could it be that from the midst of these reveries he was hoping that solutions would emerge for the twists and turns of his plots? Daydreaming, then, rather than boredom?

What really convinces me that daydreaming is the responsible agent in the creative shower is this: there seems to be well-known neurological evidence indicating that there exists a link between daydreaming and creativity. This may help us understand the smaller point of showers and daydreaming. In 2009, of daydreaming, Dr. Kalina Christoff from the University of British Columbia "found that our

[2]You might want to compare Mary Mann, *Yawn: Adventures in boredom* (2017). The psychologist and long-time boredom scholar, Sandi Mann also emphasizes the creative upside of boredom in *The science of boredom: The upside (and downside) of downtime* (2017). Moreover, Eva Hoffman offers a chapter on "Creative Play" in *How to be Bored* (2016).

[3]"Residents in part of the outback [in New South Wales] have been ordered to limit their showers to three minutes a day and banned from using a washing machine more than twice a week amid the worst drought since 1900," reports Bernard Lagan in *The Times* (2019). Little chance of creative inspiration there.

brains are much more active when we daydream than previously thought [...] brain areas associated with complex problem-solving—previously thought to go dormant when we daydream—are actually more active than when we focus on routine tasks," according to the review by *UBC News* (see also Christoff et al. 2009). Until Christoff had published her findings

> the only parts of the brain thought to be active when our minds wander was the medial prefrontal cortex (PFC), the posterior cingulate cortex and the temporoparietal junction. However, these studies indicate that the areas associated with high level problem solving, including the lateral PFC and the dorsal anterior cingulate cortex, also become activated when we daydream. (*UBC News* 2009)

Here is a solution of sorts to the conundrum of creativity in the shower. The most gamble-worthy explanation for Gabriel García Márquez and Pamela Paul getting such good ideas in the shower is that they daydream while they wash. Daydreaming helps with knotty creative problems, and showers, for some people, are very good places for daydreaming. Intellectual success in the shower, if Christoff is correct, is likely not so much a matter of boredom as it is of daydreaming.[4]

There's been some more of this sort of neurological work done since 2009. The focus was not on daydreaming so much as what happens in the brain when the body and the mind are idle or in a 'restive' state—think again of those people who claim not to daydream in the shower so much as to think of nothing at all. Deniz Vatansever and his Cambridge University team "focussed on what the brain does when it's not actually 'doing stuff'" (James 2018; see also Vatansever et al. 2017). To achieve this, they gave their attention to the regions of the brain known as the 'default mode network' (DMN). These areas are known to be very active, in a coordinated way, when people are in an inactive state. In such instances, "the brain is highly active in the background, but not carrying out any specific tasks" (James 2018). Vatansever and his colleagues reached these conclusions by having their research subjects learn to and to play a new card game. They observed the DMN "kick into action as their subjects switched from learning the rules of the card game to applying the rules of the card game" (James 2018). Deniz Vatanseter explains that what is happening in the DMN at such times is, "we might be trying to make sense of the world around us by using what we already know" (James 2018). The Cambridge team do not use term boredom in their article to describe these inactive states. Vatanseter does suggest (2017, p. 12825),

> this proactive framework of brain function may provide an all-important scaffold to explain not only the DMN's ongoing activity in stable "rest" conditions, but also its contribution to social interactions (e.g., theory of mind, intuition, and stereotyping), a conscious sense-of-self, *creativity*, and a variety of other cognitive domains that all require the stable use of learned information for predicting the world around us.

[4]Christine A. Godwin and his colleagues from the Georgia Tech took the argument a little further to maintain, we "found that those who scored higher on the ability tests daydreamed more than their less intellectual, less creative peers" (McCall 2017; see also Godwin et al. 2017).

Creativity, therefore, may be linked with these states of inactivity in just the same way that it might be linked to daydreaming according to Kalina Christoff. There is no need to bring up the emotion of boredom in this instance at all.

Daydreaming and inactive or just plain idle states are not the same thing as boredom. And, while daydreaming and inactivity can sometimes be linked to boredom (something John Eastwood will speak to in this volume concerning daydreaming), there is no special reason to claim that daydreaming and inactivity are boring. Many people daydream when they are in otherwise enjoyable but unvarying situations that don't require much mental exertion: jogging, walking, playing with small children and with animals, waiting to go to sleep, or waiting for a well-liked friend to arrive in F.A.T.S. for a shared coffee. I have read that most people spend 46.9% of their waking time daydreaming (*BBC News* 2010; see also Killingsworth and Gilbert 2010). If this is true—and I admit it is a hard statistic to swallow—then for some of this time many people may be bored and they may be using daydreaming to medicate the boredom—but for an awful lot of this time, they may also be contentedly daydreaming. They will also perhaps be relatively inactive (taking a shower, a hot bath, attending a routine meeting, or work talk). Do you daydream and become inactive because you are bored, or do you daydream because it's satisfying, helpful, and even enjoyable? The answer, I suppose, is both. When Pamela Paul praises the opportunities afforded by boredom, perhaps she really should as well be praising the opportunities afforded daydreaming and inactivity.

Let's take this discussion a step further and turn our attention back to boredom. A great deal of the current concern about the relationship between boredom and creativity stems from smart phone use.[5] The argument seems to be this, that individuals spend so much time checking their phones, that they never get a chance to experience that fruitful, creativity-inducing boredom. Here is what Jason Farman thinks of the matter. This is in his thoughtful book, *Delayed response: The art of waiting from the ancient to the instant world* (2018), a study on waiting and modes of communication. Farman tells us of one of his experiments with his students that captured the, can I say, canonical interpretation of the link between boredom and mobile phones. I "asked [my undergraduate students]," explains Farman,

> to spend one week of the semester charting [...] what they did from the moment they woke up until they fell asleep. What each student in this class of 35 had in common was that there wasn't a minute of the day when they weren't occupying themselves with *something* [...] Even standing in line meant taking out their phones to respond to text messages or check email or play games. If boredom peeked around the corner, these students ran the other way by keeping themselves busy; and if not 'busy' with some kind of task or reading the latest updates on social media news sites, they occupied their time by playing a game on their mobile devices. (2018, p. 13)

[5]The most stimulating of the many contributions on this topic, in my opinion, is Susan Maushart *The winter of our disconnect* (2011).

"Let children get bored again," we might conclude. But—could it be that boredom—deprivation isn't really the problem. Could it be instead that Jason Farman's undergraduate students are vigorously depriving themselves of the 46% of the day that is purportedly devoted to daydreaming? Now I realize that this may seem to be a strange and even frivolous assertion that smart phones are depriving people of the productive daydreaming time. But then again linking smart phone use to boredom–deprivation and increased stupidity is pretty frivolous as well. Lots of Jason Farman's students from New York University (NYU) are, I am sure, A-grade candidates and are not stupid at all when it comes to creativity or to problem solving. My point has nothing to do with the human need for daydreaming, which may or may not be true, or with the human need for boredom, which also may or may not also be true. It is to say simply that the confusion between boredom and daydreaming and inactivity suggests that when people invoke boredom in their essays, they frequently do not have a clear definition in mind of what they mean by boredom or daydreaming or even inactivity. Let me add quickly that I am not always sure of what I mean by boredom either. But I don't intend to claim that it is one of life's great and unsung virtues. Nor should you.

The devil really is in the definition. If we knew how to define boredom and if we could all agree on such a definition, then we might know if it is a good thing to be bored or if it is in fact not. As for the subject of definitions, just look at this excellent book that Dr. Josefa Ros Velasco has generously put together. As far as I can tell it exhibits no agreed-upon definition for boredom—though that, I am sure, was one of the reasons that she chose to compile *Boredom is in your mind*. You could say that her book, in the best of ways, exemplifies the confusion and the challenges and the vagueness of the attempt to define boredom. But there are hints among her contributors' essays that there is some commonality concerning the formulations of a definition. It appears from these definitions, furthermore, that boredom is not always viewed as a great intellectual fructifier. I'll highlight just three of these definitions and then add a description of my own.

John Eastwood and his team provide, I believe, the most widely accepted definition: Boredom is "an aversive state of wanting but being unable to engage in satisfying activity" (2012, p. 483). Perhaps sensing that this works as well as an emotional description of sexual impotence, as of boredom, Eastwood modifies his definition in this collection as follows, "boredom […] is an aversive emotional concomitant of 'unused cognitive potential'." John Eastwood believes that boredom is a "regulatory alarm to the presence of cognitive slack and serves to keep us moving toward meaningful engagement and the accomplishment of critical imperatives." Boredom, you could paraphrase, is an unpleasant state and one that drives its victim into productive action that will remedy this unpleasant sense of downtime, this cognitive slack. Eastwood's formulation is, therefore, the direct opposite of those who see the experience of boredom as, in and of itself, valuable.

For James Danckert, another Canadian in this collection, "boredom may provide the signal to switch between exploration [exploring one's environs for resources] and exploitation [exploiting those resources once found] […] boredom may function to minimize opportunity costs." The element of the "aversive" is still important.

The unpleasantness of the experience of boredom aims to force its victim into exploitive action, to pursue creaturely advantage. But, and this is worth stressing, most creatures do not require the experience of boredom to explore and exploit their circumstances. It just helps, that's all.

A third definition comes from Wijnand A. P. van Tilburg and Eric R. Igou who link boredom with "the search for meaningful engagement." Failing to achieve such meaningful engagement and becoming bored can result in "impulsiveness, unhealthy consumption, and, plausibly, mental health issues." The search is triggered by the aversive nature of the emotion of boredom. Van Tilburg has written another fascinating article, "Eaten up by boredom: consuming food to escape awareness of the bored self" (2015). The association of boredom with food and with disgust and satiety has a very long lexical and visual history. A 2000-year-old Latin term for boredom is *satietas vitae*, satiety of life (Seneca 1970, ep. 24.26). The point, I suppose, is that boredom is well recognized as a very unpleasant condition. It is not one that we would necessarily wish upon our children.

Perhaps I could dwell just for a moment longer on the link between satiety, disgust, and boredom made by Wijnand A. P. van Tilburg and in doing so I might offer a fourth description of boredom. This will provide another example of the aversive nature of boredom and it will also have a child, or a near child, as part of the illustration. I'll draw this description from the painting, *La tailleuse de soupe*, by the short-lived Swiss artist, Francois Barraud (1899–1934) (Fig. 1.1). It features his wife, Marie, on the right, and her younger sister Louise, on the left.[6] The title translates as *The soup cutter*. The cutter is Marie and she cuts bread into hers and her sister's soup.[7] Marie seems to enjoy her task. Louise, dressed in flapper style and with a bow in her hair, is not at all contented. In my opinion, she is bored. In fact, in my opinion, she embodies what you might term a typical visual phenotype for boredom.

The following six elements are often to be found in visual representations of boredom. You will recognize five of these in *La tailleuse de soupe*. It is my conviction that to create or to enact a visual phenotype for the emotion of boredom, you need at least three of these elements. Disgust and satiety are also prominent in this aversive landscape.

1. Food may be prominent (the bread in the soup which seems to offer little pleasure to the young woman) and it frequently seems to offer little pleasure to the bored individual.
2. The bored head is usually rested on the left palm (the gesture is as old as the ancient Greeks; if the person is right handed, then the head is on the left palm; this leaves the right hand free to fiddle; if the head rests on the right palm, you are probably looking at a painting about depression). Louise's right hand is free.

---

[6]She appears as well in Barraud's *La séance de painture* (1933) and *Les songes creux* (1933).

[7]There is another version of this scene, but without a Louise, hence without boredom, by Francois Bonvin, *La tailleuse de soupe* (c. 1886).

Fig. 1.1 François Barraud. *La tailleuse de soupe*. 1933. Oil on canvas: 15.3 × 14.6 in. (38.7 × 37 cm). Private Collection. Public Domain

3. The posture, the slouch, the leaning on the arm, offers a reaction to something that is happening right now. Boredom is about a specific and present constraining situation. Depression, which uses some of the same gestures, looks to something permanent and something not bound to a specific situation. Louise is reacting to what is going on right now.
4. Temporary entrapment or constraint is obvious—this is something common to most experiences of boredom. You can't get away—for now at least. Louise really does give the impression that she'd like to escape from her sister and from the soup.
5. The bored individual is often painted on their own, but if they are in company they stare away, over or beyond their company, the so-called Arctic gaze (Louise looks at us—but we don't count as we are not in the painting. She does not look at her sister, *la tailleuse*).

6. Yawning—this one is not to be found in *La tailleuse de soupe* but as you'd expect it is a common reaction to boredom. It is not something that is easily painted or photographed, however. People find it offensive.

As I have indicated, you need several indicators (palm, gaze, food, for example) to evoke the visual phenotype of boredom. One indicator is not enough. A gloomy face doesn't really say too much without a few more accompanying clues. Franz Xaver Messerschmidt sculpted many beautiful 'character heads' that dramatized various emotional states. But without a phenotypical context they can be confusing. In François Barraud's painting of his wife and her sister, he evokes boredom by using five of the six visual clichés I have listed above. I could, if there were sufficient space, show you many comparable examples. What they would all have in common is the stress on the aversive nature of boredom, with an additional emphasis on the unpleasantness of the experience and on its temporary constraint. There is, however, no inactivity in this evocation and there is no daydreaming either. What there is instead is a stress on the unpleasantness of the experience—though what evokes this in Louise we will never know for certain. It may be provoked by the food. Maybe she doesn't like bread in her soup. The visualization of this emotion offers a commentary of sorts on the idea of "Let children get bored." Louise is our child. Leaving her to wallow in the situation of boredom is the very last reaction that you'd want to have to the adolescent in this picture.

Boredom has very little to do with daydreaming and creativity. Its link to creativity, strengthened more by enthusiasm than by evidence, is exaggerated. And, for what it is worth, boredom may not be the biggest casualty of excessive cell phone use. That is probably daydreaming. Although there seems to be no cut and dried way of defining the emotion, the concept of aversion is something that keeps coming up in the various attempts at the lexical task. Boredom is an unpleasant emotion to undergo. Its sufferers will do what they can to escape it. If benefits accrue to the experience of boredom, it is because its victims will do their level best to escape the experience and to move on to something worthwhile (Danckert's point). Their remedy may or may not be creative. It only has to be successful. I am sure that's what Louise would tell you. Maybe I could put this another way and use the illustration of Gabriel García Márquez again. Unhappy childhoods are often associated with literary ability and literary creativity. I doubt that anyone would choose literary preeminence over a happy childhood. Gabriel García Márquez may have been grateful for a difficult childhood as he climbed the Nobel podium in Stockholm in 1982, aged 83. Perhaps he really did feel grateful on that occasion for having been abandoned by his mother and father to his grandparents in Aracataca, Colombia, as a small child. But for most of the rest of his life, he seems to have wished his parents had made a different decision. Maybe you could think about boredom in the same way. If it is true that it is linked with creativity (and for all I know people who have had an unhappy childhood are more prone to boredom), then it provides this bounty at some cost. Lars Svendsen's examination of emotions in animals (in this book) will evaluate the possibility of the presence of boredom (among other emotions) in animals. If animals get bored, it does not say much for the contribution of boredom to creativity. Like anything that is painful, boredom is an emotion that calls out for remediation and for relief. In my experience, the greatest sufferers are the very young and the very old. Their boredom, you could say, is a plea for assistance, a remediation that does not always come as readily as it should do. I am not so sure that we should "let children get bored again." Whatever boredom really is, it is something that aims to drive a person away from the situation in which they find themselves and on into more fruitful activity. It isn't an emotion or an emotional situation that should be coddled as the cradle of the next *Love in a time of cholera.*

One last query: Does experiencing boredom tough children up? Who could say? But I think that one of the jobs both parents and teachers should seriously take on themselves is to teach children how to cope with boredom. I stress teachers as well as parents, for now that education is increasingly orientated toward STEM instruction, children's capacity to cope with boredom may be severely tried, especially if their instruction is substandard. Learning to cope with boredom, anyhow, is probably an important life skill. How else could you end up with a Ph.D.? Perhaps the best way to prepare children to cope with the inevitable boredom of the working life is to teach them how to self-medicate using alleviations such as daydream. That might improve their creativity, their problem solving, and give them something to do while they are bored. Who in their right mind would want to be bored?

References

BBC News. (2010, November 12). People spend 'half their waking hours daydreamin'. *BBC News*. https://www.bbc.com/news/health-11741350. Accessed March 20, 2019.

Brodsky, J. (1995). In praise of boredom (adapted from Dartmouth College commencement address). *Harper's Magazine, 290*(1738), 11.

Christoff, K., Gordon, A. M., Smallwood, J., Smith, R., & Schooler, J. W. (2009). Experience sampling during fMRI reveals default network and executive system contributions to mind wandering. *PNAS, 106*(21), 8719–8724. https://doi.org/10.1073/pnas.0900234106.

Eastwood, J. D., Frischen, A., Fenske, M. J., & Smilek, D. (2012). The unengaged mind. *Perspectives on Psychological Science, 7*(5), 482–495. https://doi.org/10.1177/1745691612456044.

Farman, J. (2018). *Delayed response: The art of waiting from the ancient to the instant world.* New Haven, CT: Yale University Press.

Godwin, C. A., Hunter, M. A., Bezdek, M. A., Lieberman, G., Elkin-Frankston, S., Romero, V. L., et al. (2017). Functional connectivity within and between intrinsic brain networks correlates with trait mind wandering. *Neuropsychologia, 103,* 140–153. https://doi.org/10.1016/j.neuropsychologia.2017.07.006.

Hoffman, E. (2016). Creative play. *How to be bored* (pp. 149–156). New York, NY: Picador.

James, V. (2018). On boredom. *CAM (Cambridge Alumni Magazine)*, 84. https://www.cam.ac.uk/cammagazine/benefitsofboredom. Accessed March 20,2019.

Killingsworth, M. A., & Gilbert, D. T. (2010). A wandering mind is an unhappy mind. *Science, 330*(6006), 932. https://doi.org/10.1126/science.1192439.

Lagan, B. (2019, March 4). Long showers banned as Australia's dry spell worsens. *The Times*. https://www.thetimes.co.uk/article/long-showers-banned-as-australia-s-dry-spell-worsens-ntv8jzfd8. Accessed March 21, 2019.

Mann, M. (2017a). *Yawn: Adventures in boredom*. New York, NY: FSG Originals.

Mann, S. (2017b). *The science of boredom: The upside (and downside) of downtime*. London, UK: Hachette.

Maushart, S. (2011). *The winter of our disconnect*. London, UK: Profile Books.

McCall, R. (2017, October 25). A new study says daydreaming is a sign of creativity and intelligence. *IFLScience*. https://www.iflscience.com/brain/science-says-daydreaming-is-a-sign-of-creativity-and-intelligence/. Accessed March 21, 2019.

Moynihan, A. B., Van Tilburg, W. A. P., Igou, E. R., Wisman, A., Donnelly, A. E., & Mulcaire, J. B. (2015). Eaten up by boredom: Consuming food to escape awareness of the bored self. *Frontiers in psychology, 6*, 369. https://doi.org/10.3389/fpsyg.2015.00369.

Paul, P. (2019, February 2). Let children get bored again. *New York Times*, p. SR3.

Seneca. (1970). *Epistles 1–65*. Cambridge, MA: Harvard University Press.

Streitfeld, D. (1994, April 10). The intricate solitude of Gabriel Garcia Marquez. *The Washington Post*. https://www.washingtonpost.com/archive/lifestyle/1994/04/10/the-intricate-solitude-of-gabriel-garcia-marquez/4b20cf31-5ac5-4726-89e5-de30f8c7c70a/?noredirect=on&utm_term=.ff60dd4f157b. Accessed March 21, 2019.

University of British Columbia. (2009, May 12). Brain's problem-solving function at work when we daydream. *UBC News*. https://news.ubc.ca/2009/05/11/archive-media-releases-2009-mr-09-054/. Accessed March 20, 2019.

Vatansever, D., Menon, D. K., & Stamatakis, E. A. (2017). Default mode contributions to automated information processing. *PNAS, 114*(48), 12821–12826. https://doi.org/10.1073/pnas.1710521114.

Zomorodi, M. (2017). *Bored and brilliant: How spacing out can unlock your most productive and creative self*. New York, NY: St. Martin's Press.

Peter Toohey was born in Seymour, Victoria, and taught for many years in his native Australia, at the University of New England, Armidale. He is currently a Professor of Classics in the Department of Classics and Religion at the University of Calgary in Canada. He was educated at Monash University in Melbourne, Australia, and at the University of Toronto. He is particularly interested in the nature, representation, and the history of difficult emotional and physical conditions, how people cope with these, and how individuals sometimes turn these to their own advantage. His most recent books are *Jealousy* (Yale University Press, 2014) and *Boredom: A lively history* (Yale University Press, 2011). He is also the author of academic papers on boredom such as "Some ancient notions of boredom" (*Illinois Classical Studies*, 1988) and "Acedia in late classical antiquity" (*Illinois Classical Studies*, 1990). His works have been translated into seven languages and quoted worldwide. He is considered a leading figure in the field of boredom.

Chapter 2
The Unbearable Lightness of Boredom: A Pragmatic Meaning-Regulation Hypothesis

Wijnand A. P. van Tilburg and Eric R. Igou

Introduction

> Since boredom advances and boredom is the root of all evil, no wonder, then, that the world goes backwards, that evil spreads. This can be traced back to the very beginning of the world. The gods were bored; therefore they created human beings.
>
> Kierkegaard (1852)

It is not pleasant to be bored. Those who are bored feel restless yet unchallenged (Leary et al. 1986; Van Tilburg and Igou 2012), and long for excitement (Blaszczynski et al. 1990), stimulation (Fromm 1973; Mikulas and Vodanovich 1993; Wilson et al. 2014), and purpose (Van Tilburg and Igou 2011a). Unsurprisingly, boredom triggers attempts to avoid this adverse state, prompting a disengagement with current behavior in favor of temporary distraction (Cummings et al. 2013; Fromm 1968; Moynihan et al. 2015, 2017) or a search for what is presumably thought of as enduring solutions (Elpidorou 2018a; Struk et al. 2016; Van Tilburg and Igou 2011a, 2012).

One might think that boredom plays a minor role in people's lives, representing an annoyance when one needs to wait or cannot do what seems more important. The reader may even know people who assert to be too busy for such an experience, proclaiming, rather dramatically with a touch of despair, their longing for times of utter boredom. Regardless of whether these beliefs are genuine or serve to enhance perceived importance through humble-bragging, they are probably misguided. Rest assured, boredom is not trivial. According to Kierkegaard (1852), it can even move the gods themselves.

W. A. P. van Tilburg (✉)
King's College London, London, UK
e-mail: Wijnand.van_tilburg@kcl.ac.uk

E. R. Igou
University of Limerick, Limerick, Ireland

J. Ros Velasco (ed.), *Boredom Is in Your Mind*,
https://doi.org/10.1007/978-3-030-26395-9_2

Literature on boredom demonstrates the importance of this experience in the lives of many individuals and groups (e.g., Vodanovich 2003; Vodanovich and Watt 2016). For example, boredom is present in the lives of substance abusers (Iso-Ahola and Crowley 1991), those struggling with eating disorders (Zeeck et al. 2011), joyriders (Kellett and Gross 2006), narcissists (Wink and Donahue 1997), students (Larson and Richards 1991; Mann and Robinson 2009), the employed and the unemployed (Weinberg 2016), and both children and adults (Ferrari et al. 2005). Assuming that everyone belongs to at least one of these groups, it is fair to say that boredom is probably part of most people's lives.

Indeed, Chin et al. (2017) estimated that 63% of USA adults experience boredom at least once every 10 days. Boredom was the seventh most frequently experienced emotion and featured in 2.8% of any 30 min period during waking hours. For a day with 8 h of sleep, that equates to approximately 54 min of boredom every day, and over 2 years of some level of boredom over the course of an 80-year-long life. To make matters worse, boredom is associated with a wide range of potentially detrimental personal and interpersonal correlates and consequences, including aggression (Dahlen et al. 2004; Rupp and Vodanovich 1997; Fromm 1973; Van Tilburg et al. 2019a), depression (Goldberg et al. 2011), school dropout (Weybright et al. 2017), intergroup bias (Van Tilburg and Igou 2011a), attentional problems (Eastwood et al. 2012; Hunter and Eastwood 2018; Malkovsky et al. 2012), and poor health and diet (Denny et al. 2013; Moynihan et al. 2015; Sommers and Vodanovich 2000). Clearly, boredom matters.

After having highlighted the dark side of boredom—including drug abuse, aggression, and poor health behavior—literature on boredom reflects a bright side, too. For example, it may enhance creativity (Mann and Robinson 2009), prosociality (Van Tilburg and Igou 2017b), and self-soothing nostalgic reverie (Van Tilburg et al. 2013b). Boredom is not intrinsically 'bad' (or 'good,' for that matter). Rather, we propose that boredom serves self-regulatory functions that ultimately guide people's behaviors, for better or worse. By understanding the processes through which boredom operates, it becomes possible to develop strategies that are effective at preventing boredom itself or its negative consequences while also promoting positive outcomes. We identify a key psychological process to explain the consequences of boredom: pragmatic meaning-regulation. Before we detail this function and discuss the empirical basis for its development, we first review the origins of boredom's alleged connection with meaning.

Boredom and Meaning: Historical Roots

The empirical study of boredom has a relatively brief history of psychological science. Most of what we know about this emotion has been examined in the past few decades, with few exceptions (for more details, see Leary et al. 1986; Vodanovich 2003). Much of the early work on boredom focused on the psychometric properties of its measurement and the correlations expressing people's proneness to experience boredom with a range of social and psychological variables (Farmer and Sundberg 1986; Gordon et al. 1997; Vodanovich 2003; Vodanovich et al. 1991). The study of 'state' boredom—that is, boredom as an acute and situated affective experience (e.g., Fahlman et al. 2013; Van Tilburg and Igou 2011a, 2012)—gained momentum only very recently, typically using experimental methods to examine causal relations.

Despite the absence of a long-standing empirical research tradition on boredom in psychology, this does not mean that boredom has been entirely neglected. To the contrary, eminent philosophers had plenty to say about boredom (for a review, see Svendsen 2005); often in a tone of depreciation, if not outright hostility. Heidegger referred to it as the "monstrosity" within existence (quoted in Thiele 1997, p. 491) and Sartre denounced it as "leprosy of the soul" (quoted in Martin et al. 2006, p. 195). Besides accusing boredom of being "the root of all evil" and attributing human existence to the gods merely being bored, Kierkegaard contended that human procreation and cultural advance was merely inspired by the desperation to escape their own perpetual boredom, and ultimately paved the way for humans' alleged fall from grace: "And what consequences this boredom had: humankind stood tall and fell far, first through Eve, then from the Babylonian tower" (Kierkegaard 1852, p. 1). Kierkegaard's gloom seems only rivaled by that of Schopenhauer, who proclaimed that the human capacity for boredom is nothing less than evidence of life's ultimate emptiness (1851 [trans. 2009], p. 357):

> Human life must be some kind of mistake. The truth of this will be sufficiently obvious if we only remember that man is a compound of needs and necessities hard to satisfy; and that even when they are satisfied, all he obtains is a state of painlessness, where nothing remains to him but abandonment to boredom. This is direct proof that existence has no real value in itself; for what is boredom but the feeling of the emptiness of life?

What is it about boredom that caused such a negative portrayal? Is there any truth to boredom being the monstrous, immoral, or nihilistic sentiment that these philosophers made it out to be? It seems tempting to dismiss these claims as an overly simplistic and untenable 'boredom = bad' narrative, especially given that recent empirical work reveals a much more complicated, and possibly far more interesting, role for boredom than the boogeyman it was made out to be (Elpidorou 2014, 2017, 2018a, b; Leary et al. 1986; Van Tilburg and Igou 2011a, 2012; 2017a, b; Westgate and Wilson 2018). Yet, there are important lessons to be learned from these philosophers' beliefs. One of these lessons is that boredom supposedly relates to perceptions of meaning and purpose in life. Another one is that boredom supposedly causes potent attempts to change course. We address these two suggestions, boredom's existential connotation and its motivational significance, next.

Boredom's Existential Connotation

Psychological research has recognized that it is very important for people to perceive their lives and actions as meaningful (e.g., Greenberg et al. 2004; Heine et al. 2006; Heintzelman and King 2014; Steger et al. 2006). Indeed, having a sense of meaningfulness correlates with many positive factors, including life satisfaction, happiness, and work enjoyment (Bonebright et al. 2000; Debats et al. 1993; Steger et al. 2006, 2008), whereas lacking meaningfulness involves decreased well-being, depression, anxiety, and substance abuse, to name a few (e.g., Adler and Fagley 2005; Steger et al. 2009).

Making Sense of Meaning in Psychology

Given the apparent psychological significance of meaning, clear definitions, and operationalizations of this concept should be key in research. Yet definitions of meaning diverge are somewhat vague. For example, Heine et al. (2006) suggest that meaning is "what connects things to other things in expected ways" (pp. 90–91), and Baumeister (1992) stated that meaning is a "shared mental representation of possible relationships among things, events, and relationships" (p. 15), while Heintzelman and King contend that meaning is a subjective experience of coherence (2014). Other researchers emphasize the connection between meaning and concepts such as personal growth, self-transcendence, and fulfilling personal possibilities (e.g., Deci and Ryan 2000; Kasser and Sheldon 2004; Ryan and Deci 2004).

Meaning-Regulation

Unfortunately, many situations in life challenge people's sense of meaningfulness, be it at a specific level (e.g., feeling devoid of meaning in the activity at hand) or at a more general level (seeing one's entire life as meaningless). As an example, a 'classic' meaning-threat is mortality salience—a condition in which people are implicitly or explicitly reminded that they will inevitably die (Greenberg et al. 2004). Next to mortality salience as a threat to meaning, several other factors have been identified that are detrimental to people's current sense of meaningfulness or meaning in life, including uncertainty (Van den Bos et al. 2005), ostracism (e.g., Case and Williams 2004), and various expectancy violations (e.g., Proulx and Inzlicht 2012; Randles et al. 2011; Maher et al. 2013, 2019), including disillusionment (e.g., Maher et al. 2018).

Unsurprisingly, people attempt to combat these threats. For example, terror management theory (e.g., Greenberg et al. 2004) proposes that people try to protect life's perceived meaningfulness, in particular in the face of mortality salience, by boosting adherence to cultural worldviews such as religion, ideologies, or group-held values. People are proposed to do so because these beliefs subsequently protect meaningfulness by offering a sense of symbolic immortality that helps people to 'transcend' their individual and limited existence. For example, mortality salience has been found to increase the adherence to meaning-laden worldviews such as religion (Norenzayan and Hansen 2006), political ideology (Jost et al. 2004), and ingroup beliefs (Castano et al. 2002). When purpose in one's individual, temporary life is under threat, one might find refuge in the seemingly enduring survival of ideologies, beliefs, groups, or, quite literally, through the immortality that some sort of afterlife might promise.

In the attempt to formulate a 'meaning-regulation' model applicable beyond just mortality salience, Heine et al. (2006) proposed their 'meaning maintenance model.' People try to maintain and re-establish meaning by using a variety of strategies, including revision of existing meaning-structures and reappraising meaning-inconsistent targets (for an overview see Proulx and Inzlicht 2012). An important maintenance strategy that they propose is 'fluid compensation:' Threats in one domain (e.g., mortality salience) can lead to the bolstering meaning in another domain (e.g., self-esteem). Beyond the specifics of this model or similar models, particularly important in the context of the current chapter is the notion that loss of meaning can trigger compensatory responses that are not directly related to the cause of meaning loss, but may boost meaning through alternative, intact sources of meaning.

Boredom and Meaning

How is boredom related to lack of meaning? To explain the relationship between boredom and meaning, it is useful to distinguish between *epistemic* and *teleological* meaning (Van Tilburg and Igou 2013).[1] Teleological meaning is concerned with the functional aspects of a phenomenon, or the goals that it might serve; it relates to questions regarding 'why' one might perform an activity, or what purpose a particular action serves. This type of meaning is typically challenged when people lack purpose in their activity or life in general, for example, through experiencing loneliness or reduced self-worth (Burrow and Rainone 2017; Sjöberg et al. 2018). Key factors that determine whether people assign high teleological meaning to a particular activity are the *value of the goal* that is served by the behavior (e.g., an important outcome) and the *instrumentality* of the particular behavior in question in pursuit of that goal (e.g., probability of the behavior facilitating the goal, speed of incremental approach to the goal). Only when both instrumentality of the behavior and value of the goal are high do people perceive the particular behavior as meaningfulness (Van Tilburg and Igou 2013). For example, in Kafka's famous novel *Das Schloß* [The Castle], protagonist 'K.' is required to navigate through dense bureaucracy to initiate his surveying services for the town. The utter ineffectiveness (i.e., low instrumentality) of this bureaucratic system renders K.'s quest a seemingly meaningless exercise.

[1]Part of the ambiguity in psychological definitions of meaning might be resolved by using more specific terms, such as *sense making* (epistemic meaning) and *purposefulness* (teleological meaning).

Indeed, the phenomenology of boredom is replete with features that could indicate a lack of behavioral instrumentality or goal value. For example, the unchanging repetitiveness, monotony, and lack of challenge that characterizes many boring tasks (e.g., Cleary et al. 2016; Sansone et al. 1992; Van Tilburg and Igou 2012) suggest that the behavior at hand does not progress (sufficiently) toward the desired goal. Furthermore, the typical lack of interest, engagement, and attention under boredom (e.g., Hunter and Eastwood 2018; Struk et al. 2016; Sulea et al. 2015) might signal that the value of the goal, which the current behavior supposedly serves, is low. In this way, boredom likely involves a lack of perceived teleological meaning.

Epistemic meaning is conceptually distinct from teleological meaning. It "concerns the meaning of concepts, how these meanings are created, and how they are validated or protected" (Van Tilburg and Igou 2013, p. 374). Epistemic meaning is typically studied in the context of expectancy violation or difficulties in comprehension (Janoff-Bulman and Yopyk 2004; Proulx and Inzlicht 2012; Proulx and Heine 2010), where disruptions of existing schemas trigger compensatory responses (e.g., Maher et al. 2013, 2018; Randles et al. 2011). Perhaps, at least to some degree, the role of boredom in school dropout and lack of class attendance (Reid 2006; Sahin et al. 2016) indicates an inconsistency between people's expectations of life and its reality. Although lack of epistemic meaning might be involved for some instances of boredom, we reason that for this emotion challenges to teleological meaning are typically more central than challenges to epistemic meaning. This is different for other emotions, such as doubt, confusion, meta-cognitive uncertainty, and disillusionment, where lack of insights or inconsistencies to people's expectations are at the center (Maher et al. 2019).[2]

As light is salient in darkness, we reason that the possibility of boredom involving a lack of purpose opens the opportunity for its antagonist: meaning. After all, the literature on meaning-regulation suggests that threats to perceptions of meaning elicit compensatory responses (e.g., fluid compensation; Heine et al. 2006) to maintain or re-obtain a sense of meaning. If boredom can indeed join the ranks of other meaning-threats, then this opens the possibility for boredom having consequences that are more diverse than 'merely' the negative correlates and consequences typically ascribed to it. Furthermore, it would hold the promise of consequences of boredom that lie outside the specific context that caused acute boredom. For example, boredom elicited by, say, a school activity might cause

[2]While it is conceptually helpful to distinguish between teleological and epistemic meaning, this should not be interpreted as evidence that these 'forms' of meaning are independent of each other. Rather, these forms of meaning may empirically be hard to distinguish (see Cantarero et al. *The need for sense-making: Development and validation of a new measure* and *Some people just need to make more sense: An exploratory study of individual differences in the need for sense-making*, both manuscripts under review, 2019) and threats to either tend to elicit compensatory responses (e.g., Maher et al. 2018).

meaning-regulation attempts in the domain of affirmation of values attached to one's social identity.

Boredom as a Motivational Force

In order to understand why one might speculate about a motivational role for boredom, it is useful to reflect on the connection between emotion and motivation. Both terms (specifically, 'emotion' and 'motive') find their origins in the Latin *movere*, meaning to *move*. Past and contemporary emotion theories honor these origins: Scherer's (2001) sequential check theory of emotion, for example, proposes that the cognitive appraisals that characterize specific emotions can elicit behavioral responses directed at moving toward or away from stimuli. For example, *joy* and *nostalgia* encourage approaching toward or engaging with the cause of these emotions (see Van Tilburg et al. 2019b), whereas emotions such as *shame* and *fear* tend to cause avoidance (Lerner and Keltner 2001; Schmader and Lickel 2006).

The motivational role of emotion is particularly evident in models of *self-regulation* "efforts by the human self to alter any of its own inner states or responses" (Baumeister and Vohs 2004, p. 2). An important assumption in self-regulation theorizing is the presence of psychological 'feedback loops' that inform the self about discrepancies between a perceived value (e.g., current state) relative to some internal reference standard (e.g., a personal goal; Carver 2004). This psychological feedback process triggers responses aimed at either reducing or avoiding the difference between the current state and the internal reference, and emotion plays a key role in this process. Specifically, positive emotions serve as a cue that one is making progress in moving toward the internal reference standard, whereas negative emotions serve as a cue that one is not (or not sufficiently; Rasmussen et al. 2006). By facilitating self-regulation, emotions can thus serve psychological homeostasis (e.g., Van Tilburg et al. 2019d) and do so through motivating behavioral approach or avoidance (Frijda et al. 1989; Van Tilburg et al. 2018).

Self-regulatory Effects of Boredom

Boredom is likely no exception to the above important role of emotions in self-regulation. Indeed, research suggests that people who experience boredom at the moment (i.e., state boredom) report that they continuously think about what alternative engagements or activities exist that prove more challenging or meaningful (Van Tilburg and Igou 2011b). Consistently, work by Csíkszentmihályi (1990) suggests that a mismatch between the perceived low challenges of a task relative to one's ability, present under boredom, triggers attempts to increase that challenge in the attempt to escape boredom.

A select amount of early studies confirms the presence of motivated consequences of boredom. In an early set of experiments, Sansone et al. (1992) observed that state boredom—induced using a repetitive task—increased the use of strategies to facilitate interest in the boring task at hand. For example, boredom made people try to come up with reasons why the task might nevertheless be important and interesting (e.g., adopting the belief that the task served health benefits). In another set of experiments, Smith et al. (2009) observed that the engagement in a boring task makes people more likely to adopt small task variations in their attempt to remain interested, especially when people adopted a promotion focus. Specifically, participants who focused on attaining positive outcomes were more likely to creatively vary the use of capitalized and non-capitalized letters in the boring task of copying letters.

The recognition of boredom's profound motivational character offers promising new directions into understanding the consequences of boredom. Importantly, research on experiences associated with a lack of meaning, such as boredom, indicates that regulatory processes are evoked by the experience with the focus on gleaning meaning from one's activities or life in general. Indeed, the research by Sansone et al. (1992) and Smith et al. (2009) suggests that boredom signals to people that there is a need to engage in responses that are helpful to remain interested and to search for the underlying value in the boring activity, reflecting an overall attempt to re-establish a sense of meaningfulness that is lacking when people are bored.

A Pragmatic Meaning-Regulation Hypothesis

Based on the notion that boredom has existential connotations with strong links to perceptions of meaning and functions as motivating force, our research builds on the notion of pragmatic meaning-regulation or the *pragmatic meaning-regulation hypothesis* (Van Tilburg and Igou 2011a). According to this account, boredom has the potential to aid people's pursuit of meaning. Boredom involves an acute awareness of the lack of meaning or purpose in one's current engagements, triggers a search for alternative courses of action that seem more meaningful, and then commits the individual to those behaviors that are perceived as offering a sense of purpose. This account casts boredom in a role akin to Socrates' proverbial gadfly, whose strings would cause the local Athenians to question the status quo and reconsider their behavior and convictions. Boredom rouses people from their proverbial slumber, awakening a desire for something more worthwhile than current affairs. Boredom thus helps to regulate or maintain the engagement in behavior that is perceived as meaningful.

Over the years, research has tested the tenets of this pragmatic meaning-regulation hypothesis, which can be partitioned in three main constituents: (1) boredom thrives in environments that are appraised as meaningless; (2) boredom triggers a search for meaningful alternatives; (3) sources of meaning prevent boredom. In the following sections, we review experimental and correlational work that sheds light on these processes.

Constituent 1: Low Meaning Is Boredom's Habitat

The first constituent of our pragmatic meaning-regulation account of boredom is that a lack of perceived meaning or purpose is a necessary (but probably not a sufficient) condition for boredom to occur. Supporting this notion, MacDonald and Holland (2002) found that people prone to boredom reported less meaning and purpose in their lives. Consistently, Melton and Schulenberg (2007) report an inverse relationship between boredom proneness and perceived life purpose. Since then, this association between dispositional boredom on the one hand and indicators for meaning or purpose in life on the other hand has been replicated on numerous occasions (Coughlan et al. 2019; Fahlman et al. 2009; Van Tilburg and Igou 2012, 2016; Van Tilburg et al. 2013b, 2019a).

Of course, based solely on the existence of an association between (lack of) meaning in life and boredom proneness one should not directly infer that *state* boredom tends to occur when meaning is lacking; after all, these correlations merely indicate covariance in dispositions or tendencies, not between actual experiences. Fortunately, several studies investigated the association between meaning and state boredom. Fahlman et al. (2009), for example, found in an experiment that boredom decreased when meaning in life was experimentally elevated, relative to a low-meaning control. Furthermore, experiments indicate that highly boring activities (vs. a low or no boredom control) involve a lack of perceived meaning (Van Tilburg and Igou 2011a; Moynihan et al. 2017). Thus, it seems that boredom tends to occur when meaning is lacking.

Perhaps the most convincing evidence of the intimate link between boredom and a lack of perceived meaning comes from studies that sought to identify the key characteristics of boredom, and in particular relative to other states of affect. One of the first investigations of this distinct 'psychological profile' of boredom compared characteristics of dispositional boredom, measured state boredom, and manipulated state boredom against frustration, anger, and sadness (Van Tilburg and Igou 2012). While distinct from boredom, these three negative states have either been found or are theoretically likely to correlate positively with boredom; they might therefore co-occur in situations where boredom emerges (e.g., Rupp and Vodanovich 1997; Smith et al. 2009; see also Van Tilburg and Igou 2011a). We found that boredom was uniquely characterized by thoughts about the lack of meaning or purpose of the situation in which boredom occurred. This distinguished boredom from the other three emotions, which featured a lack of perceived meaning too far lesser extent. Furthermore, this finding was observed for emotional events that participants recalled from memory (Study 1), correlations between dispositions (Study 2), correlations between state experiences (Study 3), and state experience in response to experimental induction (Study 4).

Findings consistent with the previous were reported by Chan et al. (2018), who examined the role of meaning in recollected past situations that caused boredom (Study 1) and in a diary study of current situations (Study 2). These researchers found that those situations that elicited boredom were also strongly characterized by a perceived lack of meaning. This characteristic meaninglessness of boring situations was found in comparisons with situations that were instead deemed not boring, engaging, or saddening. Furthermore, the association between situational boredom and meaninglessness remained significant after controlling for sadness and various personality factors, including trait boredom.

A further investigation of boredom's distinct profile, and the role of meaning therein, evidenced the importance of low meaning as key characteristic of boredom relative to other forms of negative affect (Van Tilburg and Igou 2017a). Using a multidimensional scaling approach (Kruskal and Wish 1978; Maher et al. 2019; Van Tilburg et al. 2018), we investigated (1) if boredom can be empirically distinguished from a range of other forms of negative affect, and (2) what cognitive and affective features of boredom characterize these differences. We simultaneously examined this at three levels: lay conceptions of boredom and other emotions (e.g., people's perceptions and believes about boredom; Study 1), state experiences of boredom and the other emotions (Study 2), and individual differences in people's tendencies to experience boredom and the other emotions (Study 3).

For the investigation of lay perceptions, we asked participants to evaluate the perceived similarity between any pair of emotions among boredom, sadness, anger, frustration, fear, disgust, feeling depressed, guilt, shame, regret, and disappointment. We then used these similarity ratings to statistically construct a two-dimensional 'emotion space' in which the proximity between any two emotions revealed their perceived similarity. A similar procedure was used for the state and trait emotions, with the exception that here we relied on correlations between their actual occurrence in response to an emotion induction, or on the basis of frequency of experiencing them in the past, respectively. In a second empirical step, we statistically fitted to these two-dimensional emotion spaces a number of characteristics that past research had attributed to boredom—(negative) valence, (low) arousal, (high) relevance to morality, (low) attention, (low) challenge, and, finally, (low) meaning. The results indicated that boredom was associated with less perceived meaning than any of the other emotions, in conjunction with lack of attention. The perception of low meaning explained exceptionally well the differences between boredom and the other emotions. As we found that meaning played this key characterizing role of boredom across the levels of lay perceptions, state experiences, and individual differences (see Fig. 2.1 for state boredom as an example), it can be concluded that lack of meaning plays a defining role in boredom.

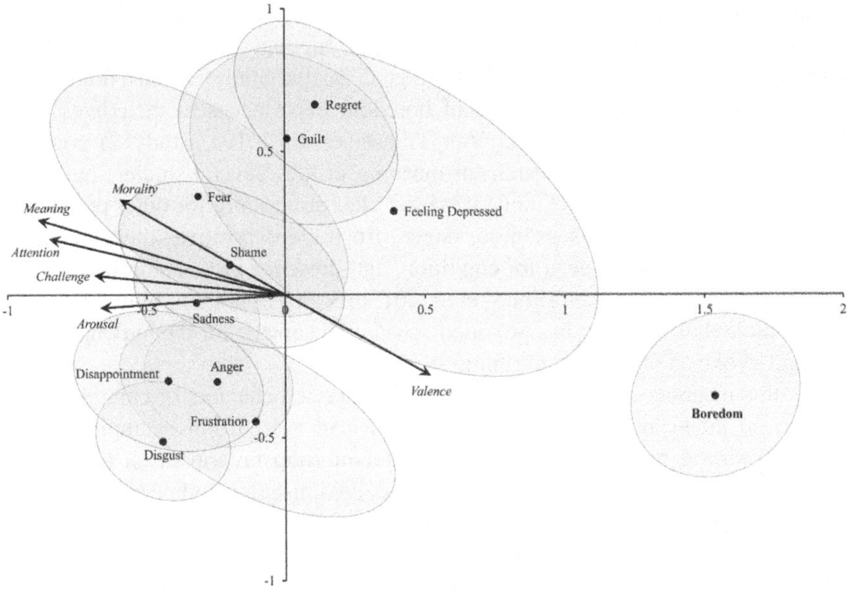

Fig. 2.1 State boredom's relative position as low-meaning emotion. Note: Greater distance between two emotions reflects that they are more distinct; they occur in relative isolation. Grey areas represent 95% confidence regions. Vector orientation indicates the direction in the space that is characterized by emotions that score comparatively high on that feature; emotions located opposite to its direction score relatively low of that feature. Vector length is analogous to its usefulness for characterizing differences between the emotions. The length of *meaning* and *attention* vectors is substantially reduced in the absence of boredom, rendering these particularly essential for understanding what uniquely characterizes boredom. Van Tilburg, W. A. P., & Igou, E. R. (2017). Boredom begs to differ: Differentiation from other negative emotions. *Emotion, 17*(2), 309–322. American Psychology Association. Reprinted with permission

Constituent 2: Boredom Instigates a Search for Meaningful Engagement

The second constituent of our meaning-regulation account is that boredom evokes a search for meaning. Evidence for this process comes in two forms: (1) findings indicating that boredom predicts or increases a self-reported search for meaningful engagement, and (2) findings indicating that boredom predicts adoption of meaning-laden beliefs or engagement in behavior that is perceived as meaningful.

A range of studies indicates that boredom increases a search for meaning. For example, experiments show that highly versus little boring tasks (e.g., transcribing literature on concrete or lawnmowers, watching agricultural instruction videos; e.g., Van Tilburg and Igou 2012, 2017b; Van Tilburg et al. 2019c) increases people's desire to do something more purposeful (Van Tilburg and Igou 2012), and increases a search for meaning (Van Tilburg and Igou 2011a; Van Tilburg et al. 2013b). In addition, correlational studies show that state boredom is associated with the desire to find purposeful and meaningful activities (Van Tilburg and Igou 2011a, Study 3). Consistently, people's disposition to feel bored (Coughlan et al. 2019; Van Tilburg and Igou 2016, Study 2 and 3; Van Tilburg et al. 2019a, Study 2; Van Tilburg et al. 2013, Study 5) and the prominence of boredom experiences in their lives (Van Tilburg and Igou 2012, Study 2; Van Tilburg et al. 2019c, Study 2) correlate positively with self-reported search for meaning in life. Several studies found that these causal effects and correlations persisted after controlling for other potentially relevant variables, such as sadness, anger, frustration, positive affect, negative affect, need for structure, need for cognition, and presence of meaning in life (Van Tilburg and Igou 2012; Van Tilburg et al. 2013b; Van Tilburg and Igou 2016). We can conclude that literature has provided substantial support for the hypothesis that boredom evokes a search for meaning.

Can this meaning-search manifest itself in concrete behaviors or commitments? The second theme in our studies shows that it can indeed. For example, experimentally induced boredom resulted in stronger ingroup favoritism (at the cost of outgroups), which is an established source perceived meaning and purpose (Reicher et al. 1995; Spears et al. 2004) and mitigates meaning-threats (Castano et al. 2002). Specifically, Van Tilburg and Igou (2011a) found that Irish participants who felt highly (vs. little) bored subsequently expressed a greater preference for the Irish spelling of the name *Eoin* over its anglicized equivalent, *Owen*. Furthermore, highly bored participants identified more strongly with their groups and were more lenient in their recommendations of the duration for which a racist ingroup offender needed to be incarcerated, relative to the same crime committed by a racist outgroup member. In a final experiment, Irish participants attributed greater beauty to the Shamrock, an Irish symbol, but not to other images—an effect that was mediated by participants' intensified search for meaning.

Besides the impact of boredom on social identification, through meaning-search, other consequences of boredom have been identified that can be interpreted from the perspective that they follow from a search for meaning. Among these is nostalgia (Van Tilburg et al. 2013b)—a self-relevant emotion characterized as a sentimental and wistful affection for the past (Van Tilburg et al. 2018). Nostalgia is a bittersweet sentiment (Hepper et al. 2012) that mixes positive with negative affect. It is a distinct emotion that shares superficial similarities especially with positive emotions such as love and pride (Van Tilburg et al. 2019b). Nostalgia psychologically reconnects people with their past (Sedikides et al. 2015) and inspires and propels creativity (Stephan et al. 2015; Van Tilburg et al. 2015). Importantly, nostalgia boosts people's sense of meaning in life and thwarts meaning-threats (Routledge et al. 2012). It does this by invigorating a sense of connectedness with valued others and uniting past and present selves (Van Tilburg et al. 2019e). Indeed, boredom triggers nostalgic reverie, which in turn enhances the sense of meaning that bored individuals are otherwise lacking (Van Tilburg et al. 2013). Furthermore, people's use of nostalgia in the face of boredom is indeed mediated by the search for meaning that boredom engenders (Fig. 2.2).

Another important source of meaning in life is people's political beliefs. Consistently, we found that boredom strengthens people's political beliefs contributing to political polarization (Van Tilburg and Igou 2016, Study 1). Similarly, those who are more easily bored affirm their heroes (Coughlan et al. 2019), which serve as sources of meaning (Kinsella et al. 2019). Also for these sources of meaning, the effects of state boredom and boredom proneness were statistically mediated by people's search for meaningful engagement or purpose.

Likewise, a prominent source of meaning in everyday life is helping other people (Jonas et al. 2002). Consistently, we found that the pursuit of meaning explains such behavior intentions when people experience boredom (Van Tilburg and Igou 2017b). In an initial experiment, we found that experimentally induced boredom increased people's willingness to donate money to a charity. Importantly, in a follow-up experiment we found that this effect of boredom was qualified by the instrumentality of the charity for making a meaningful impact. Specifically, boredom only increased charitable intentions when the charitable cause was framed and perceived as a meaningful endeavor. Thus, boredom promoted prosocial intentions only if the charity might serve as a vehicle to do something meaningful.

Constituent 3: Sources of Meaning Prevent Boredom

As boredom serves, at least in part, to regulate meaningful engagement one might wonder whether boredom is likely or unlikely to occur when people glean meaning from their activities and life in general. Consistent with the notion that boredom might serve the enhancement of meaning via a search for meaning, we propose that meaning gained from these regulatory responses should counteract or prevent subsequent boredom, thus closing the self-regulatory circle. To our knowledge, this third constituent has been addressed by very few studies thus far.

Initial evidence that sources of meaning can prevent boredom was found by Van Tilburg et al. (2019c), who investigated religiosity as one repository of perceived meaning (Steger et al. 2006). In a first experiment (Study 1), we found that those who were religious (vs. non-religious) became less bored in a subsequent task that required participants to transcribe references to literature on lawn mowers. Furthermore, the strength of religious belief, operationalized as continuous variable, was negatively correlated with the intensity of subsequent state boredom. Another experiment (Study 3) replicated these findings and showed that the link between religiosity and state boredom was statistically mediated by participants' perceived meaning in life: Religious participants perceived life to be more meaningful, which in turn predicted a reduced level of state boredom. These studies furthermore found that the prevention of boredom through the perceived meaning that religious belief offered in turn resulted in a subdued search for meaning. Thus, religiosity, as an important source of meaning, prevented the meaning-regulation process that boredom would otherwise instigate (Fig. 2.3).

Further support, be it tentative, for the proposition that meaning-laden behaviors or beliefs prevent subsequent boredom comes from research by Coughlan et al. (2019). We found that dispositional boredom was associated with the increased

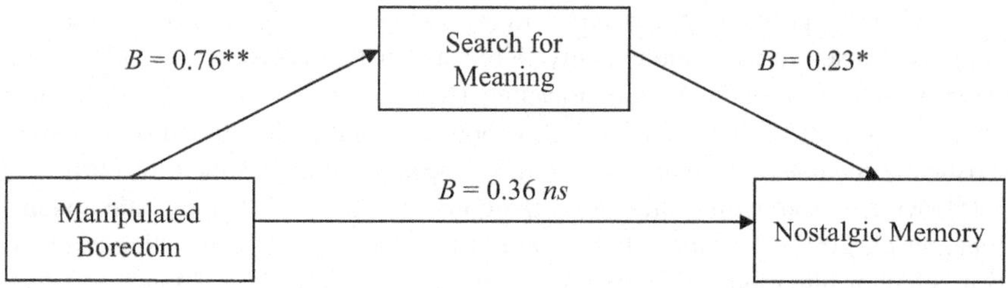

Fig. 2.2 Experimentally induced boredom causes nostalgia, through meaning-search. Note: * $p \leq 0.05$; ** $p \leq 0.01$. Regression coefficients indicate relationships between manipulated boredom, measured search for meaning, and measured nostalgia. Search for meaning significantly mediates the effect of boredom on nostalgia, $0.04 < B_{95} < 0.40$, $SE = 0.09$ (estimated with 5.000 bootstraps). Van Tilburg, W. A. P., Igou, E. R. & Sedikides, C. (2013). In search of meaningfulness: Using nostalgia as an antidote to boredom. *Emotion, 13*(3), 450–461. American Psychology Association. Adapted with permission

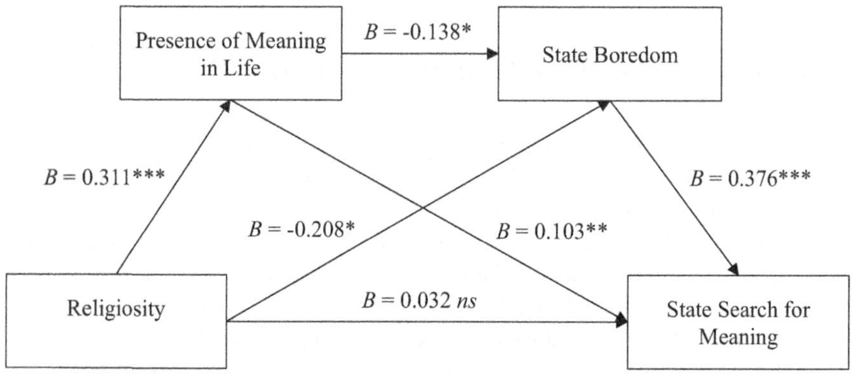

Fig. 2.3 Religiosity prevents boredom through meaning in life. Note: * $p \leq 0.05$; ** $p \leq 0.01$, *** $p \leq 0.001$. Meaning presence significantly mediates the effect of religiosity on state boredom, −0.09< B95 < −0.01, SE = 0.02 (estimated with 5.000 bootstraps). Van Tilburg, W. A. P., Igou, E. R., Maher, P. J., Moynihan, A. B., & Martin, A. (2019). Bored like hell: Religiosity reduces boredom and tempers the quest for meaning. *Emotion, 19*(2), 255–269. American Psychology Association. Reprinted with permission

affirmation of heroes, a known source of a perceived meaning in life (e.g., Green et al. 2017; Kinsella et al. 2019). In a recursive process, the meaning in life that hero affirmation provided in turn predicted a reduction in boredom. Converging findings for the boredom-preventing nature of meaningful behavior and belief comes from research in which we found that the state boredom experienced in the context of a repetitive experiment was lower if this experiment was introduced to participants as being highly (vs. little) instrumental for our understanding a highly (vs. little) valued scientific question (Van Tilburg and Igou 2019a).[3] These two features of goal pursuit, instrumentality of behavior and goal value, are fundamental components of the perceived meaningfulness of behavior (Van Tilburg and Igou 2013). Indeed, the meaningfulness attributed to this task mediated these factors' reductions of boredom. Overall, the research into the third constituent process of the pragmatic meaning-regulation proposition, while still in its adolescence, is generally encouraging.

The Notion of Pragmatism

Boredom features as a protagonist in the regulation of purpose; boredom triggers a search for meaning, which results in behaviors that are (perceived to be) more meaningful, and in turn prevent boredom. The *pragmatic* aspect of the meaning-regulatory process is central and warrants greater emphasis. Clearly, there are some situations in which finding meaning is all but impossible, undesirable, or overshadowed by other motives.[4] People are likely *pragmatic* when searching for meaning. If a source of meaning is readily available, then boredom may cause one to pursue it. If not, then alternative actions may take place. For example, Moynihan et al. (2015) found that participants who had to endure a boring management video on the topic of aquaculture simply distracted themselves through snacking. This indicates that boredom may cause impulsive behavior, not oriented toward a source of meaning, to temporarily withdraw from the meaning-threat posed in that situation (Moynihan et al. 2017).

Support for the notion that people are somewhat pragmatic in their meaning-regulation attempts is evident from experiments on nostalgia and prosocial intentions in response to boredom. For example, we found that nostalgia—a potent remedy against meaning-threats (Routledge et al. 2012)—increased in response to boredom when people were prompted to retrieve a memory (Van Tilburg et al. 2013, Study 1). Providing bored people with an opportunity for meaning-regulation (e.g., a memory retrieval task) thus facilitated the use of nostalgia. Likewise, we found that boredom can increase prosocial tendencies (in particular expressing a willingness to donate money to charity) only if this charity is perceived as useful for

[3]See the manuscript in preparation *Increasing perceived behavioural instrumentality and goal value reduces boredom: A pragmatic meaning-regulation approach.*

[4]To give an example, as part of a recently and compulsory 'data protection' training, this chapter's first author was required to pass a long, repetitive test with unexciting questions such as 'Which of these devices might contain data?' Having postponed this uninspiring work before, and the training deadline now drawing near, the response to this boring situation was to get a snack to eat to alleviate the hardship (and then complain about it for years, of course). By the way, the answer to this particular question was multiple-choice option D: *a banana*. I kid you not.

making a (meaningful) difference (Van Tilburg and Igou 2017b, see Footnote 4). Thus, people are pragmatic in their commitment to potentially meaningful behaviors under boredom.

Synopsis, Outstanding Matters, and Future Directions

Research on boredom over the last decades demonstrates clearly boredom's intimate relationship with meaning in life: Boredom is associated with a lack of perceived meaning (e.g., Chan et al. 2018; Fahlman et al. 2013; Van Tilburg and Igou 2012). This includes the meaninglessness of tasks (Van Tilburg et al. 2019c) and can rise up to the level of lacking meaning in life (Van Tilburg et al. 2016). The link between boredom and meaninglessness exists for boredom as a trait (Moynihan et al. 2017) as well as for boredom as a state (Van Tilburg and Igou 2017a). Our approach to boredom focuses on the regulatory processes that serve the goal to maintain or re-establish an overall sense of meaning (Heine et al. 2006; Proulx and Inzlicht 2012). We distinguish two paths in this regard. Bored people search for sources of meaning to re-establish it (Van Tilburg and Igou 2011a), and sources of meaning can counteract the emergence of boredom (Van Tilburg et al. 2013, 2019c).

The empirically demonstrated links between boredom and meaning take the conceptualizations of boredom beyond the philosophical reasoning that paved the way for this research. By demonstrating these links, boredom research also supports the overarching notion that meaning is central in people's lives; it is a psychological variable of tremendous importance (Heine et al. 2006; King et al. 2016; Van Tilburg and Igou 2012; Steger et al. 2006, 2008, 2009). Perhaps, boredom is a crucial variable that—among other variables—takes on the prestigious role of capturing meaning-regulation dynamics involved in everyday life activities.

Boredom's Future Is Meaningful: Some Unexamined Directions

Our pragmatic meaning-regulation hypothesis is one among several approaches to boredom. For example, research by Eastwood and Danckert, and their colleagues (e.g., Eastwood et al. 2012; Malkovsky et al. 2012) identified the essential connection between attention (failures) and boredom. Elpidorou (2014, 2017, 2018a, b) proposes an account to boredom focused on its behavior-guiding aspects. Furthermore, Westgate and Wilson (2018) proposed a *meaning and attentional components* (MAC) model of boredom. How does our pragmatic meaning-regulation hypothesis sit with these other accounts? We believe that, while individual emphases within each of these approaches might differ, their converging view is one that places boredom consistently in a position of self-regulation. Where approaches diverge, they seem complementary. For example, while our pragmatic meaning-regulation hypothesis does not primarily focus on attention, attentional disengagement from a boring activity might facilitate the search for meaningful alternatives by shifting attention elsewhere (see also Van Tilburg and Igou 2017a). Furthermore, we suggest that the behaviors that follow from boredom's guiding function (e.g., Elpidorou 2014) likely are those that people perceive as meaningful (Van Tilburg and Igou 2013).

Research has yet to examine the conditions under which boredom evokes a search for meaning process versus the conditions under which boredom evokes attempted avoidance of the meaningless situation altogether (Goldenberg et al. 2006). We assume that contextual variables such as the availability of meaning sources from which people can glean meaning are central in this regard, but also the ease with which people can turn to distractors from meaning (Moynihan et al. 2015, 2017, 2019). Additional variables might be associated with people's individual differences in motivational orientations such as approach versus avoidance orientations or individual differences in regulatory focus (e.g., Smith et al. 2009).

Boredom's Regulation of Symbolic Resources: Meaning as a Case in Point

Boredom is involved in basic self-regulatory processes; managing interest, challenge, and perhaps arousal (e.g., Sansone et al. 1992; Van Tilburg and Igou 2012; Westgate et al. 2018). Yet, at the same time, boredom appears linked to nothing less than the regulation of perceived meaning in life (Van Tilburg and Igou 2011a; Van Tilburg et al. 2013; Van Tilburg et al. 2019c), and, if we were to take some philosophers' words at face value, its reality might even cause us to doubt the value of existence itself (Schopenhauer 1851 [trans. 2009]). It seems that, on the one hand, boredom regulates some of the most basic of psychological and physiological processes, while, on the other hand, it is a grave existential threat. What is going on? How can this emotion be accused of such divergent roles at the same time?

We want to first clarify that the involvement of the same emotion in the regulation of 'basic' and 'symbolic' resources is not uncommon. Take disgust for example. This emotion is surely essential for regulating consumption; and the rejection of foul-tasting food in particular (e.g., Rozin 1996). Yet, at the same time, disgust serves to regulate responses to perceived moral transgressions (Russell and Giner-Sorolla 2011). Transcending its, presumably initial, basic origins, disgust seems to have been incorporated through cultural evolution as an emotion that more broadly regulates 'distaste' at a symbolic level (Rozin 1996).

Might boredom have been similarly hijacked for its utility in humans' symbolic words, transcending its more basic functions? Of course, this is a question that is difficult to answer, especially given the relatively recent entrance that boredom made on the stage of psychological science. Nonetheless, some initial evidence indicates that, depending on availability, boredom can cause the pursuit of both 'pre-symbolic' (basic) resources and symbolic resources (Moynihan et al. 2015; 2017). Speculatively, the basic self-regulatory function of boredom is one that serves exploration (e.g., Geana, et al. 2016); encouraging one to venture into unknown territories, with the (risky) prospect of access to new or uncontested resources. Within a world of symbolic resources, this basic 'exploration' motive might have been adapted for meaning-search, perhaps facilitating the acquisition of knowledge, encouraging unconventional learning, and promoting creativity (e.g., Mann and Robinson 2009). A caged animal might try to escape its dull existence by breaking free and finding play, food, and mates; the chained human, trapped in Plato's Cave (Plato, *Republic*), might break free from perpetual dull shadow play by venturing into the light in search of meaning. What unites these prisoners is perhaps their boredom.

References

Adler, M. G., & Fagley, N. S. (2005). Appreciation: Individual differences in finding value and meaning as a unique predictor of subjective well-being. *Journal of Personality, 73*(1), 79–114. https://doi.org/10.1111/j.1467-6494.2004.00305.x.

Baumeister, R. F. (1992). *Meaning of life*. New York, NY: The Guilford Press.

Baumeister, R. F., & Vohs, K. D. (2004). *Handbook of self-regulation: Research, theory, and applications*. New York, NY: The Guilford Press.

Blaszczynski, A., McConaghy, N., & Frankova, A. (1990). Boredom proneness in pathological gambling. *Psychological Reports, 67*(1), 35–42. https://doi.org/10.2466/pr0.67.5.35-42.

Bonebright, C. A., Clay, D. L., & Ankenmann, R. D. (2000). The relationship of workaholism with work-life conflict, life satisfaction, and purpose in life. *Journal of Counseling Psychology, 47*(4), 469–477. https://doi.org/10.1037/0022-0167.47.4.469.

Burrow, A. L., & Rainone, N. (2017). How many likes did I get? Purpose moderates links between positive social media feedback and self-esteem. *Journal of Experimental Social Psychology, 69*, 232–236. https://doi.org/10.1016/j.jesp.2016.09.005.

Carver, C. S. (2004). Negative affects deriving from the behavioral approach system. *Emotion, 4* (1), 3–22. https://doi.org/10.1037/1528-3542.4.1.3.

Case, T. I., & Williams, K. D. (2004). Ostracism: A metaphor for death. In J. Greenberg, S. L. Koole, & T. Pyszczynski (Eds.), *Handbook of experimental existential psychology* (pp. 336–368). New York: Guilford Press.

Castano, E., Yzerbyt, V., Paladino, M. P., & Sacchi, S. (2002). I belong, therefore, I exist: Ingroup identification, ingroup entitativity, and ingroup bias. *Personality and Social Psychology Bulletin, 28*(2), 135–143. https://doi.org/10.1177/0146167202282001.

Chan, C. S., Van Tilburg, W. A. P., Igou, E. R., Poon, C. Y. S., Tam, K. Y. Y., Wong, W., et al. (2018). Situational meaninglessness and state boredom: Cross-sectional and experience-sampling findings. *Motivation and Emotion, 42*(471), 555–565. https://doi.org/10.1007/s11031-018-9693-3.

Chin, A., Markey, A., Bhargava, S., Kassam, K. S., & Loewenstein, G. (2017). Bored in the USA: Experience sampling and boredom in everyday life. *Emotion, 17*(2), 359–368. https://doi.org/10.1037/emo0000232.

Cleary, M., Sayers, J., Lopez, V., & Hungerford, C. (2016). Boredom in the workplace: Reasons, impact, and solutions. *Issues in Mental Health Nursing, 37*(2), 83–89. https://doi.org/10.3109/01612840.2015.1084554.

Coughlan, G., Igou, E. R., Van Tilburg, W. A. P., Kinsella, E. L., & Ritchie, T. D. (2019). On boredom and perception of heroes: A meaning-regulation approach to heroism. *Journal of Humanistic Psychology, 59*, 455–473. https://doi.org/10.1111/jtsb.12094.

Csíkszentmihályi, M. (1990). *The domain of creativity*. Thousand Oaks, CA: Sage Publications Inc.

Cummings, M. L., Mastracchio, C., Thornburg, K. M., & Mkrtchyan, A. (2013). Boredom and distraction in multiple unmanned vehicle supervisory control. *Interacting with Computers, 25* (1), 34–47. https://doi.org/10.1093/iwc/iws011.

Dahlen, E. R., Martin, R. C., Ragan, K., & Kuhlman, M. M. (2004). Boredom proneness in anger and aggression: Effects of impulsiveness and sensation seeking. *Personality and Individual Differences, 37*(8), 1615–1627. https://doi.org/10.1016/j.paid.2004.02.016.

Debats, D. L., Van der Lubbe, P. M., & Wezeman, F. R. A. (1993). On the psychometric properties of the Life Regard Index (LRI): A measure of meaningful life. *Personality and Individual Differences, 14*(2), 337–345. https://doi.org/10.1016/0191-8869(93)90132-M.

Deci, E. L., & Ryan, R. M. (2000). The "what" and "why" of goal pursuits: Human needs and the self-determination of behavior. *Psychological Inquiry, 11*(4), 227–268. https://doi.org/10.1207/S15327965PLI1104_01.

Denny, K. N., Loth, K., Eisenberg, M. E., & Neumark-Sztainer, D. (2013). Intuitive eating in young adults. Who is doing it, and how is it related to disordered. *Appetite, 60*(1), 13–19. https://doi.org/10.1016/j.appet.2012.09.029.

Eastwood, J. D., Frischen, A., Fenske, M. J., & Smilek, D. (2012). The unengaged mind: Defining boredom in terms of attention. *Perspectives on Psychological Science, 7*(5), 482–495. https://doi.org/10.1177/1745691612456044.

Elpidorou, A. (2014). The bright side of boredom. *Frontiers in Psychology, 5*, 1245. https://doi.org/10.3389/fpsyg.2014.01245.

Elpidorou, A. (2017). The moral dimensions of boredom: A call for research. *Review of General Psychology, 21*(1), 30–48. https://doi.org/10.1007/s10746-013-9298-5.

Elpidorou, A. (2018a). The bored mind is a guiding mind: Toward a regulatory theory of boredom. *Phenomenology and the Cognitive Sciences, 17*(3), 455–484. https://doi.org/10.1007/s11097-017-9515-1.

Elpidorou, A. (2018b). The good of boredom. *Philosophical Psychology, 31*(3), 323–351. https://doi.org/10.1080/09515089.2017.1346240.

Fahlman, S. A., Mercer, K. B., Gaskovski, P., Eastwood, A. E., & Eastwood, J. D. (2009). Does a lack of life meaning cause boredom? Results from psychometric, longitudinal, and experimental analyses. *Journal of Social and Clinical Psychology, 28*, 307–340. https://doi.org/10.1521/jscp.2009.28.3.307.

Fahlman, S. A., Mercer-Lynn, K. B., Flora, D. B., & Eastwood, J. D. (2013). Development and validation of the multidimensional state boredom scale. *Assessment, 20*(1), 68–85. https://doi.org/10.1177/1073191111421303.

Farmer, R., & Sundberg, N. D. (1986). Boredom proneness—The development and correlates of a new scale. *Journal of Personality Assessment, 50*(1), 4–17. https://doi.org/10.1207/s15327752jpa5001_2.

Ferrari, J. R., O'Callaghan, J., & Newbegin, I. (2005). Prevalence of procrastination in the United States, United Kingdom, and Australia: Aarousal and avoidance delays among adults. *North American Journal of Psychology, 7*, 1–6.

Frijda, N. H., Kuipers, P., & Ter Schure, E. (1989). Relations among emotion, appraisal, and emotional action readiness. *Journal of Personality and Social Psychology, 57*(2), 212–228. https://doi.org/10.1037/0022-3514.57.2.212.

Fromm, E. (1968). *The revolution of hope. Toward a humanized technology*. New York, NY: Harper & Row.

Fromm, E. (1973). *The anatomy of human destructiveness*. New York, NY: Holt, Rinehart, & Winston.

Geana, A., Wilson, R., Daw, N. D., & Cohen, J. (2016). Boredom, information-seeking and exploration. In A. Papafragou, D. Grodner, D. Mirman, & J. C. Trueswell (Eds.), *Proceedings of the Cognitive Science Society* (pp. 1751–1756). Austin, TX: Cognitive Science Society.

Goldberg, Y. K., Eastwood, J. D., LaGuardia, J., & Danckert, J. (2011). Boredom: An emotional experience distinct from apathy, anhedonia, or depression. *Journal of Social and Clinical Psychology, 30*(6), 647–666. https://doi.org/10.1521/jscp.2011.30.6.647.

Goldenberg, J. L., Kosloff, S., & Greenberg, J. (2006). Existential underpinnings of approach and avoidance of the physical body. *Motivation and Emotion, 30*(2), 127–134. https://doi.org/10.1007/s11031-006-9023-z.

Gordon, A., Wilkinson, R., McGown, A., & Jovanoska, S. (1997). The psychometric properties of the Boredom Proneness Scale: An examination of its validity. *Psychological Studies, 42,* 85–97. https://doi.org/10.2466/PMS.71.7.963-966.

Green, J., Van Tongeren, D., Cairo, A., & Hagiwara, N. (2017). Heroism and the pursuit of meaning. In S. T. Allison, G. R. Goethals, & R. M. Kramer (Eds.), *Handbook of heroism and heroic leadership* (pp. 507–524). New York, NY: Routledge.

Greenberg, J., Koole, S. L., & Pyszczynski, T. (2004). *Handbook of experimental existential psychology*. New York, NY: The Guilford Press.

Heine, S. J., Proulx, T., & Vohs, K. D. (2006). The meaning maintenance model: On the coherence of social motivations. *Personality and Social Psychology Review, 10*(2), 88–110. https://doi.org/10.1207/s15327957pspr1002_1.

Heintzelman, S. J., & King, L. A. (2014). (The feeling of) meaning-as-information. *Personality and Social Psychology Review, 18*(2), 153–167. https://doi.org/10.1177/1088868313518487.

Hepper, E. G., Ritchie, T. D., Sedikides, C., & Wildschut, T. (2012). Odyssey's end: Lay conceptions of nostalgia reflect its original Homeric meaning. *Emotion, 12*(1), 102–119. https://doi.org/10.1037/a0025167.

Hunter, A., & Eastwood, J. D. (2018). Does state boredom cause failures of attention? Examining the relations between trait boredom, state boredom, and sustained attention. *Experimental Brain Research, 236*(9), 2483–2492. https://doi.org/10.1007/s00221-016-4749-7.

Iso-Ahola, S. E., & Crowley, E. D. (1991). Adolescent substance abuse and leisure boredom. *Journal of Leisure Research, 23*(3), 260–271. https://doi.org/10.1080/00222216.1991.11969857.

Janoff-Bulman, R., & Yopyk, D. K. (2004). Random outcomes and valued commitments: Existential dilemmas and the paradox of meaning. In J. Greenberg, S. L. Koole, & T. Pyszczynski (Eds.), *Handbook of experimental existential psychology* (pp. 122–138). New York, NY: The Guilford Press.

Jonas, E., Schimel, J., Greenberg, J., & Pyszczynski, T. (2002). The Scrooge effect: Evidence that mortality salience increases prosocial attitudes and behavior. *Personality and Social Psychology Bulletin, 28*(10), 1342–1353. https://doi.org/10.1177/014616702236834.

Jost, J. T., Fitzsimons, G., & Kay, A. C. (2004). The ideological animal. In J. Greenberg, S. L. Koole, & T. Pyszczynski (Eds.), *Handbook of experimental psychology* (pp. 263–283). New York, NY: The Guilford Press.

Kasser, T., & Sheldon, K. M. (2004). Nonbecoming, alienated becoming, and authentic becoming: A goal-based approach. In J. Greenberg, S. L. Koole, & T. Pyszczynski (Eds.), *Handbook of experimental existential psychology* (pp. 480–493). New York, NY: The Guilford Press.

Kellett, S., & Gross, H. (2006). Addicted to joyriding? An exploration of young offenders' accounts of their car crime. *Psychology, Crime and Law, 12*(1), 39–59. https://doi.org/10.1080/10683160512331316343.

Kierkegaard, S. (1852). The rotation of crops: A venture in a theory of social prudence. *Søren Kierkegaard*. https://www.sorenkierkegaard.nl/. Accessed 26 Feb 2019.

King, L. A., Heintzelman, S. J., & Ward, S. J. (2016). Beyond the search for meaning: A contemporary science of the experience of meaning in life. *Current Directions in Psychological Science, 25*(4), 211–216. https://doi.org/10.1177/0963721416656354.

Kinsella, E. L., Igou, E. R., & Ritchie, T. D. (2019). Heroism and the pursuit of a meaningful life. *Journal of Humanistic Psychology, 59*, 474–498. https://doi.org/10.1177/0022167817701002.

Kruskal, J. B., & Wish, M. (1978). *Multidimensional scaling*. Newbury Park, CA: Sage Publications Inc.

Larson, R. W., & Richards, M. H. (1991). Boredom in the middle school years: Blaming schools versus blaming students. *American Journal of Education, 99*(4), 418–443. https://doi.org/10.1086/443992.

Leary, M. R., Rogers, P. A., Canfield, R. W., & Coe, C. (1986). Boredom in interpersonal encounters: Antecedents and social implications. *Journal of Personality and Social Psychology, 51*(5), 968–975. https://doi.org/10.1037/0022-3514.51.5.968.

Lerner, J. S., & Keltner, D. (2001). Fear, anger, and risk. *Journal of Personality and Social Psychology, 81*(1), 146–159. https://doi.org/10.1037//O022-3514.81.1.146.

MacDonald, D. A., & Holland, D. (2002). Spirituality and boredom proneness. *Personality and Individual Differences, 32*(6), 1113–1119. https://doi.org/10.1016/S0191-8869(01)00114-3.

Maher, P. J., Van Tilburg, W. A. P., & Van Den Tol, A. J. M. (2013). Meaning in music: Deviations from expectations in music prompt outgroup derogation. *European Journal of Social Psychology, 43*(6), 449–454. https://doi.org/10.1002/ejsp.1969.

Maher, P. J., Igou, E. R., & Van Tilburg, W. A. P. (2018). Brexit, Trump, and the polarizing effect of disillusionment. *Social Psychological and Personality Science, 9*(2), 205–213. https://doi.org/10.1177/1948550617750737.

Maher, P. J., Van Tilburg, W. A. P., & Igou, E. R. (2019). Lost in multidimensional space: Epistemic motivations define and distinguish negative affect. *Personality and Social Psychology Bulletin, 45*, 1409–1424. https://doi.org/10.1177/0146167219833395 .

Malkovsky, E., Merrifield, C., Goldberg, Y., & Danckert, J. (2012). Exploring the relationship between boredom and sustained attention. *Experimental Brain Research, 221*(1), 59–67. https://doi.org/10.1007/s00221-012-3147-z.

Mann, S., & Robinson, A. (2009). Boredom in the lecture theatre: An investigation into the contributors, moderators and outcomes of boredom amongst university students. *British Educational Research Journal, 35*(2), 243–258. https://doi.org/10.1080/01411920802042911.

Martin, M., Sadlo, G., & Stew, G. (2006). The phenomenon of boredom. *Qualitative Research in Psychology, 3*(3), 193–211. https://doi.org/10.1191/1478088706qrp066oa.

Melton, A. M., & Schulenberg, S. E. (2007). On the relationship between meaning in life and boredom proneness: Examining a logotherapy postulate. *Psychological Reports, 101*(3 Pt 2), 1016–1022. https://doi.org/10.2466/pr0.101.4.1016-1022.

Mikulas, W. L., & Vodanovich, S. J. (1993). The essence of boredom. *The Psychological Record, 43*, 3–12.

Moynihan, A. B., Van Tilburg, W. A. P., Igou, E. R., Wisman, A., Donnelly, A. E., & Mulcaire, J. B. (2015). Eaten up by boredom: Consuming food to escape awareness of the bored self. *Frontiers in psychology, 6*, 369. https://doi.org/10.3389/fpsyg.2015.00369.

Moynihan, A. D., Igou, E. R., & Van Tilburg, W. A. P. (2017). Boredom increases impulsiveness: A meaning-regulation perspective. *Social Psychology, 48*(5), 293–309. https://doi.org/10.1027/1864-9335/a000317.

Moynihan, A. B., Igou, E. R., & Van Tilburg, W. A. P. (2019). Lost in the crowd: Conformity as escape following disbelief in free will. *European Journal of Social Psychology, 49*(3), 504–520. https://doi.org/10.1002/ejsp.2499.

Norenzayan, A., & Hansen, I. G. (2006). Belief in supernatural agents in the face of death. *Personality and Social Psychology Bulletin, 32*(2), 174–187. https://doi.org/10.1177/0146167205280251.

Proulx, T., & Heine, S. J. (2010). The Frog in Kierkegaard's Beer: Finding meaning in the threat-compensation literature. *Social and Personality Psychology Compass, 4*(10), 889–905. https://doi.org/10.1111/j.1751-9004.2010.00304.x.

Proulx, T., & Inzlicht, M. (2012). The five "A" s of meaning maintenance: Finding meaning in the theories of sense-making. *Psychological Inquiry, 23*(4), 317–335. https://doi.org/10.1080/1047840X.2012.702372.

Randles, D., Proulx, T., & Heine, S. J. (2011). Turn-frogs and careful-sweaters: Non-conscious perception of incongruous word pairings provokes fluid compensation. *Journal of Experimental Social Psychology, 47*(1), 246–249. https://doi.org/10.1016/j.jesp.2010.07.020.

Rasmussen, H. N., Wrosch, C., Scheier, M. F., & Carver, C. S. (2006). Self-regulation processes and health: The importance of optimism and goal adjustment. *Journal of Personality, 74*(6), 1721–1748. https://doi.org/10.1111/j.1467-6494.2006.00426.x.

Reicher, S. D., Spears, R., & Postmes, T. (1995). A social identity model of deindividuation phenomena. *European Review of Social Psychology, 6*(1), 161–198. https://doi.org/10.1080/14792779443000049.

Reid, K. (2006). Raising school attendance: A case study of good practice in monitoring and raising standards. *Quality Assurance in Education, 14*(3), 199–216. https://doi.org/10.1108/09684880610678531.

Routledge, C., Wildschut, T., Sedikides, C., Juhl, J., & Arndt, J. (2012). The power of the past: Nostalgia as a meaning-making resource. *Memory, 20*(5), 452–460. https://doi.org/10.1080/09658211.2012.677452.

Rozin, P. (1996). Towards a psychology of food and eating: From motivation to module to model to marker, morality, meaning, and metaphor. *Current Directions in Psychological Science, 5* (1), 18–24. https://doi.org/10.1111/1467-8721.ep10772690.

Rupp, D. E., & Vodanovich, S. J. (1997). The role of boredom proneness in self-reported anger and aggression. *Journal of Social Behavior and Personality, 12*(4), 925–936.

Russell, P. S., & Giner-Sorolla, R. (2011). Moral anger, but not moral disgust, responds to intentionality. *Emotion, 11*(2), 233–240. https://doi.org/10.1037/a0022598.

Ryan, R. M., & Deci, E. L. (2004). Autonomy is no illusion: Self-determination theory and the empirical study of authenticity, awareness, and will. In J. Greenberg, S. L. Koole, & T. Pyszczynski (Eds.), *Handbook of experimental existential psychology* (pp. 449–479). New York, NY: The Guilford Press.

Sahin, S., Arseven, Z., & Kiliç, A. (2016). Causes of student absenteeism and school dropouts. *International Journal of Instruction, 9*(1), 195–210. https://doi.org/10.12973/iji.2016.9115a.

Sansone, C., Weir, C., Harpster, L., & Morgan, C. (1992). Once a boring task always a boring task? Interest as a self-regulatory strategy. *Journal of Personality and Social Psychology, 63* (3), 379–390. https://doi.org/10.1037/0022-3514.63.3.379.

Scherer, K. R. (2001). Appraisal considered as a process of multilevel sequential checking. In K. R. Scherer, A. Schorr, & R. Johnstone (Eds.), *Appraisal processes in emotion. Theory, Methods, Research* (pp. 92–120). New York, NY: Oxford University Press.

Schmader, T., & Lickel, B. (2006). The approach and avoidance function of guilt and shame emotions: Comparing reactions to self-caused and other-caused wrongdoing. *Motivation and Emotion, 30*(1), 42–55. https://doi.org/10.1007/s11031-006-9006-0.

Schopenhauer, A. (1851 [2009]). The essays of Arthur Schopenhauer. *BiblioBazaar*. https://books.google.ie/books?id=5eWCI1UjvikC&lpg=PP1&pg=PP1#v=onepage&q&f=false Accessed 26 Feb 2018.

Sedikides, C., Wildschut, T., Routledge, C., & Arndt, J. (2015). Nostalgia counteracts self-discontinuity and restores self-continuity. *European Journal of Social Psychology, 45* (1), 52–61. https://doi.org/10.1002/ejsp.2073.

Sjöberg, M., Beck, I., Rasmussen, B. H., & Edberg, A. K. (2018). Being disconnected from life: meanings of existential loneliness as narrated by frail older people. *Aging and Mental Health, 22*(10), 1357–1364. https://doi.org/10.1080/13607863.2017.1348481.

Smith, J. L., Wagaman, J., & Handley, I. M. (2009). Keeping it dull or making it fun: Task variation as a function of promotion versus prevention focus. *Motivation and Emotion, 33,* 150–160. https://doi.org/10.1007/s11031-008-9118-9.

Sommers, J., & Vodanovich, S. J. (2000). Boredom proneness: Its relationship to psychological-and physical-health symptoms. *Journal of Clinical Psychology, 56*(1), 149–155. https://doi.org/10.1002/(SICI)1097-4679(200001)56:13.0.

Spears, R., Scheepers, D., Jetten, J., Doosje, B., Ellemers, N., & Postmes, T. (2004). Entitativity, group distinctiveness, and social identity: Getting and using social structure. In V. Yzerbyt, C. M. Judd, & O. Corneille (Eds.), *The psychology of group perception: Perceived variability, entitativity, and essentialism* (pp. 293–316). New York, NY: Psychology Press.

Steger, M. F., Frazier, P., Oishi, S., & Kaler, M. (2006). The meaning in life questionnaire: Assessing the presence of and search for meaning in life. *Journal of Counseling Psychology, 53*(1), 80–93. https://doi.org/10.1037/0022-0167.53.1.80.

Steger, M. F., Kashdan, T. B., Sullivan, B. A., & Lorentz, D. (2008). Understanding the search for meaning in life: Personality, cognitive style, and the dynamic between seeking and experiencing meaning. *Journal of Personality, 76*(2), 199–228. https://doi.org/10.1111/j.1467-6494.2007.00484.x.

Steger, M. F., Oishi, S., & Kashdan, T. B. (2009). Meaning in life across the life span: Levels and correlates of meaning in life from emerging adulthood to older adulthood. *The Journal of Positive Psychology, 4*(1), 43–52. https://doi.org/10.1080/17439760802303127.

Stephan, E., Sedikides, C., Wildschut, T., Cheung, W. Y., Routledge, C., & Arndt, J. (2015). Nostalgia-evoked inspiration: Mediating mechanisms and motivational implications. *Personality and Social Psychology Bulletin, 41*(10), 1395–1410. https://doi.org/10.1177/0146167215596985.

Struk, A. A., Scholer, A. A., & Danckert, J. (2016). A self-regulatory approach to understanding boredom proneness. *Cognition and Emotion, 30*(8), 1388–1401. https://doi.org/10.1080/02699931.2015.1064363.

Sulea, C., Van Beek, I., Sarbescu, P., Virga, D., & Schaufeli, W. B. (2015). Engagement, boredom, and burnout among students: Basic need satisfaction matters more than personality traits. *Learning and Individual Differences, 42*, 132–138. https://doi.org/10.1016/j.lindif.2015.08.018.

Svendsen, L. (2005). *A philosophy of boredom*. London: Reaktion Books.

Thiele, L. P. (1997). Postmodernity and the routinization of novelty: Heidegger on boredom and technology. *Polity, 29*, 489–517.

Van den Bos, K., Poortvliet, P. M., Maas, M., Miedema, J., & Van den Ham, E. J. (2005). An enquiry concerning the principles of cultural norms and values: The impact of uncertainty and mortality salience on reactions to violations and bolstering of cultural worldviews. *Journal of Experimental Social Psychology, 41*(2), 91–113. https://doi.org/10.1016/j.jesp.2004.06.001.

Van Tilburg, W. A. P., & Igou, E. R. (2011a). On boredom and social identity: A pragmatic meaning-regulation approach. *Personality and Social Psychology Bulletin, 37*(12), 1679–1691. https://doi.org/10.1177/0146167211418530.

Van Tilburg, W. A. P., & Igou, E. R. (2011b). On the meaningfulness of existence: When life salience boosts adherence to worldviews. *European Journal of Social Psychology, 41*(6), 740–750. https://doi.org/10.1002/ejsp.819.

Van Tilburg, W. A. P., & Igou, E. R. (2012). On boredom: Lack of challenge and meaning as distinct boredom experiences. *Motivation and Emotion, 36*(2), 181–194. https://doi.org/10.1007/s11031-011-9234-9.

Van Tilburg, W. A. P., & Igou, E. R. (2013). On the meaningfulness of behavior: An expectancy x value approach. *Motivation and Emotion, 37*(3), 373–388. https://doi.org/10.1007/s11031-012-9316-3.

Van Tilburg, W. A. P., Igou, E. R., & Sedikides, C. (2013). In search of meaningfulness: Using nostalgia as an antidote to boredom. *Emotion, 13*(3), 450–461. https://doi.org/10.1037/a0030442.

Van Tilburg, W. A. P., Sedikides, C., & Wildschut, T. (2015). The mnemonic muse: Nostalgia fosters creativity through openness to experience. *Journal of Experimental Social Psychology, 59*, 1–7. https://doi.org/10.1016/j.jesp.2015.02.002.

Van Tilburg, W. A. P., & Igou, E. R. (2016). Going to political extremes in response to boredom. *European Journal of Social Psychology, 46*(6), 687–699. https://doi.org/10.1002/ejsp.2205.

Van Tilburg, W. A. P., & Igou, E. R. (2017a). Boredom begs to differ: Differentiation from other negative emotions. *Emotion, 17*(2), 309–322. https://doi.org/10.1037/emo0000233.

Van Tilburg, W. A. P., & Igou, E. R. (2017b). Can boredom help? Increased prosocial intentions in response to boredom. *Self and Identity, 16*(1), 82–96. https://doi.org/10.1080/15298868.2016.1218925.

Van Tilburg, W. A. P., Wildschut, T., & Sedikides, S. (2018). Nostalgia's place among self-relevant emotions. *Cognition and Emotion, 32*(4), 742–759. https://doi.org/10.1080/02699931.2017.1351331.

Van Tilburg, W. A. P., Igou, E. R., Maher, P. J., & Lennon, J. (2019a). Various forms of existential distress are associated with aggressive tendencies. *Personality and Individual Differences, 144,* 111–119. https://doi.org/10.1016/j.paid.2019.02.032.

Van Tilburg, W. A. P., Bruder, M., Wildschut, T., Sedikides, C., & Göritz, A. (2019b). An appraisal profile of nostalgia. *Emotion, 19*(1), 21–36. https://doi.org/10.1037/emo0000417.

Van Tilburg, W. A. P., Igou, E. R., Maher, P. J., Moynihan, A. B., & Martin, A. (2019c). Bored like hell: Religiosity reduces boredom and tempers the quest for meaning. *Emotion, 19*(2), 255–269. https://doi.org/10.1037/emo0000439.

Van Tilburg, W. A. P., Sedikides, C., & Wildschut, T. (2019d). Adverse weather evokes nostalgia. *Personality and Social Psychology Bulletin, 44*(7), 984–995. https://doi.org/10.1177/0146167218756030.

Van Tilburg, W. A. P., Sedikides, C., Wildschut, T., & Vingerhoets, A. J. J. M. (2019e). How nostalgia infuses life with meaning: From social connectedness to self-continuity. *European Journal of Social Psychology, 49*(3), 521–532. https://doi.org/10.1002/ejsp.2519.

Vodanovich, S. J. (2003). Psychometric measures of boredom: A review of the literature. *The Journal of Psychology, 137*(6), 569–595. https://doi.org/10.1080/00223980309600636.

Vodanovich, S. J., & Watt, J. D. (2016). Self-report measures of boredom: An updated review of the literature. *The Journal of Psychology, 150*(2), 196–228. https://doi.org/10.1080/00223980.2015.1074531.

Vodanovich, S. J., Verner, K. M., & Gilbride, T. V. (1991). Boredom proneness: Its relationship to positive and negative affect. *Psychological Reports, 69*(3 Pt 2), 1139–1146. https://doi.org/10.2466/PR0.69.8.1139-1146.

Weinberg, A. (2016). When the work is not enough: The sinister stress of boredom. Stress: Concepts. *Cognition, Emotion, and Behavior, 1,* 195–201. https://doi.org/10.1016/B978-0-12-800951-2.00023-6.

Westgate, E. C., & Wilson, T. D. (2018). Boring thoughts and bored minds: The MAC model of boredom and cognitive engagement. *Psychological Review, 125*(5), 689–713. https://doi.org/10.1037/rev0000097.

Weybright, E. H., Caldwell, L. L., Xie, H., Wegner, L., & Smith, E. A. (2017). Predicting secondary school dropout among South African adolescents: A survival analysis approach. *South African Journal of Education, 37*(2), 1353. https://doi.org/10.15700/saje.v37n2a1353.

Wilson, T. D., Reinhard, D. A., Westgate, E. C., Gilbert, D. T., Ellerbeck, N., Hahn, C., et al. (2014). Just think: The challenge of the disengaged mind. *Science, 345*(6192), 75–77. https://doi.org/10.1126/science.1250830.

Wink, P., & Donahue, K. (1997). The relation between two types of narcissism and boredom. *Journal of Research in Personality, 31*(1), 136–140. https://doi.org/10.1006/jrpe.1997.2176.

Zeeck, A., Stelzer, N., Linster, H. W., Joos, A., & Hartmann, A. (2011). Emotion and eating in binge eating disorder and obesity. *European Eating Disorders Review, 19*(5), 426–437. https://doi.org/10.1002/erv.1066.

Wijnand A. P. van Tilburg received his Bachelors and Research Masters degrees in psychology from Tilburg University in 2006 and 2008, respectively. In 2011, he completed his Ph.D. degree at the University of Limerick, investigating the psychological signature and consequences of boredom in collaboration with Dr. Eric Igou. This was followed by a post as a lecturer (Assistant Professor) in Psychology, lecturing mainly on statistics and economic psychology. In April 2013, he joined the School of Psychology of the University of Southampton as Research Fellow working primarily with Prof. Constantine Sedikides and Dr. Tim Wildschut. Since September 2015, he is a lecturer at King's College London. He is a social cognition researcher. His research mainly concerns decision-making, emotion, and motivation, using experimental methods. A major part of his research involves the study of nostalgia and boredom, and how these experiences affect phenomena such as economic behavior, intergroup processes, and self-regulation. In addition to the above, he is also involved in research on game theory and existential psychology. A selection of his work on boredom: "On boredom and social identity: A paradigmatic meaning-regulation approach" (*Personality and Social Psychology Bullet*, 2011), "On boredom: Lack of challenge and meaning as distinct boredom experiences" (*Motivation and Emotion*, 2012), "In search of meaningfulness: Nostalgia as an antidote to boredom" (*Emotion*, 2013), "Eaten up by boredom: consuming food to escape awareness awareness of the bored self" (*Frontiers in Psychology*, 2015), and "Boredom begs to differ: Differentiation from other negative emotions" (*Emotion*, 2017).

Eric R. Igou received his Ph.D. from the University of Heidelberg in 2000 (summa cum laude; supervisor and mentor: Herbert Bless). Since then, he worked at the University of Mannheim, the New School University (fellowship), New York University (fellowship; mentor: Yaacov Trope), Tilburg University (tenured), and now the University of Limerick. He joined the University of Limerick in 2008 to become part of a newly formed and growing Department of Psychology. Here, he led the development of two postgraduate courses (M.Sc. in Psychological Science and MA in Psychology), served for a number of years as their Course Director, Head of Department, and Transnational Coordinator Psychology Education. He is currently the Academic Coordinator of the Psychology Department. In general terms, he investigates social judgments from a social cognitive perspective as well as existential concerns triggered by mortality and life salience, boredom, and disillusionment, and how people respond to these threats motivationally and cognitively. He is the co-author of all the above-mentioned publications with an h-index of 19.

Chapter 3
Boredom: Managing the Delicate Balance Between Exploration and Exploitation

James Danckert

Introduction

> Man is the only animal that can be *bored*.
>
> Eric Fromm (1955)

In the modern world, we have little opportunity to forage for food. At pick-your-own fruit farms, we can reconnect with a behavior common across the animal kingdom and reveal ourselves to be more similar to animals than we might want to admit. As you stand in front of a blueberry bush, you don't pick it clean before moving on. Instead, at some point you decide that this bush is no longer worth the effort and you move on in search of a more plentiful bounty. This describes the tension between two drives: to exploit known resources and to explore the environment to minimize opportunity costs (Charnov 1976). This tension between exploiting resources and exploring the world need not be limited to foraging. Minimizing opportunity costs—making sure we explore sufficiently to ensure that optimal rewards/resources don't go begging—applies to a broad range of adaptive decision-making contexts (Kurzban et al. 2013; see Box 1 for a computational approach). But how does it relate to boredom?

Boredom is an unpleasant state of wanting, but failing, to engage with the world–what Tolstoy called 'a desire for desires' (1899; Danckert et al. 2018b; Eastwood et al. 2012). When bored, we are dissatisfied by what we are currently doing—whether that is due to monotony, a lack of meaning, or because we feel compelled to do something we'd rather not (see Danckert et al. 2018b for review). Beyond those contingencies, when bored we are incapable of *satisfying* the need to be engaged—we can't find a thing to do, and nothing seems like it will suffice. Ultimately, this is the paradox of boredom, the uncomfortable feeling that we want

J. Danckert (✉)
University of Waterloo, Waterloo, Canada
e-mail: jdancker@uwaterloo.ca

J. Ros Velasco (ed.), *Boredom Is in Your Mind*,
https://doi.org/10.1007/978-3-030-26395-9_3

something to be engaged in (something to exploit), coupled with a failure to find something that will satisfy (a failure launch into exploration mode).

This chapter first outlines the value of exploration as a basic need evident across many species. The signal to explore may itself be borne of failures to maintain engagement—that is, a failure to fully deploy our skills and talents in the service of the current task. This frames state boredom within the context of the dual drives of exploration and exploitation. The second half of the chapter explores failures to heed this signal characteristic of the highly boredom prone. In doing so, I outline some novel hypotheses concerning the profile of highly boredom prone individuals from behaviors unsuited to engagement, to genetic associations with foraging and neurotransmitter systems critical for value/reward processing, to brain activity associated with being bored.

The Value of Exploration

Humans and animals alike can be crudely characterized by basic drives that satisfy our need for survival as individuals (i.e., hunger and thirst) and as a species (i.e., reproduction). But are these the only drives that shape behavior? Writing in the late 1950s, White (1959) suggested that humans (and animals) have a drive to explore. This flew in the face of conventional wisdom built not only on decades of animal research but on the very methodology used to study animal behavior—a method largely unaltered to this day. Animals work for rewards. A typical experiment first places the animal on a mild starvation diet prior to testing. As they perform the task, desired behaviors are rewarded with a sip of juice or pellet of food. The deprivations of a basic need prime the animal to work in a desired way. But there are myriad examples of animals working to achieve goals independent of appetitive needs. Monkeys learn a repertoire of discriminatory abilities with the simple goal of opening a door to expose a novel view of the world (Butler and Harlow 1957). Such exploratory behavior is evident even when appetitive (i.e., thirst, hunger) drives are sated. Just giving monkeys a problem to solve (e.g., opening a clasp on a box) is enough to engender activity (Harlow et al. 1950; Harlow 1953). Clearly, there is a drive toward exploration in even some of the most basic behaviors—as White puts it "Even Pavlov, whose theory of behaviour was one of Spartan simplicity, could not do without an investigatory or orienting reflex" (1959, p. 298).

What function does exploration serve? White (1959) suggests is satisfies the need for effectance—turning the notion of stimulus–response relations on their head. We are not passive responders to stimuli but are driven to explore how our own actions influence the world—from response to effect (or stimulus). This drive to explore satisfies more than curiosity. Exploration is a powerful learning tool. By examining the consequences of our own actions on the world, we can successfully build mental models that accurately represent regularities (Filipowicz et al. 2016). Observation of infants provides ample evidence of this exploratory drive. An initial, automatic grasp reflex is quickly turned toward object-oriented action, which in turn allows the infant to explore their world—bringing objects to their mouths, banging them on available surfaces, and dropping them repeatedly only to immediately pick them up again. This serves no appetitive need, but is vital for learning the physical properties of the infant's world (Collard 1971; Sim and Xu 2017; Twomey and Westermann 2018).

Exploration represents one example of effectance motivation; the need to influence our surroundings also drives our desire for mastery, manipulation of objects within our world, and ultimately, a general need to maintain an optimal level of activity (a kind of homeostasis between mania and lethargy; White 1959). The outcomes toward which effectance motivation is driven cast it as an evolutionary need, vital for learning, adapting and, according to White, building self-esteem. The notion here is that the development of a robust sense of self depends to some extent on early success in effecting change in one's environs. For our understanding of boredom, failures to engage with the world characteristic of highly boredom prone individuals can be cast as frustrated attempts at effectance—or thwarted exploration. In adults, we do find that self-esteem and boredom proneness are negatively correlated (Fig. 3.1). What drives this correlation is a matter for future research, but persistent failures to exert influence in one's world—failures of the effectance drive—represent one potential candidate.

The need to effect change in our environment represents a powerful drive that serves a range of functional outcomes, one of which is exploration. Failing to satisfy that 'urge' may be a potent antecedent of boredom. This brings us back to opportunity costs and a functional account of boredom. Boredom signals rising opportunity costs (Kurzban et al. 2013; Gomez-Ramirez and Costa 2017). What we are doing now is not rewarding, too monotonous, or lacks meaning (Chan et al.

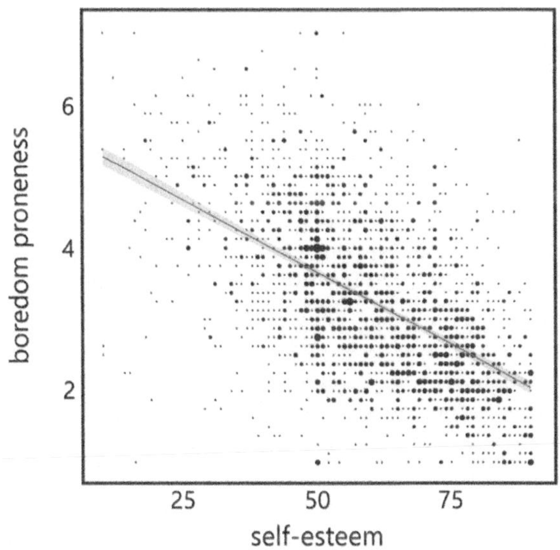

Fig. 3.1 Boredom proneness and self-esteem. Note: In a large sample (n = 2191) collected from Winter 2017, self-esteem is negatively correlated with boredom proneness. In repeated samples, this correlation ranges from −0.55 to −0.59. Circle size represents numbers of respondents—larger circles = more respondents

2018; Van Tilburg and Igou 2012, 2017), signaling the need to explore (Bench and Lench 2013; Elpidorou 2014, 2018). White makes the direct association between boredom and effectance motivation in this way:

> Boredom, the unpleasantness of monotony, the attraction of novelty, the tendency to vary behaviour rather than repeating it rigidly, and the seeking of stimulation and mild excitement stand as inescapable facts of human existence and clearly have their parallels in animal behaviour. (1959, pp. 314–315)

While it seems plausible that man is not alone in harboring a drive to explore, is there any evidence that animals do experience boredom?

Can Animals Be Bored?

As the quote from Fromm that begins this chapter highlights, many see boredom as uniquely human. In the context of the pursuit of self-knowledge, this seems plausible. As Fromm claims, humans see life as a problem demanding a solution and in pursuit of that solution we risk experiencing things as meaningless and boring. For Fluffy the cat this seems an unlikely existential crisis. She doesn't seem capable of questioning her place in the world and the value in her daily routine of eating, sleeping, scratching, and chasing a laser pointer. But in the context of effectance motivation, it seems plausible that animals can be bored—certainly for those in captivity. In other words, an animal—human or otherwise—prevented from effectively interacting with their world could become bored.

We have long known that rearing animals in impoverished environs has detrimental effects on health, leading to increased stress and poor coping strategies (Bolhuis et al. 2006; Carlstead 1996; Stevenson 1983). The flipside is also true, with increased neuroplasticity evident in animals reared in enriched environs (e.g., Kemperman et al. 2002, 1997; Young et al. 1999). But do impoverished environs lead to boredom in animals? Perhaps the most obvious sign of ennui in animals is increased rates of sleeping in captivity. Beyond sleep, animals in captivity demonstrate decreases in exploratory behavior, stereotypical actions such as pacing, and increased aggressive or fearful reactions to novel stimuli, all evidence of increased stress (Wemelsfelder 1993). More extreme behaviors including self-mutilation (birds plucking their own feathers out) have also been attributed to boredom (Burn 2017). But how does one determine whether these behaviors represent boredom and not some other state like depression or anxiety?

To address this question, Meagher and Mason (2012) examined the behavior of caged mink with one group of animals experiencing typical, non-enriched environs and a second group housed in more enriching cages that enabled exploratory behaviors. The intention was to distinguish between anhedonia (the inability to experience pleasure), apathy, and boredom in the animals (see Goldberg et al. 2011 for comparison of these emotions in humans). To do this, both groups—after having spent several weeks in their respective environs—were exposed to stimuli, including aversive stimuli (e.g., the odor of bobcat urine), rewarding stimuli (i.e., apparently a toothbrush is to a mink what a laser pointer is to a cat), and ambiguous or neutral stimuli (e.g., a plastic bottle). Using time to contact and duration of contact as metrics, the authors hypothesized that an anhedonic animal would fail to approach rewarding stimuli, an apathetic animal would show no interest in all stimulus types, and a bored animal would rapidly engage with all objects indiscriminately. Indeed, the mink housed in non-enriched cages more rapidly interacted with all stimulus types when compared with animals housed in enriched cages. Furthermore, the animals housed in non-enriched cages consumed significantly more treats at the end of the experiment than did animals housed in enriched cages, despite the fact that both groups had not experienced any prior restriction of diet. In other words, the bored animals were not hungry, just bored (overconsumption of food is a common response to boredom in humans too; Abramson and Stinson 1977; Crockett et al. 2015; Havermans et al. 2015).

It seems clear then that animals experience boredom, at least for animals in captivity (Burn 2017). It seems unlikely that wild animals, unconstrained by cages, would be as prone to the experience of boredom. But that is the point: Boredom is likely exacerbated for those animals *prevented* from engaging in species typical behaviors, normally effective in the wild. Linking effectance motivation (or the hindrance of satisfying effectance motivation) directly to boredom in man and animal casts boredom as a self-regulatory signal with a long evolutionary history. In some sense then Fromm is right—man is the only animal capable of being bored *despite* the fact that a full suite of possible actions remains available to him. This raises the question of why is it that some people are more prone to the experience than others?

A Failure to Launch and a Failure to Focus

How we choose to respond to the boredom signal can be either adaptive or not. For those high in boredom proneness, maladaptive responses may reflect dysfunctional exploration *and* exploitation. To highlight this state/trait distinction, on the exploration side state boredom signals the *need for* effectance, but does not signal *how* to satisfy that need. On the exploitation side, state boredom may arise in moments in which we become aware that we are failing to maintain attention/engagement on the task at hand. For those high in trait boredom, failures to engage may simply be experienced more frequently and intensely.[1] There are many

[1]In our own samples (n = 2.195), we asked how frequently and intensely people experienced boredom and correlated that with responses on the 8-item short version of the BPS. Frequency correlated at 0.64 and intensity at 0.49, both highly significant.

external contingencies, factors inherent to a particular environment or task that make boredom more likely. When things are repetitive or monotonous (Davies 1926; Thackray et al. 1977; Wyatt and Fraser 1929; Wyatt and Langdon 1937), when we see little value or purpose to a task (Van Tilburg and Igou 2012), or when we feel as though we lack autonomy, being forced to do things we would prefer not to (Watt and Vodanovich 1999), boredom takes hold. Similarly, there is a broad swathe of consequences for those who fail to adaptively respond when boredom strikes, from increased levels of depression, anxiety, and aggression (Dahlen et al. 2004; Farmer and Sundberg 1986; Goldberg et al. 2011; Isacescu et al. 2017), to problems with drugs of addiction and impulsive behaviors (Dahlen et al. 2004; Moynihan et al. 2017; Patterson and Pegg 1999). Finally, there are numerous individual characteristics more prominently associated with high boredom proneness, including higher levels of narcissism (Wink and Donahue 1997) and neuroticism (Mercer-Lynn et al. 2013).

Despite this body of research, we are left with the question of what it is that prevents some people from adaptively responding to the boredom signal. If boredom signifies rising opportunity costs that prompt exploration, why do the highly boredom prone fail to explore? Before addressing this question, it is worth asking whether or not there is any evidence that highly boredom prone individuals *do* indeed fail to launch into activities. We recently explored this by examining the relationship between two self-regulatory profiles and boredom proneness (Mugon et al. 2018). Kruglanski et al. (2000) outline two distinct regulatory modes—locomotion and assessment. The locomotion or 'just do it' mode is characterized by the propensity to move rapidly from one action to another, to 'get on with things.' People adopting the assessment mode are characterized by a tendency to consider possible avenues for action, weighing up pros and cons to ensure they 'do the right thing.' Research shows that we tend to favor one mode over another (e.g., Zee et al. 2018). For our purposes, the tendency to adopt a locomotion mode acts as a prophylactic against boredom, whereas adopting an assessment mode is associated with higher levels of boredom proneness (Mugon et al. 2018). These associations do suggest that the highly boredom struggle to launch into action and highlights a key paradox in boredom proneness. The state signals the need to act. But it is this demand for action that is precisely what highly boredom prone individuals find difficult to satisfy.

As yet the reasons for this failure to launch are underspecified. It may be that highly boredom prone individuals are less willing to exert effort, or at least *perceive* things to be more effortful. Highly boredom prone individuals may fail to accurately represent reward values. In other words, perhaps everything seems to be of little value, or at the very least equal value, making it impossible to choose one option for action among many. Fear of failure may keep the highly boredom prone rooted to the spot. If one lacks the confidence to believe a goal *can* be achieved, then why start in the first place? Indeed, self-esteem and boredom proneness are strongly negatively correlated and the highly boredom prone do tend to procrastinate more (Blunt and Pychyl 1998; Ferrari 2000). All of these challenges represent a hindrance toward both exploration and exploitation—a challenge to effective engagement.

The troubles for the highly boredom prone don't stop there. Even when an activity has been engaged, research shows that highly boredom prone people struggle to maintain focus, to stay engaged (Hunter and Eastwood 2018; Malkovsky et al. 2012). Rates of unintentional (and to a much lesser extent intentional) mind-wandering are higher in high boredom prone individuals (Isacescu et al. 2017). Trait boredom uniquely predicts failures of sustained attention (Hunter and Eastwood 2018). Furthermore, the psychophysical profile of boredom mirrors that of a disengaged attentional state, with heart rate rising and skin conductance levels dropping (Merrifield and Danckert 2014; Jang et al. 2015), a profile also seen in ADHD (Hermens et al. 2004). Higher boredom prone individuals have also been shown to have higher blink rates (Danckert et al. 2018a) which in turn are associated with increased mind-wandering (Smilek et al. 2010). All this points to a challenge in maintaining focus. The highly boredom prone individual struggles to launch into action despite acutely recognizing the need/desire to do so. Even when they do engage, they experience difficulty in maintaining that engagement.

A Boredom Prone Phenotype: Foraging and Beyond

As mentioned above, boredom proneness is associated with distinct profiles of goal pursuit (Mugon et al. 2018). This distinction in humans between locomotion and assessment has a parallel in the fruit fly, *Drosophila melanogaster* (de Belle and Sokolowski 1987; Hughson et al. 2018). When examining the so-called *foraging* gene, researchers show distinct phenotypes labeled rovers and sitters (see Sokolowski 2001 for review). Among myriad characteristics, rovers explore an environment more extensively in search of food than do sitters who hug the boundary of their environs even after 24 h of food deprivation (Hughson et al. 2018). In this analogy, human locomotors are akin to fruit fly rovers and assessors are similar to sitters. We explored whether or not these distinctions are conserved in the human equivalent of the *foraging* gene, *PRKG1* (Struk et al. 2019). We had people swipe a touch screen through a large environment, tapping on 'berries' to collect them. We characterized search paths into three patterns labeled boundary-biased, systematic, and mixed (Fig. 3.2). The presence of an A allele on *PRKG1* was associated with a preference for adopting an assessment regulatory mode and a boundary-biased search strategy—precisely what is seen in fruit fly sitters (Hughson et al. 2018; Struk et al. 2019).

Beyond associations with regulatory mode on *PRKG1*, we also observed differences on boredom proneness and self-control on other single-nucleotide polymorphisms (SNPs). On the dopamine transporter gene DAT1, the presence of the T allele was associated with higher levels of boredom proneness and lower levels of self-control (Fig. 3.2). Similarly, on catechol-*O*-methyltransferase (COMT), a gene involved in the breakdown of catecholamines such as dopamine, the presence of the T allele was associated with higher levels of boredom and lower levels of self-control (Fig. 3.2). The strong association between dopamine and reward

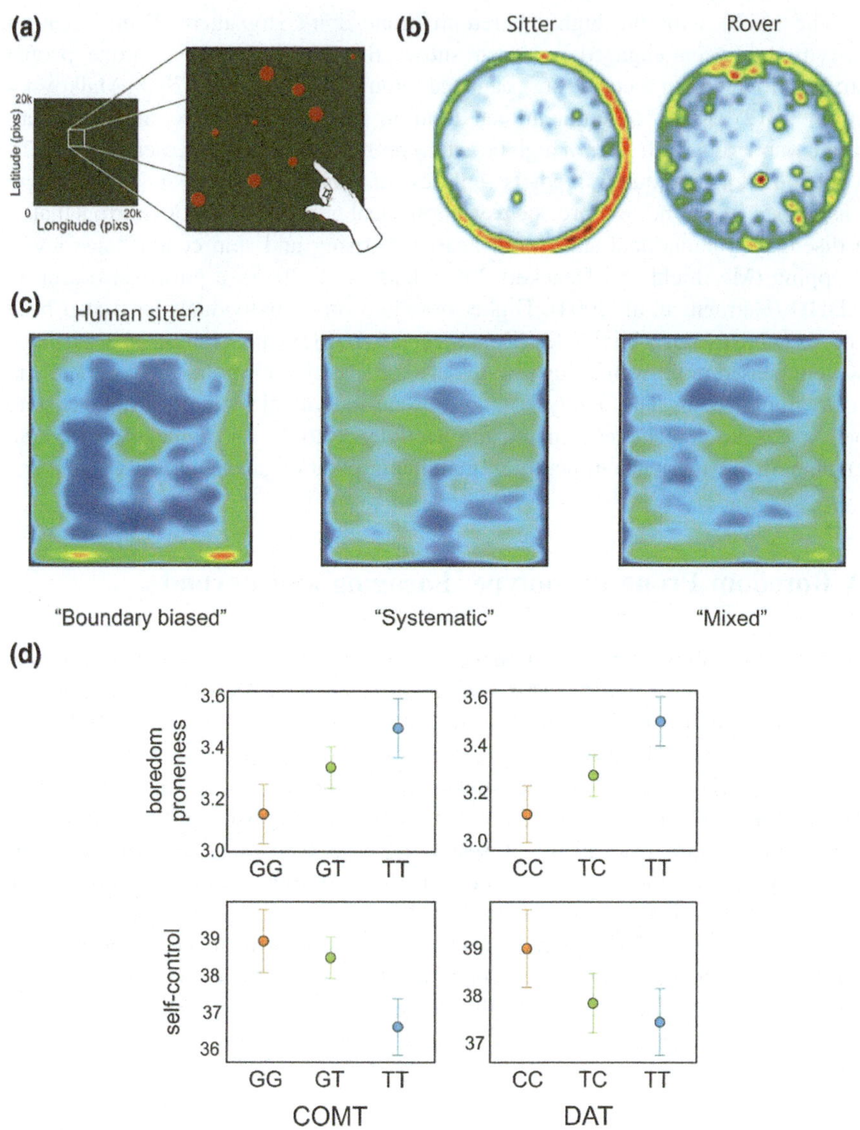

Fig. 3.2 Catechol-*O*-methyltransferase (COMT). Note: **a** Virtual foraging task: people swiped a touch screen tapping on berries to collect them. **b** Heat maps of search paths for fruit fly sitters and rovers in a dish with four food sources (adapted from Hughson et al. 2018). **c** Heat maps of search paths for humans on our foraging task. **d** Patterns of responses on boredom proneness and self-control questionnaires split by genotype on the COMT and DAT genes

processing (Cohen et al. 2005) may suggest that highly boredom prone individuals present with dysfunctional regulation of dopamine, a hypothesis clearly warranting further research.

The Neural Profile of Boredom

Research exploring the neural signature of boredom remains in its infancy. Although some work using EEG has been done (e.g., Tabatabaie et al. 2014), my focus here is on results from the handful of studies making use of functional MRI (Dal Mas and Wittman 2017; Danckert and Merrifield 2018; Danckert and Isacescu 2017; Ulrich et al. 2014, 2016). Ulrich et al. (2014; 2016) explored what some consider the opposite of boredom—the state of flow (Csíkszentmihályi 1990). Flow has a complex operationalization (e.g., nine components including time distortion, resistance to distraction, etc.) that might best be thought of as *extreme* engagement. Ulrich et al. (2014, 2016) manipulated the challenge level of math problems to engage either a state of flow (skill-challenge fit was optimized), or frustration (the task was beyond participants' capabilities), or boredom (the task was facile). In contrast to flow, activation during the bored state was seen in posterior components of the default mode network (DMN; Buckner et al. 2008). That is, activity was higher in the medial prefrontal cortex (mPFC; Ulrich et al. 2014) and posterior cingulate cortex (PCC; Ulrich et al. 2016).

Similarly, in two separate samples, we had people watch movies intended to make people sad, engaged, or bored while we scanned their brains (Danckert and Merrifield 2018; Danckert and Isacescu 2017). When bored, activity was correlated in the mPFC and PCC. In addition, we found that during the boredom mood induction activity in the anterior insular cortex was anticorrelated with the DMN (Danckert and Merrifield 2018; Danckert and Isacescu 2017). Dal Mas and Wittman (2017) had people indicate how much money they would be prepared to pay for a music download after having done boring or challenging tasks. People were willing to pay more for music after the boring task, which in turn was associated with increased activity in the insular. The involvement of the anterior insula in these studies is intriguing. Theories regarding the insular cast it in many roles, from representing salience (Uddin 2015), to exploring novel hypotheses to explain ambiguous stimuli (Stöttinger et al. 2015, 2018). Further work is needed to delineate the role this region plays in both the state of boredom (Danckert and Merrifield 2018) and in goal-directed behavior necessary for avoiding the state (i.e., engagement; Dal Mas and Wittman 2017).

Conclusion

Boredom pushes us to engage our minds in ways that allow us to effectively deploy our skills and talents. This doesn't mean hitting home runs with every action we take, or writing best sellers each time we put pen to paper. Rather, the call to action that is boredom is driven by a need to feel that whatever we are doing is impactful in some demonstrable way. In other words, boredom signals the need for effectance (White 1959). At any given moment that need may manifest as a drive to explore options for engagement or to exploit fully what we are doing right now. The conundrum for the highly boredom prone arises in the recognition of the desire to engage coupled with the failure to launch. This failure may be driven by many things, some of which we have evidence for (e.g., lack of meaning; Chan et al. 2018; Van Tilburg and Igou 2012) and some of which we don't (e.g., higher threshold for effort expenditure).

The challenge ahead in understanding boredom proneness is to understand the forces behind the conundrum of wanting but failing to satisfy the 'desire for desires.' The highly boredom prone individual may be searching not only for *something/anything* satisfying to engage with, but the *perfect* thing. The highly boredom prone may feel that nothing perfectly fits their needs—a kind of unrealistic Goldilocks ultimatum. Alternatively, the highly boredom prone may fail to stay engaged because they oscillate too readily between exploration and exploitation. Here too, there will be a Goldilocks zone for balancing the two drives, and the highly boredom prone may fail to achieve that balance. This notion has some bearing on the debate regarding boredom as either a high or low arousal state (Danckert et al. 2018). In the course of any given day, arousal naturally fluctuates. Perhaps for the highly boredom prone, such fluctuations are more rapid making engagement more challenging.

As hinted at, this ultimately places boredom proneness as a struggle to find a Goldilocks zone—the just right level for engagement. This idea is not new. Klapp (1986) suggested that boredom can be cast in terms of information theory–too little information signals a high level of redundancy/monotony—a ripe condition for boredom. Too much information ultimately impedes our ability to extract signal from noise rendering things meaningless and boring. I suggest that the drives of exploration and exploitation function to deal with this scale of information flow. When there is too little or too much for us to process—Klapp's redundancy and noise—we seek to explore new opportunities for engagement (see Gomez-Ramirez and Costa 2017 for a computational account that bears some resemblance to Klapp's ideas). When we find just the right amount of information for the goal(s) at hand, we buckle down and exploit the circumstances in service of that goal(s). The highly boredom prone struggle in both phases. One final thought is worth raising: It may be unreasonable to expect that any organism could *continuously* oscillate between exploration and exploitation, that we could immediately initiate the pursuit of one goal upon the completion of another. There is a case to be made for a refractory period–down time. We still have much to learn about cognitive effort and fatigue, but it seems plausible to suggest that the concepts capture something real about everyday experience. Perhaps for the boredom prone, people we know who tend to be impulsive (Kass and Vodanovich 1990; Watt and Vodanovich 1992), there is a kind of discomfort with the refractory period that typically follows the achievement of a goal. Clearly, a great deal of what is raised here is speculative. No time to be bored though, there's research to be done.

Box 1: Boredom, AI and the Dark room Problem

In our age of increasing automation and influence of artificial intelligence, it is worth asking whether such systems are (or should be) capable of experiencing boredom? In one sense, assembly line automation ought to *avoid* boredom assiduously. If a machine with one job—attach widget *X* to panel *Y*—were capable of boredom, it might fail to execute the job, or at least not do so indefinitely. This is precisely what drives automation–the need to remove humans from repetitive, monotonous tasks, to improve accuracy. But what of artificially intelligent systems? Might we want to imbue them with drives, including boredom? Such systems are undergirded by machine learning algorithms hungry for training data, in order to flexibly execute some function. Often, such systems become highly efficient at things once thought intractable (e.g., facial recognition; Ioannou et al. 2005). But does that equate to a drive? Can we imagine facial recognition software ever *wanting* to create portraits of the faces it takes as inputs?

This question can be turned on its head somewhat—why, beyond appetitive drives—does the human algorithm bother with such things as creating art, expressing ourselves in ways not directly tied to survival? One notion is that we do so to avoid the dark room problem (Gomez-Ramirez and Costa 2017; Yu et al. 2019). That is, humans have been characterized as predictive machines (Friston 2010). We create mental models of our world that enable us to predict the consequences of our actions. The success of our models depends on how accurately they represent environmental contingencies and on how well they update when contingencies change (Filipowicz et al. 2016). Successful updating, in turn, depends on comparative processes highlighting when new information does not conform to model predictions–prediction error. Computational models suggest that our brains seek to minimize prediction error (Friston 2010, 2012). Ultimately, the optimal way to do this would be to find ourselves a dark corner, curl up in a ball, and go nowhere–the dark room problem (Friston et al. 2012). The environment would be fully predictable, and prediction error would approach zero. Clearly, we don't do this. In a recent computational model, Gomez-Ramirez and Costa (2017) suggest that boredom represents one solution to the dark room problem. When a circumstance is monotonous, as surely a dark room would be, we get bored and seek other activities. Interestingly, in another computational approach, Yu et al. (2019) showed that learning algorithms driven by boredom outperformed those driven by curiosity.

Box 2: Sensory Deprivation, Incarceration, and Boredom

A serendipitous meeting with intelligence services from the USA, UK, and Canada led Donald O. Hebb and colleagues to test an unusual hypothesis—would sensory deprivation lead a person to change their beliefs? (see Brown 2007 for details of the meeting and Heron, 1957 for discussion of methods used). The Western intelligence agencies were concerned that prisoners of war returning home from the Korean theater were espousing communist beliefs—how had the Koreans brought about this change? Hebb and colleagues thought that depriving an individual of their normal capacity to interact with the world (depriving them of opportunities to satisfy the effectance drive) might facilitate belief change. They had people placed in a small, well-lit room with opaque goggles and the constant hum of an air conditioner—not the absence of stimulation, but a constant, unchanging environment. People wore specially fitted gloves that both minimized haptic sensations and prevented active exploration. They didn't find what they were looking for—the only belief that changed even slightly was an increased belief in the supernatural! But what they observed most was that people quickly became restless, often slept despite the time of day, and commonly reported struggling to maintain a stream of thought. It seems that humans need the thrust and parry of interacting with *things in the world* to maintain a stable state of mind. More recently, Wilson et al. (2014) had people sit in a room with nothing but their thoughts for 15 min. Many reported being bored. In their final experiment, they gave people the option to self-administer an electric shock. Despite having experienced the shock beforehand and stating they would pay to avoid it, many participants chose to shock themselves rather than sit idle with only their thoughts as entertainment.

We routinely limit the capacity for some individuals to interact with the world via incarceration and, in its extreme, solitary confinement. While the latter is known to have serious mental health consequences, more routine forms of incarceration are also associated with prolonged periods of boredom (Arrig and Bullock 2008; Bengtsson 2012; Smith 2006; see also Palinkas 2003 and Palinkas et al. 2000 for effects of isolation on polar expeditions and an analogy with space). Even the language used by inmates of 'doing time' or 'killing time' highlights a sense of waiting and of time dragging on, itself a critical component of boredom (e.g., Danckert and Allman 2005). With the imposition of strict routines and constraints on autonomous control of one's actions, it is perhaps not surprising that boredom is a common experience in prisons.

References

Abramson, E. E., & Stinson, S. G. (1977). Boredom and eating in obese and non-obese individuals. *Addictive Behaviors, 2*(4), 181–185. https://doi.org/10.1016/0306-4603(77)90015-6.

Arrigo, B. A., & Bullock, J. L. (2008). The psychological effects of solitary confinement on prisoners in supermax units. *International Journal of Offender Therapy and Comparative Criminology, 52,* 622–640. https://doi.org/10.1177/0306624X07309720.

Bench, S. W., & Lench, H. C. (2013). On the function of boredom. *Behavioural Sciences, 3*(3), 459–472. https://doi.org/10.3390/bs3030459.

Bengtsson, T. T. (2012). Boredom and action — experiences from youth confinement. *Journal of Contemporary Ethnography, 41,* 526–553. https://doi.org/10.1177/0891241612449356.

Blunt, A., & Pychyl, T. A. (1998). Volitional action and inaction in the lives of undergraduate students: State orientation, procrastination and proneness to boredom. *Personality and Individual Differences, 24*(6), 837–846. https://doi.org/10.1016/S0191-8869(98)00018-X.

Bolhuis, J. E., Schouten, W. G. P., Schrama, J. W., & Wiegant, V. M. (2006). Effects of rearing and housing environment on behaviour and performance of pigs with different coping characteristics. *Applied Animal Behavioral Science, 101*(1), 68–85. https://doi.org/10.1016/j.applanim.2006.01.001.

Brown, R. E. (2007). Alfred McCoy, Hebb, The CIA and torture. *Journal of the History of the Behavioral Sciences, 43,* 205–213. https://doi.org/10.1002/jhbs.

Buckner, R. L., Andrews-Hanna, J. R., & Schacter, D. L. (2008). The brain's default network: Anatomy, function, and relevance to disease. *Annals of the New York Academy of Sciences, 1124,* 1–39. https://doi.org/10.1196/annals.1440.011.

Burn, C. C. (2017). Bestial boredom: A biological perspective on animal boredom and suggestions for its scientific investigation. *Animal Behaviour, 130,* 141–151. https://doi.org/10.1016/j.anbehav.2017.06.006.

Butler, R. A., & Harlow, H. F. (1957). Discrimination learning and learning sets to visual exploration incentives. *Journal of General Psychology, 57*(2), 257–264. https://doi.org/10.1080/00221309.1957.9920369.

Carlstead, K. (1996). Effects of captivity on the behavior of wild mammals. In D. G. Kleiman, M. E. Allen, K. V. Thompson, & S. Lumpkin (Eds.), *Wild Mammals in Captivity* (pp. 317–333). Chicago, IL: University of Chicago Press.

Chan, C. S., Van Tilburg, W. A. P., Igou, E. R., Poon, C. Y., Tam, K. Y., Wong, V. U., et al. (2018). Situational meaninglessness and state boredom: Cross-sectional and experience-sampling findings. *Motivation and Emotion, 42*(471), 555–565. https://doi.org/10.1007/s11031-018-9693-3.

Charnov, E. L. (1976). Optimal foraging, the marginal value theorem. *Theoretical Population Biology, 9*(2), 129–136. https://doi.org/10.1016/0040-5809(76)90040-X.

Cohen, M. X., Young, J., Baek, J. M., Kessler, C., & Ranganath, C. (2005). Individual differences in extraversion and dopamine genetics predict neural reward responses. *Cognitive Brain Research, 25*(3), 851–861. https://doi.org/10.1016/j.cogbrainres.2005.09.018.

Collard, R. R. (1971). Exploratory and play behaviors of infants reared in an institution and in lower-and middle-class homes. *Child Development, 42,* 1003–1015.

Crockett, A. C., Myhre, S. K., & Rokke, P. D. (2015). Boredom proneness and emotion regulation predict emotional eating. *Journal of Health Psychology, 20*(5), 670–680. https://doi.org/10.1177/1359105315573439.

Csíkszentmihályi, M. (1990). *Flow: The psychology of optimal experience*. New York, NY: Harper Collins.

Dahlen, E. R., Martin, R. C., Ragan, K., & Kuhlman, M. M. (2004). Boredom proneness in anger and aggression: Effects of impulsiveness and sensation seeking. *Personality and Individual Differences, 37*(8), 1615–1627. https://doi.org/10.1016/j.paid.2004.02.016.

Dal Mas, D. E., & Wittmann, B. C. (2017). Avoiding boredom: Caudate and insula activity reflects boredom-elicited purchase bias. *Cortex, 92,* 57–69. https://doi.org/10.1016/j.cortex.2017.03.008.

Danckert, J. A., & Allman, A. A. A. (2005). Time flies when you're having fun: Temporal estimation and the experience of boredom. *Brain and Cognition, 59*(3), 236–245. https://doi.org/10.1016/j.bandc.2005.07.002.

Danckert, J., & Isacescu, J. (2017). The bored brain: Insular cortex and the default mode network. *PsyArXiv*. https://doi.org/10.17605/osf.io/aqbcd.

Danckert, J., & Merrifield, C. (2018). Boredom, sustained attention and the default mode network. *Experimental Brain Research, 236*(9), 2507–2518. https://doi.org/10.1007/s00221-016-4617-5.

Danckert, J., Hammerschmidt, T., Marty-Dugas, J., & Smilek, D. (2018a). Boredom: Under-aroused and restless. *Consciousness and Cognition, 61,* 24–37. https://doi.org/10.1016/j.concog.2018.03.014.

Danckert, J., Mugon, J., Struk, A., & Eastwood, J. D. (2018b). Boredom: What is it good for? In H. Lench (Ed.), *The function of emotions* (pp. 93–119). Cham, Switzerland: Springer.

Davies, A. H. (1926). Discussion on the physical and mental effects of monotony in modern industry. *The British Medical Journal*, 472–479.

de Belle, J. S., & Sokolowski, M. B. (1987). Heredity of rover/sitter: alternative foraging strategies of Drosophila melanogaster larvae. *Heredity, 59,* 73–83. https://doi.org/10.1038/hdy.1987.9.

Eastwood, J. D., Frischen, A., Fenske, M. J., & Smilek, D. (2012). The unengaged mind: Defining boredom in terms of attention. *Perspectives on Psychological Science, 7*(5), 482–495. https://doi.org/10.1177/1745691612456044.

Elpidorou, A. (2014). The bright side of boredom. *Frontiers in Psychology, 5,* 1245. https://doi.org/10.3389/fpsyg.2014.01245.

Elpidorou, A. (2018). The good of boredom. *Philosophical Psychology, 31*(3), 323–351. https://doi.org/10.1080/09515089.2017.1346240.

Farmer, R., & Sundberg, N. D. (1986). Boredom proneness — The development and correlates of a new scale. *Journal of Personality Assessment, 50*(1), 4–17. https://doi.org/10.1207/s15327752jpa5001_2.

Ferrari, J. R. (2000). Procrastination and attention: Factor analysis of attention deficit, boredom, intelligence, self-esteem, and task delay frequencies. *Journal of Social Behaviour and Personality, 15,* 185–196.

Filipowicz, A., Anderson, B., & Danckert, J. (2016). Adapting to change: The role of the right hemisphere in mental model building and updating. *Canadian Journal of Experimental Psychology, 70*(3), 201–218. https://doi.org/10.1037/cep0000078.

Friston, K. (2010). The free-energy principle: A unified brain theory? *Nature Reviews Neuroscience, 11*(2), 127. https://doi.org/10.1038/nrn2787.

Friston, K. (2012). Prediction, perception and agency. *International Journal of Psychophysiology, 83*(2), 248–252. https://doi.org/10.1016/j.ijpsycho.2011.11.014.

Friston, K., Thornton, C., & Clark, A. (2012). Free-energy minimization and the dark-room problem. *Perception Science, 3,* 130. https://doi.org/10.3389/fpsyg.2012.00130.

Fromm, E. (1955). *The sane society*. New York, NY: Rinehart & Company Inc.

Goldberg, Y. K., Eastwood, J. D., LaGuardia, J., & Danckert, J. (2011). Boredom: An emotional experience distinct from apathy, anhedonia, or depression. *Journal of Social and Clinical Psychology, 30*(6), 647–666. https://doi.org/10.1521/jscp.2011.30.6.647.

Gomez-Ramirez, J., & Costa, T. (2017). Boredom begets creativity: A solution to the exploitation–exploration trade-off in predictive coding. *Biosystems, 162,* 168–176. https://doi.org/10.1101/104521.

Harlow, H. F. (1953). Mice, monkeys, men, and motives. *Psychological Review, 60*(1), 23–32. https://doi.org/10.1037/h0056040.

Harlow, H. F., Harlow, M. K., & Meyer, D. R. (1950). Learning motivated by a manipulation drive. *Journal of Experimental Psychology, 40*(2), 228–234. https://doi.org/10.1037/h0056906.

Havermans, R. C., Vancleef, L., Kalamatianos, A., & Nederkoorn, C. (2015). Eating and inflicting pain out of boredom. *Appetite, 85,* 52–57. https://doi.org/10.1016/j.appet.2014.11.007.

Hermens, D. F., Williams, L. M., Lazzaro, I., Whitmont, S., Melkonian, D., & Gordon, E. (2004). Sex differences in adult ADHD: A double dissociation in brain activity and autonomic arousal. *Biological Psychology, 66*(3), 221–233. https://doi.org/10.1016/j.biopsycho.2003.10.006.

Heron, W. (1957). The pathology of boredom. *Scientific American, 196,* 52–57. https://doi.org/10.1038/scientificamerican0157-52.

Hughson, B. N., Anreiter, I., Chornenki, N. L. J., Murphy, K. R., William, W. J., Huber, R., et al. (2018). The adult foraging assay (AFA) detects strain and food-deprivation effects in feeding-related traits of Drosophila melanogaster. *Journal of Insect Physiology, 106*(Pt 1), 20–29. https://doi.org/10.1016/j.jinsphys.2017.08.011.

Hunter, A., & Eastwood, J. D. (2018). Does state boredom cause failures of attention? Examining the relations between trait boredom, state boredom, and sustained attention. *Experimental Brain Research, 236*(9), 2483–2492. https://doi.org/10.1007/s00221-016-4749-7.

Ioannou, S. V., Raouzaiou, A. T., Tzouvaras, V. A., Mailis, T. P., Karpouzis, K. C., & Kollias, S. D. (2005). Emotion recognition through facial expression analysis based on a neurofuzzy network. *Neural Networks, 18*(4), 423–435. https://doi.org/10.1016/j.neunet.2005.03.004.

Isacescu, J., Struk, A. A., & Danckert, J. (2017). Cognitive and affective predictors of boredom proneness. *Cognition and Emotion, 31*(8), 1741–1748. https://doi.org/10.1080/02699931.2016.1259995.

Jang, E. H., Park, B. J., Park, M. S., Kim, S. H., & Sohn, J. H. (2015). Analysis of physiological signals for recognition of boredom, pain, and surprise emotions. *Journal of physiological anthropology, 34*(1), 25. https://doi.org/10.1186/s40101-015-0063-5.

Kass, S. J., & Vodanovich, S. J. (1990). Boredom proneness: Its relationship to Type A behaviour pattern and sensation seeking. *Psychology: Journal of Human Behavior, 27*(3), 7–16. https://doi.org/10.2466/pr0.1991.69.3f.1139.

Kempermann, G., Kuhn, H. G., & Gage, F. H. (1997). More hippocampal neurons in adult mice living in an enriched environment. *Nature, 386*(6624), 493–495. https://doi.org/10.1038/386493a0.

Kempermann, G., Gast, D., & Gage, F. H. (2002). Neuroplasticity in old age: sustained fivefold induction of hippocampal neurogenesis by long-term environmental enrichment. *Annals of Neurology, 52*(2), 135–143. https://doi.org/10.1002/ana.10262.

Klapp, O. E. (1986). *Overload and boredom: Essays on the quality of life in the information society*. Santa Bárbara, CA: Greenwood Publishing Group Inc.

Kruglanski, A. W., Thompson, E. P., Higgins, E. T., Atash, M., Pierro, A., Shah, J. Y., et al. (2000). To "do the right thing" or to "just do it": Locomotion and assessment as distinct self-regulatory imperatives. *Journal of Personality and Social Psychology, 79*(5), 793–815. https://doi.org/10.1037/0022-3514.79.5.793.

Kurzban, R., Duckworth, A., Kable, J. W., & Myers, J. (2013). An opportunity cost model of subjective effort and task performance. *Behavioral and Brain Sciences, 36*(6), 661–679. https://doi.org/10.1017/S0140525X12003196.

Malkovsky, E., Merrifield, C., Goldberg, Y., & Danckert, J. (2012). Exploring the relationship between boredom and sustained attention. *Experimental Brain Research, 221*(1), 59–67. https://doi.org/10.1007/s00221-012-3147-z.

Meagher, R. K., & Mason, G. J. (2012). Environmental enrichment reduces signs of boredom in caged mink. *PLoS ONE, 7*(11), e49180. https://doi.org/10.1371/journal.pone.0049180.

Mercer-Lynn, K. B., Hunter, J. A., & Eastwood, J. D. (2013). Is trait boredom redundant? *Journal of Social and Clinical Psychology, 32*(8), 897–916. https://doi.org/10.1521/jscp.2013.32.8.897.

Merrifield, C., & Danckert, J. (2014). Characterizing the psychophysiological signature of boredom. *Experimental Brain Research, 232*(2), 481–491. https://doi.org/10.1007/s00221-013-3755-2.

Moynihan, A. B., Igou, E. R., & Van Tilburg, W. A. P. (2017). Boredom increases impulsiveness. *Social Psychology, 48*(5), 293–309. https://doi.org/10.1027/1864-9335/a000317.

Mugon, J., Struk, A., & Danckert, J. (2018). A failure to launch: Regulatory modes and Boredom Proneness. *Frontiers in Psychology, 9,* 1126. https://doi.org/10.3389/fpsyg.2018.01126.

Palinkas, L. (2003). The psychology of isolated and confined environments: Understanding human behavior in Antarctica. *American Psychologist, 58,* 353–363. https://doi.org/10.1037/0003-066X.58.5.353.

Palinkas, L., Gunderson, E. K., Holland, A. W., Miller, C., & Johnsen, J. C. (2000). Predictors of behavior and performance in extreme environments: the Antarctic space analogue program. *Aviation, Space and Environmental Medicine, 71,* 619–625.

Patterson, I., & Pegg, S. (1999). Nothing to do: the relationship between 'leisure boredom' and alcohol and drug addiction: Is there a link to youth suicide in rural Australia? *Youth Studies Australia, 18*(2), 24–29.

Sim, Z. L., & Xu, F. (2017). Infants preferentially approach and explore the unexpected. *British Journal of Developmental Psychology, 35*(4), 596–608. https://doi.org/10.1111/bjdp.12198.

Smilek, D., Carriere, J. S., & Cheyne, J. A. (2010). Out of mind, out of sight: Eye blinking as indicator and embodiment of mind wandering. *Psychological Science, 21*(6), 786–789. https://doi.org/10.1177/0956797610368063.

Smith, P. S. (2006). The effects of solitary confinement on prison inmates: A brief history and review of the literature. *Crime and Justice, 34*(1), 441–528. https://doi.org/10.1086/500626.

Sokolowski, M. B. (2001). Drosophila: Genetics meets behaviour. *Nature Reviews Genetics, 2* (11), 879–890. https://doi.org/10.1038/35098592.

Stevenson, M. F. (1983). The captive environment: Its effect on exploratory and related behavioural responses in wild animals. In J. Archer & L. I. A. Birke (Eds.), *Exploration in animals and man* (pp. 176–197). London, UK: Van Nostrand Reinhold.

Stöttinger, E., Filipowicz, A., Valadao, D., Culham, J. C., Goodale, M. A., Anderson, B., et al. (2015). A cortical network that marks the moment when conscious representations are updated. *Neuropsychologia, 79*(Pt A), 113–122. https://doi.org/10.1016/j.neuropsychologia.2015.10.037.

Stöttinger, E., Aichhorn, M., Anderson, B., & Danckert, J. (2018). The neural systems for perceptual updating. *Neuropsychologia, 112,* 86–94. https://doi.org/10.1016/j.neuropsychologia.2018.03.017.

Struk, A., Mugon, J., Huston, A., Scholer, A., Stadler, G., Higgins, E. T., et al. (2019). Self-regulation and the foraging gene (PRKG1) in humans. *Proceedings of the National Academy of Sciences, 116*(10), 4434–4439. https://doi.org/10.1073/pnas.1809924116.

Tabatabaie, A. F., Azadehfar, M. R., Mirian, N., Noroozian, M., Yoonessi, A., Saebipour, M. R., et al. (2014). Neural correlates of boredom in music perception. *Basic and Clinical Neuroscience, 5*(4), 259–266.

Thackray, R. I., Bailey, J. P., & Touchstone, R. M. (1977). Physiological, subjective, and performance correlates of reported boredom and monotony while performing a simulated radar control task. In R.R. Mackie (Ed.), *Vigilance. NATO Conference Series*, (Vol. 3, pp. 203–215). Boston, MA: Springer.

Tolstoy, L. N. (1899). *Anna Karénina.* New York, NY: Thomas Y. Crowell Co.

Twomey, K. E., & Westermann, G. (2018). Curiosity-based learning in infants: a neurocomputational approach. *Developmental Science, 21*(4), e12629. https://doi.org/10.1111/desc.12629.

Uddin, L. Q. (2015). Salience processing and insular cortical function and dysfunction. *Nature Reviews Neuroscience, 16,* 55–61. https://doi.org/10.1038/nrn385.

Ulrich, M., Keller, J., Hoenig, K., Waller, C., & Grön, G. (2014). Neural correlates of induced flow experiences. *NeuroImage, 86,* 194–202. https://doi.org/10.1016/j.neuroimage.2013.08.019.

Ulrich, M., Keller, J., & Grön, G. (2016). Neural signatures of experimentally induced flow experiences identified in a typical fMRI block design with BOLD imaging. *Social Cognitive and Affective Neuroscience, 11*(3), 496–507. https://doi.org/10.1093/scan/nsv133.

Van Tilburg, W. A. P., & Igou, E. R. (2012). On boredom: Lack of challenge and meaning as distinct boredom experiences. *Motivation and Emotion, 36*(2), 181–194. https://doi.org/10.1007/s11031-011-9234-9.

Van Tilburg, W. A. P., & Igou, E. R. (2017). Boredom begs to differ: Differentiation from other negative emotions. *Emotion, 17*(2), 309–322. https://doi.org/10.1037/emo0000233.

Watt, J. D., & Vodanovich, S. J. (1992). Relationship between boredom proneness and impulsivity. *Psychological Reports, 70*(3), 688–690. https://doi.org/10.2466/pr0.1992.70.3.688.

Watt, J. D., & Vodanovich, S. J. (1999). Boredom proneness and psychosocial development. *The Journal of Psychology, 133*(3), 303–314. https://doi.org/10.1080/00223989909599743.

Wemelsfelder, F. (1993). The concept of animal boredom and its relationship to stereotyped behaviour. In A. B., & J. Rushen (Eds), *Stereotypic behavior: Fundamentals and applications to animal welfare* (pp. 95–96). Wallingford, UK: CAB International.

White, R. W. (1959). Motivation reconsidered: The concept of competence. *Psychological Review, 66*(5), 297–333. https://doi.org/10.1037/h0040934.

Wilson, T. D., Reinhard, D. A., Westgate, E. C., Gilbert, D. T., Ellerbeck, N., Hahn, C., et al. (2014). Just think: The challenges of the disengaged mind. *Science, 345,* 75–77. https://doi.org/10.1126/science.1250830.

Wink, P., & Donahue, K. (1997). The relation between two types of narcissism and boredom. *Journal of Research in Personality, 31*(1), 136–140. https://doi.org/10.1006/jrpe.1997.2176.

Wyatt, S., & Fraser, J. A. (1929). The effects of monotony in work-a preliminary enquiry. *IHRB Report*, 56.

Wyatt, S., & Langdon, J. N. (1937). Fatigue and boredom in repetitive work. *IHRB Report*, 77.

Young, D., Lawlor, P. A., Leone, P., Dragunow, M., & During, M. J. (1999). Environmental enrichment inhibits spontaneous apoptosis, prevents seizures and is neuroprotective. *Nature Medicine, 5*(4), 448–453. https://doi.org/10.1038/7449.

Yu, Y., Chang, A. Y. C., & Kanai, R. (2019). Boredom-driven curious learning by homeo-heterostatic value gradients. *Frontiers in Neurorobotics*, 12. https://doi.org/10.3389/fnbot.2018.00088.

Zee, K. S., Cavallo, J. V., Flores, A. J., Bolger, N., & Higgins, E. T. (2018). Motivation moderates the effects of social support visibility. *Journal of Personality and Social Psychology, 114*(5), 735–765. https://doi.org/10.1037/pspi0000119.

Dr. James Danckert received his master's in clinical neuropsychology and Ph.D. in psychology from La Trobe University in Melbourne, Australia. He completed a Postdoctoral Fellowship under the guidance of Professor Mel Goodale at Western University in 2002. During that time, he also worked with Dr. Yves Rossetti in Lyon, France. He was awarded a Tier II Canada Research Chair in Cognitive Neuroscience in 2002. He has been Professor in the Psychology Department at the University of Waterloo since that time, achieving Full Professor status in 2013. He has published over 80 articles in peer-reviewed journals, garnering more than 3000 citations, with an h-index of 35. His research has broadly examined the cognitive and neural bases of behavior focusing on the control of attention, visuomotor control, and more recently, the cognitive and affective components of the experience of boredom. His work on boredom regularly attracts popular media attention with articles in *The New York Times, The Washington Post, Toronto Star*, and *The Globe and Mail.* Some of his academic papers on boredom include 'Time flies when you're having fun: Temporal estimation and the experience of boredom' (*Brain and Cognition*, 2005), 'Boredom: An emotional experience distinct from apathy, anhedonia, or depression' (*Journal of Social and Clinical Psychology*, 2011), 'Exploring the relationship between boredom and sustained attention' (*Experimental Brain Research*, 2012), 'Characterizing the psychophysiological signature of boredom' (*Experimental Brain Research*, 2014), and 'Boredom, sustained attention and the default mode network' (*Experimental Brain Research*, 2016).

Chapter 4
Boredom Is a Feeling of Thinking and a Double-Edged Sword

John D. Eastwood and Dana Gorelik

None of the other patrons noticed when emergency personnel arrived. Already stiff, hands still on the console, he had been dead for 10 h. Other than a brief bathroom and food break, he hadn't moved from his chair for five days straight. They say thrombosis or a cardiac event was the likely culprit.[1]

Lost playing video games, unable to escape the *machine zone*—that's where he died. The *machine zone,* induced by an action-reward cycle, is a tranquil trance-like mental state in which time, space, and even a sense of self and body disappear. Awareness of daily worries, social demands, and even pain drop away; all that remains is the doing, a positive feedback loop with the machine (Hsu 2013; Schüll 2014). Our evolutionary history has not prepared us to cope with the machine zone, or as others have called it *dark flow* (Dixon et al. 2017); we are vulnerable. In fact, it might be more accurate to say our evolutionary history has precisely prepared us to be easy victims (Madrigal 2013; Schüll 2014).

As we will see, the possibility of boredom makes us vulnerable to the machine zone. And yet the possibility of boredom also saves us from the damage of stagnation. Boredom then is a double-edged sword; we must master so as to avoid its dangers and maximize its benefits. In this chapter, we articulate a psychological model of boredom. In so doing, we situate boredom as an instance of the *feeling of thinking,* and we explore the functional role played by boredom, and other feelings of thinking, in our day-to-day lives.

[1]This is a fictitious story based on an amalgamation of news accounts of deaths related to excessive video game playing.

J. D. Eastwood (✉) · D. Gorelik
York University, Toronto, Canada
e-mail: johneast@yorku.ca

J. Ros Velasco (ed.), *Boredom Is in Your Mind*,
https://doi.org/10.1007/978-3-030-26395-9_4

What Is Boredom?

Boredom is the *aversive feeling of wanting but being unable to engage in satisfying activity*. That's the subjective experience of being bored—what it feels like. We anchor our definition of boredom in terms of this feeling (Fahlman et al. 2013). Two psychological factors underpin the feeling; namely a *desire bind* and an *unoccupied mind* (Danckert et al. 2018). When bored, we want to do something but are incapable of wanting to do what is available. And when bored, our cognitive capacities are underused; our mind is unoccupied.

Our view on the underlying cognitive mechanism of boredom has evolved since our previous publications. In the past, we put the emphasis on boredom being underpinned by a *failure of attention* (Eastwood et al. 2012). We now see that such characterization unhelpfully puts the emphasis on success of performance rather than underutilization of cognitive potential and the state of being unengaged. For example, during a sustained attention task, a person may make no task errors yet still experience boredom because they have not become mentally engaged with the task at hand. Thus, we now emphasize the *under-utilization* of cognitive capacity rather than a failure of those capacities.

The two factors that underpin boredom—a desire bind and an unoccupied mind—could be described as proximal causes of boredom, or part and parcel of the definition of boredom. Either way, we contend that these two factors are necessary and sufficient for boredom.

These two factors also give rise to four additional experiences that are very closely associated with boredom; so much so that they are often seen as being part of boredom. Namely, when bored: *time drags*, we *struggle to concentrate*, our current *activity lacks meaning*, and our *arousal levels fluctuate or fractionate* (Eastwood et al. 2012; Zakay 2014; Damrad-Frye and Laird 1989; Van Tilburg and Igou 2012; Merrifield and Danckert 2014; Danckert et al. 2018). We would argue that these four experiences are not strictly speaking part of the definition of boredom because they can occur when we are not bored (i.e., a desire bind and an unoccupied mind are sufficient, but not necessary for these four associated experiences). We contend that these four additional experiences should be seen as proximal consequences of boredom or closely associated features of boredom.

Boredom feels bad. It is an inherently aversive feeling. We don't like it. While there are healthy debate and discussion about how best to define boredom, it is near-universally conceptualized as an uncomfortable feeling (Fahlman et al. 2013). While some of us may cherish quiet moments of downtime when there is nothing to do—a reprieve from the onslaught of external stimulation and demands—this is not the same as being bored. In our view, such a state is better characterized as something like relaxed daydreaming.[2] We think it is conceptually incoherent to say

[2]However, the capacity to do nothing without succumbing to boredom is a critical life skill that is seemingly in short supply in our society of hyperstimulation.

boredom has a positive valence, further in our view, such conceptualization lacks utility. Thus, we define boredom as an inherently uncomfortable feeling.

Boredom Is the Feeling of a Particular Mode of Thinking

Given we have defined boredom as an uncomfortable feeling; we next need to unpack the concept *feeling*. What is a feeling? We feel our emotions. Perhaps less recognized, we also feel our thinking. It's not merely *what* we think that is important for feeling—although, for example, thoughts of past failure or belief in one's inadequacy will certainly lead to negative feelings—but rather, *how* we think is also associated with a feeling. For example, thinking in a rapid and variable way, such as when we brainstorm ideas to solve a problem, independent of the content, will make us feel good. Whereas thinking in a slow and repetitive way, such as when experiencing writers' block, will make us feel bad (Pronin and Jacobs 2008). Other examples of the feeling of thinking include that positive feeling we get when information is easily evaluated or we know we are close to solving a problem or when we become so absorbed with a mental task that we fail to notice the passing of time. What these examples all have in common is that regardless of *what* we are thinking about, the process of thinking is also experienced as a feeling. As Frijda (2005) noted: feelings arise from the "functioning of one's information processes" (p. 483); and "pleasure and pain […] stem from thinking proceeding smoothly or unsuccessfully" (p. 481).

In our view, boredom can be usefully thought of as a feeling arising from information processing—it's the feeling associated with a particular mode of thinking. As we claimed earlier, boredom is underpinned by wanting, but being unable to become mentally engaged (i.e., desire bind and unoccupied mind). It's not the frustration of trying to engage with *X* but failing to become engrossed. That is, boredom is not about thinking proceeding unsuccessfully or lacking fluency. Rather, boredom arises from the failure to deploy or engage our cognitive capacity such that our cognitive capacity remains underutilized. Boredom is the feeling of wanting to be mentally engaged but failing to find anything we want to engage).[3]

To be clear, in the previous section, we defined boredom as the *aversive feeling of wanting, but being unable to, engage in satisfying activity*. The astute reader will note that here while specifying boredom as the feeling of a particular mode of thinking, we have shifted to the claim that boredom is the *feeling associated with a failure to engage our cognitive capacity (desire bind) such that our cognitive capacity remains under-utilized (unoccupied mind)*. The first proposal defines boredom in terms of what it subjectively feels like to be bored, whereas the second articulates the underlying mode of thinking which underpins the subjective

[3]Because the bored person wants an actionable desire, and internal or external forces thwart this want, frustration surrounds the boredom of being mentally unengaged.

experience. The first puts the emphasis on the subjective experience of the external environment failing to satisfy, whereas the second puts the emphasis on the internal mental state associated with the subjective experience. When bored, we typically locate the problem outside of us (i.e., lack of satisfying activity), but clearly, the feeling is mediated by an internal state; and our claim here is that the internal state is a mode of thinking.

We are not the first to define boredom as the feeling of a particular mode of thinking. In fact, Theodor Waitz conceptualized boredom in a similar manner in 1849 (Romand 2015; Teo 2007). According to Waitz, boredom arises from how the content of our mind is flowing; that is, how mental contents encounter and combine with one another, rather than because of what we are thinking. Waitz claimed that as one mental thought flows into another, we develop unconscious expectations about how our mental life will unfold. And boredom, according to Waitz, is associated with a break in the expected flow because of a mismatch between expected and actual mental activity. For Waitz, feelings like boredom are critical to effective thinking because they provide feedback about how our thinking is operating. Feeling our thinking allows us to make adjustments—giving us control and choice. Waitz also talked about the boringness of things, which he called a *qualitative feeling* (as opposed to *formal feelings*) and here too, he thought expectations played a key role. When we find some "thing" boring, it is either because as we explore it, we have 100% or 0% confidence that our expectations will be met. While the details of our model are substantially different from Waitz's account—we put desire bind and unoccupied mind at its core rather than violated expectations—nevertheless, we fully agree with his broad-brush strokes—boredom is a feeling of thinking that provides feedback about our thinking.

Notably, in claiming that boredom is a feeling of thinking, *we are not saying boredom is an emotion*. In our view, the boredom literature has been hampered by a lack of clarity and careful analysis on this very point. It is not obvious if it is most useful and coherent to think of boredom as a feeling of thinking, a feeling of an emotion, or a mood. A detailed exposition of these thorny questions is well beyond the scope of our chapter. However, to stay oriented, we offer the following, hopefully noncontentious, definitions drawn from prominent emotion researchers (e.g., Damasio 2003; Frijda 2005; Scherer 2005) as placeholders in lieu of a more detailed exposition.

A *feeling* is a non or prelinguistic subjective experience of body-mind activity that synthesizes and situates us. Simply put, it is our positively or negatively toned experience of being ourself in the world. We can have feelings of emotions or feelings that are not related to emotions, such as feelings of heat, being satiated, or understanding.

An *emotion* possesses multiple components, only one of which is a subjective experience (i.e., feeling). The other components are often thought to be appraisals, physiological changes, a readiness for action, and overt bodily changes. An emotion is a dynamic, relatively short-lived, and intense episode that is triggered by an eliciting event that has been appraised as relevant to organismic needs. An emotion serves to synchronize a response to the triggering event.

A *mood* is a diffuse positive or negatively toned feeling of longer duration and lower intensity compared to an emotional feeling; moreover, a mood lacks a specific triggering event and appraisal.

A *thought* is the mental representation and manipulation of abstract concepts and propositions. Thought can be characterized in terms of both content and process.

In light of these provisional definitions, we put two stakes in the ground to mark the landscape for future exploration. First, the distinctions between feeling, emotion, and mood matter but have not been adequately examined in the boredom literature. Second, it's probable that a compelling case could be made to argue that boredom can be conceptualized as any or all of these neighboring affective concepts. In this chapter, however, we run with the idea that boredom is a feeling of thinking.

In summary, boredom is the aversive feeling of wanting but being unable to engage in satisfying activity. It is underpinned by a desire bind and an unoccupied mind and closely associated with feeling that: time is dragging, we can't concentrate, what we are doing is meaningless, and our arousal levels are fluctuating or fractionated. Our definition of boredom amounts to the claim that boredom is a feeling of thinking. Namely, boredom arises from the failure to deploy or engage our cognitive capacity such that our cognitive capacity remains underutilized. This failure to engage our cognitive capacity—boredom—is aversive. Thus, whenever possible, we seek to engage our cognitive capacity and thereby avoid the uncomfortable feeling of boredom.

Boredom Feels Bad; But We're Cognitive Misers Too

Although we want to engage our cognitive capacity, we typically prefer the easiest path to mental engagement. Pick up our phones, play a video game, watch that new show on Netflix, or scroll through social media. We prefer to engage in leisure activities where the focus of our attention is guided or supported by external prompts—kind of like scaffolds for the mind. For example, reading, watching television, or socializing are commonly pursued leisure activities (US Department of Labor 2012; Wilson et al. 2014). Although diverse, what these activities all have in common is that something external helps keep us mentally engaged.

The fact is, as Fiske and Taylor (1984) put it, we are *cognitive misers*. Like a person reluctant to spend money, the claim is that cognitive misers conserve cognitive resources whenever possible. A classic example of the cognitive miser theory has been illustrated with the bat and ball problem. 'A bat and a ball together cost $1.10. The bat costs $1 more than the ball. How much does the ball cost?' The answer provided by most people is '10 cents,' but that is incorrect. Because in that case, the bat would cost $1.10, and then the total cost would be $1.20, rather than $1.10 (i.e., correct answer: bat = $1.05 and ball = $0.05). The wrong answer comes quickly and easily and feels right. Perhaps substituting the 'more than' statement with the absolute statement 'the bat costs $1' we do not slow down and recognize that more careful thought is required.

Stereotypes, heuristics, and other mental shortcuts reveal our miserliness. And such shortcuts lead us to make poor decisions in spite of having the intellectual capacity to make better choices—we seem to be stingy, when it comes to using our cognitive resources. As cognitive misers, we tend to default to cognitive shortcuts whenever possible (Kool et al. 2010; Stanovich 2011). On the other hand, it may often be adaptive to use our cognitive abilities sparingly (Fiske and Taylor 1984). Time and our mental resources are limited; thus, there is only so much deep thinking we can do at any point. Yet, the information we are confronted with is immense. As the saying goes 'you can only spend a penny once'—so spend wisely. If mental shortcuts get us close enough, most of the time, they might ultimately be adaptive because they allow us to preserve resources for when we really need them. For optimal decision-making, however, it is critical that we know when to allow mental shortcuts to operate and when to rein them in so as to think more carefully.

Miserliness Revisited

On the face of it, claiming that we are cognitive misers would seem to suggest that we are reluctant to use our cognitive resources. However, in our view, this is not quite right. First, heuristic thinking and other mental short cuts are not always deliberate choices we make but automatic default ways of thinking. So, in this sense, it is a misnomer to say we are reluctant as reluctance implies a subjectively mediated process; namely, not wanting to do something. Secondly, when a subjective choice does mediate miserliness, we would claim that we are not consciously keeping track of how much cognitive capacity we are using and attempting to hoard it. Rather, in our view, we are tracking how much *mental strain* we are experiencing and attempting to limit discomfort. We are motivated to avoid mental strain—which, like boredom, is another instance of a negative feeling of thinking. Thus, cognitive miserliness is a special case of the more general principle that we avoid doing things that make us feel bad. In the case of being a cognitive miser, we avoid situations that elicit mental strain. Indeed, research shows that people quite happily use cognitive resources, and even engage in controlled, nonautomatic processing, so long as it is not associated with mental strain (e.g., Gaggioli et al. 2013; Harris et al. 2017; Ulrich et al. 2016; Helton et al. 2013). The key question for the cognitive miser is: Am I experiencing mental strain?

What Is Mental Strain?

We use the term *mental strain* rather than the more traditional term *mental effort* because the term mental effort is ambiguous and has been used in a variety of different ways in academic literature. Hsu et al. (2018), for instance, distinguish between effort as a subjective experience as opposed to effort defined in terms of objective task demands and the presumed cognitive processes required to complete tasks (i.e., simple vs. complex mathematical computations) or objective task performance (i.e., all things being equal, worse performance indicates more effort was required). Consistent with others (e.g., Westbrook and Braver 2015), we think it is more coherent and useful to define mental effort in terms of subjective experience. However, Hsu et al. (2018) further point out that even when effort is defined as a subjective experience ambiguity abounds. For example, when asked to report their level of mental effort, a research participant might respond by indicating *how hard they tried*, *how taxed they felt*, or *how difficult they think the task is*. Empirical findings support this three-part classification (e.g., Mulert et al. 2007; Otto et al. 2014). In our view, the term mental effort should be defined subjectively and deconstructed into three specific subconcepts; and we use the term mental strain to refer specifically to effort in the sense of being mentally taxed.

Mental Strain Is the Feeling of a Particular Mode of Thinking

A number of different models have been proposed to understand mental effort and mental strain more specifically. Kahneman's (1973) highly influential model was less concerned with understanding the subjective experience of effort; instead, he defined mental effort in terms of a presumed underlying cognitive process. Namely, for Kahneman mental effort is the process of allocating limited attention capacity to a possible mental activity so as to realize that activity. He proposed that the amount of effort deployed is directly determined by the intrinsic demands of the activity and, for the most part, is not under voluntary control. So the claim is we can choose what mental activity to pursue, but not how much effort to invest in the activity we choose. Historically significant and highly influential, Kahneman's model provides a useful context for thinking about mental strain. However, given he defined mental effort in nonsubjective terms; namely, in terms of task demands and cognitive processes, his model does not provide an account of mental strain per se.

In pursuing an understanding of mental fatigue, Hockey (2011) developed a somewhat different way of thinking about mental effort, which did include an account of subjective mental strain. For Hockey, mental strain (i.e., the feeling of being mentally taxed) is the subjective experience associated with the control processes required to maintain a chosen mental activity (e.g., avoid distraction). Sometimes control can be achieved through largely automatic, low-level processes and thus does not give rise to feelings of strain. On other occasions, automatic processes are not sufficient and maintaining control requires intervention from higher level, executive control systems. The failure of low-level control is subjectively experienced as mental strain and this feeling functions as a signal to elicit engagement of the executive system. At this executive level, the control options are to increase the 'effort budget' (i.e., the 'how hard I tried' kind of mental effort, which in turn will result in increased 'how strained I felt' kind of mental effort) to maintain the chosen mental activity, revise goal aspirations such as picking a new mental activity or accepting lower performance with current mental activity. Generally, the increased need for, and deployment of, cognitive control is subjectively experienced as an aversive strain and, if continued over time, results in feelings of fatigue. However, for Hockey, controllability is a key determinant of how straining and fatiguing a mental activity will be. When mental activities are self-initiated and in line with personal goals, they do not give rise to the same degree of distress. In sum, according to Hockey, mental strain is the felt sense of cognitive control processes. Hockey also proposes that subjective fatigue motivates a shift in mental activity and a preference for less effortful activities—which once again highlights how feelings of thinking provide feedback about thinking and shape subsequent thinking and behavior. The key distinguishing aspect of Hockey's model is that whereas Kahneman sees mental effort to be linked to limited attention capacity, Hockey sees it to be linked to executive control and motivation (2011; see Kurzban et al. 2013 for another, more recent account of mental strain).

Boredom and Mental Strain Can Be Beneficial

Positive and negative feelings are functional because they motivate behavior; although uncomfortable, even negative feelings generally serve us well. Boredom and mental strain are no exception.

Take physical pain for example; without it we would not be aware of damage to our body until it was too late. Pain 'says' stop what you are doing and take care of yourself. Nature, it seems, built us this way. We are programmed to experience aversive feelings when in danger. What then does boredom protect us from? The short answer is stagnation.

Our contention is that it would be bad for us as individuals and a species if we were content to be mentally unoccupied (Danckert et al. 2018). We would cease exploring, expressing our abilities, and seeking to understand and master our surroundings. To be sure boredom feels bad, but a world without boredom would be very bleak.

Boredom may even be enriching; for example, without boredom we may, not have been blessed with Goethe's creative works. In writing to his painter friend J. H. Meyer, Goethe asserted: "The day is so long that it sometimes becomes boring and this you know is very conducive to invention" (quoted in Kuhn 1976, p. 184). He even thought it necessary to give thanks to boredom in the form of a poem:

> All nine, I mean the Muses, used to beckon me often
> But I paid no note, for I had a girl on my lap.
> Then I deserted my darling: the Muses have deserted me,
> Furtively and confused I gazed about, looking for knife and noose.
> But Olympus is full of gods: you came to save me.
> Boredom, I hail you as Mother of the Muses.
> (Kuhn 1976, pp. 184–185; Bourget 1886).

More recently, others have also claimed a link between boredom and creativity (Gasper and Middlewood 2014; Mann and Cadman 2014; Vodanovich 2003; see also Larson 1990). However, taking nothing away from Goethe's poetic genius, we would say more precisely that it is *the possibility of boredom* that leads to creativity. That is, our read of the research finds no evidence to support the idea that we are more creative when in the throws of boredom (Danckert et al. 2018). We are not bored during moments of creative expression; but such moments, may at least partially, be motivated by the need to keep one step ahead of boredom.

Moreover, it is important to note that avoiding boredom does not motivate creativity per se. Nor do we think it is a sufficient cause of the variety of other things people try to pin on boredom. A search for meaning (Barbalet 1999), arousal (O'Hanlon 1981), sensation (Zuckerman 1979), and optimal challenge (Csíkszentmihályi and Csíkszentmihályi 1975), for example, are effective ways of becoming engaged; they are means to the end of becoming un-bored. In sum, our claim is that boredom, as a feeling of thinking, only directly motivates one thing, and that is to become mentally occupied. There are many ways to get there, some of which are more adaptive, easy, or effective than others. Which path we choose is likely determined by situational factors, personality, and our abilities.

It is often claimed that boredom motivates us to stop doing what we are currently doing; that is, to avoid something in particular. For example, research on academic emotions has concluded that boredom motivates students to avoid contact with the material at hand (Pekrun et al. 2010). This may indeed be the case. But if so we would argue that such research is not referring to boredom as *a feeling of thinking* but rather boredom *as an emotion* (i.e., tied to a specific triggering event that is appraised as relevant to organismic needs) *or as a preference/attitude* (i.e., judgment about the boringness of an activity) *or as enduring affective disposition* (i.e., the tendency to be bored in class). Critically, conceptualizing boredom as a feeling of thinking entails that boredom is not anchored to a specific, discrete event, and an appraisal of that event, as is the case for an emotion. Rather, boredom as a feeling of thinking is a concomitant of an ongoing cognitive state (see Scherer 2005, for a discussion of how to distinguish an emotion from neighboring affective phenomenon). To be sure, as soon as boredom is experienced, we have reactions that include appraisals, which can modulate or amplify the feeling and shape future behavior; but the initial feeling itself, as we are defining it here, is not appraisal driven in the same way as an emotion. Thus, boredom as a feeling of thinking does not motivate the avoidance of some particular thing; instead, it motivates more general attempts to become mentally engaged.

If boredom, as a negative feeling of thinking, protects us from stagnation, what about mental strain; what does it protect us from? Any good gambler knows the answer—overinvestment. When it comes to investing our precious mental capacity on a task, we need to know when it's best to fold and walk away—or run. Mental strain may also alert us to the need to 'double down' on our initial investment and try harder in the face of mental strain. However, if mental strain continues eventually, we become motivated to disengage with the task at hand.

A growing consensus suggests there are indeed costs to exerting mental effort (e.g., Kurzban 2016). In short, mental strain protects us from the costs of becoming fixated, preoccupied, and overinvested, and serves to redirect our mental capacity toward activities that have more utility. Kurzban et al. (2013) explain it thusly: Not everything that we want or need to do can be done at once; we face "the problem of simultaneity" (p. 663). The solution to the problem of simultaneity is to "prioritize" (p. 663). And the feeling of mental strain forms the biologically determined basis of our mental effort prioritization. Vigorous debate exists as to how best to characterize the costs of mental effort and the mechanisms underlying the feeling of mental strain, but there is general agreement that mental effort motivates disengagement and that this is, on balance, a good thing (Kurzban 2016). We previously touched on this function of mental strain during our discussion of the cognitive miser model. And once again, we see that our miserliness pertains to mental strain.

We can further elucidate the function of boredom and mental strain—two aversive feelings of thinking—if we compare them to a positive feeling of thinking; namely, cognitive fluency.

Cognitive fluency is the subjective experience of the ease or difficulty with which information is processed (Forster et al. 2013; Oppenheimer 2008; Winkielman et al. 2003)—we feel good when our cognitive processing is fluent. The positive feelings may motivate one to continue with and complete the task (Reber et al. 2002). Studies show that people perceive fluent statements to be superior (e.g., more truthful, more likable), and that people often choose products whose names are fluent over those that are not fluent (Oppenheimer 2008). Fluency guides many decisions and choices we make from the products we buy; to the people we find attractive; the candidates we vote for; and to the tasks we engage in. This is understandable from an evolutionary perspective. People have positive feelings about fluent things because fluency suggests safety and familiarity, which would have been a good thing for our early ancestors (Herrmann et al. 2013; Halberstadt and Rhodes 2003; Whittlesea 1993). As the psychologist Robert Zajonc has been purported to say, "if it is familiar, it has not eaten you yet" (quoted in Schwarz 2018, p. 37; see also Zajonc 1968).[4]

Boredom, mental strain, and fluency are feelings of thinking that have important functions. They provide vital feedback about the state of our mental processing and serve to motivate changes to those ongoing mental processes. Boredom motivates us to seek engagement, mental strain motivates us to disengage, and processing fluency motivates us to keep on keeping on. Together they hold us in a sweet spot of optimal engagement. If we were not subject to boredom, we would stagnate as individuals and as a society. If we did not experience the pangs of mental effort, we would overinvest our mental effort and miss out on higher utility activities. If we did not get a rush of pleasure when our thinking flowed easily and effectively, we

[4]However, when something begins to be processed so fluently such that it does not occupy our mental resources, it becomes boring and leads us to experience negative affect (Van den Bergh and Vrana 1998).

might not persist and we would flirt recklessly with the unfamiliar. We have been shaped by evolutionary forces to feel our thinking as we do. The carrot and stick of feeling of thinking, more often than not, have served us well over our long history as a species. But that was before we started engineering our environment to include things like slot machines and Instagram.

Boredom and Mental Strain Can Be Treacherous

Just as the creation of rich fatty foods puts us in danger because of our biological proclivities, so too the creation of devices that effortlessly engage and hold our attention can be our ruin. No boredom, no mental strain, lots of fluency—what's not to love? Why would anyone ever want to leave that blissful place called 'flow'?

The psychologist Mihály Csíkszentmihályi coined the term 'flow' (1975). Csíkszentmihályi became interested in how artists like painters became completely immersed in their work, to the point that they would disregard their need for food, water, and even sleep. This feeling of complete absorption in a task can occur while engaging in a wide range of activities, including chess playing, dancing, reading a book, drawing, and even skiing or mountain climbing.

Csíkszentmihályi identified several factors which are central to the experience of flow; including intense concentration on the present moment, a subjective experience of time passing quickly, low-self-awareness, a sense of high control over the activity, absorption in the task where one loses awareness of all other things including time, people, distractions, and even basic bodily needs. This occurs because all attention is on the task at hand—there is no residual attention to be allocated elsewhere—the person in a flow state is certainly not bored.

The state of flow is different from the times where we passively relax and sit in the sunshine. Flow occurs during activities that are challenging but matched in difficulty to the person's skill level. Flow-inducing situations have just the right amount of challenge, not too much and not too little. So, when in a flow state, we realize our maximal abilities and expand them at the same time. Moreover, because flow is a highly enjoyable state that involves no sense of mental strain, it often motivates us to perform difficult activities at a high level and to persist at them for long periods of time.

However, flow is not an inherently positive or negative force in our lives. One key to distinguishing negative and positive flow is recognizing what we are *not doing* when in a state of flow. Are we neglecting important activities and sacrificing other critical needs all for the sake of flow? Even activities that might be judged admirable or adaptive, like tirelessly pursuing an important scientific discovery, can be chased so obsessively that they become a destructive force. Because it is so enjoyable, being in flow can lead to addictions (Stavropoulos et al. 2018; Brailovskaia et al. 2018). Flow can certainly have negative and potentially dangerous consequences when a person finds it difficult to 'get out' of the flow-inducing activity (Dixon et al. 2017).

A second key to distinguishing negative and positive flow is identifying what skills we are expressing and developing during a state of flow. Getting yet even better at Candy Crush is a dubious accomplishment. The unfortunate reality is that most worthwhile endeavors in life require tolerating a little boredom and mental strain. Moreover, the cost of admission to a state of flow in activities that have some redeeming value is a modicum of skill. But with the advent of our ever-present entertainment and beguiling technology, we no longer have to put up with a moment of boredom or mental strain. Moreover, modern attention-grabbing devices will hook people of all skill levels. 'Don't have any skill? Can't tolerate even a bit of mental effort or boredom? No problem, we have an easy solution, you too can experience flow from the comfort of your living room sofa.'

We want desperately to be mentally engaged. We hate feeling bored. And yet, we also try to avoid the feeling of mental strain, which can arise when performing demanding tasks. Boredom and mental strain can push us toward easy ways of engaging that require little skill and arguably do not enrich our lives in any way—scrolling mindlessly through Facebook or Instagram, playing video games, watching Netflix, etc. These easy engagement outlets can control us for hours on end. Devices that have been very carefully crafted to attract and hold our attention, to optimally challenge us so that we are free of boredom and mental strain, surround us no matter where we turn. It's so easy to slip into the machine zone. We don't need much skill to get started, and before we know, it an hour has gone by or we have developed an addiction. Or, even worse, we have ignored our bodily needs to the point of putting our lives in danger—dead with the game console still in our hands.

References

Barbalet, J. M. (1999). Boredom and social meaning. *The British Journal of Sociology, 50*(4), 631–646. https://doi.org/10.1111/j.1468-4446.1999.00631.x.

Bourget, P. (1886). *Nouveaux essais de psychologie contemporaine*. Paris: Le-merre.

Brailovskaia, J., Rohmann, E., Bierhoff, H. W., & Margraf, J. (2018). The brave blue world: Facebook flow and Facebook Addiction Disorder (FAD). *PLoS ONE, 13*(7), e0201484. https://doi.org/10.1371/journal.pone.0201484.

Csíkszentmihályi, M., & Csíkszentmihályi, I. (1975). *Beyond boredom and anxiety* (Vol. 721). San Francisco, CA: Jossey-Bass.

Damasio, A. (2003). Feelings of emotion and the self. *Annals of the New York Academy of Sciences, 1001*(1), 253–261. https://doi.org/10.1196/annals.1279.014.

Damrad-Frye, R., & Laird, J. D. (1989). The experience of boredom: The role of the self-perception of attention. *Journal of Personality and Social Psychology, 57*(2), 315–320. https://doi.org/10.1037/0022-3514.57.2.315.

Danckert, J., Mugon, J., Struk, A., & Eastwood, J. (2018). Boredom—what is it good for? In H. Lench (Ed.), *The function of emotions: When and why emotions help us* (pp. 93–119). Cham, Switzerland: Springer.

Dixon, M. J., Stange, M., Larche, C. J., Graydon, C., Fugelsang, J. A., & Harrigan, K. A. (2017). Dark flow, depression and multiline slot machine play. *Journal of Gambling Studies, 34*(1), 73–84. https://doi.org/10.1007/s10899-017-9695-1.

Eastwood, J. D., Frischen, A., Fenske, M. J., & Smilek, D. (2012). The unengaged mind. *Perspectives on Psychological Science, 7*(5), 482–495. https://doi.org/10.1177/1745691612456044.

Fahlman, S. A., Mercer-Lynn, K., Flora, D. B., & Eastwood, J. D. (2013). Development and validation of the multidimensional state boredom scale. *Assessment, 20*(1), 68–85. https://doi.org/10.1177/1073191111421303.

Fiske, S. T., & Taylor, S. E. (1984). *Social cognition*. Reading, MA: Addison-Wesley Pub.

Forster, M., Leder, H., & Ansorge, U. (2013). It felt fluent, and I liked it: Subjective feeling of fluency rather than objective fluency determines liking. *Emotion, 13*(2), 280–289. https://doi.org/10.1037/a0030115.

Frijda, N. (2005). Emotion experience. *Cognition and Emotion, 19*(4), 473–497. https://doi.org/10.1080/02699930441000346.

Gaggioli, A., Cipresso, P., Serino, S., & Riva, G. (2013). Psychophysiological correlates of flow during daily activities. *Annual Review of Cybertherapy and Telemedicine, 191,* 65–69. https://doi.org/10.3233/978-1-61499-282-0-65.

Gasper, K., & Middlewood, B. L. (2014). Approaching novel thoughts: Understanding why elation and boredom promote associative thought more than distress and relaxation. *Journal of Experimental Social Psychology, 52,* 50–57. https://doi.org/10.1016/j.jesp.2013.12.007.

Halberstadt, J., & Rhodes, G. (2003). It's not just average faces that are attractive: Computer-manipulated averageness makes birds, fish, and automobiles attractive. *Psychonomic Bulletin and Review, 10*(1), 149–156. https://doi.org/10.3758/bf03196479.

Harris, D. J., Vine, S. J., & Wilson, M. R. (2017). Is flow really effortless? The complex role of effortful attention. *Sport, Exercise, and Performance Psychology, 6*(1), 103–114. https://doi.org/10.1037/spy0000083.

Helton, W. S., Green, A. L., & de Joux, N. R. (2013). Cognitive resource demands during climbing: considerations for communication technologies. *Proceedings of the Human Factors and Ergonomics Society Annual Meeting, 57*(1), 1382–1386.

Herrmann, A., Zidansek, M., Sprott, D. E., & Spangenberg, E. R. (2013). The power of simplicity: Processing fluency and the effects of olfactory cues on retail sales. *Journal of Retailing, 89*(1), 30–43. https://doi.org/10.1016/j.jretai.2012.08.002.

Hockey, G. R. (2011). A motivational control theory of cognitive fatigue. In P. L. Ackerman (Ed.), *Cognitive fatigue: Multidisciplinary perspectives on current research and future applications* (pp. 167–187). Washington, DC: American Psychological Association. https://doi.org/10.1037/12343-008.

Hsu, C., Propp, L., Panetta, L., Martin, S., Dentakos, S., Toplak, M. E., et al. (2018). Mental effort and discomfort: Testing the peak-end effect during a cognitively demanding task. *PLoS ONE, 13*(2), e0191479. https://doi.org/10.1371/journal.pone.0191479.

Hsu, H. (2013). Machine gambling in the 'zone': Natasha dow schüll's addiction by design. *Social Studies of Science, 43*(6), 952–956. https://doi.org/10.1177/0306312713507496.

Kahneman, D. (1973). *Attention and effort* (Vol. 1063). Englewood Cliffs, NJ: Prentice-Hall.

Kool, W., McGuire, J. T., Rosen, Z. B., & Botvinick, M. M. (2010). Decision making and the avoidance of cognitive demand. *Journal of Experimental Psychology: General, 139*(4), 665–682. https://doi.org/10.1037/a0020198.

Kuhn, R. (1976). *The demon of noontide: Ennui in western literature*. Princeton, NJ: Princeton University Press.

Kurzban, R., Duckworth, A., Kable, J. W., & Myers, J. (2013). An opportunity cost model of subjective effort and task performance. *Behavioral and Brain Sciences, 36*(06), 661–679. https://doi.org/10.1017/s0140525x12003196.

Kurzban, R. (2016). The sense of effort. *Current Opinion in Psychology, 7,* 67–70. https://doi.org/10.1016/j.copsyc.2015.08.003.

Larson, R. W. (1990). Emotions and the creative process: Anxiety, boredom, and enjoyment as predictors of creative writing. *Imagination, Cognition and Personality, 9,* 275–292. https://doi.org/10.2190/XT9G-WXRF-BK4M-36AK.

Madrigal, A.C. (2013, July 31). The machine zone: This is where you go when you just can't stop looking at pictures on Facebook. *The Atlantic.* https://www.theatlantic.com/technology/archive/2013/07/the-machine-zone-this-is-where-you-go-when-you-just-cant-stop-looking-at-pictures-on-facebook/278185/. Accessed February 25, 2019.

Mann, S., & Cadman, R. (2014). Does being bored make us more creative? *Creativity Research Journal, 26,* 165–173. https://doi.org/10.1080/10400419.2014.901073.

Merrifield, C., & Danckert, J. (2014). Characterizing the psychophysiological signature of boredom. *Experimental Brain Research, 232*(2), 481–491. https://doi.org/10.1007/s00221-013-3755-2.

Mulert, C., Leicht, G., Pogarell, O., Mergl, R., Karch, S., Juckel, G., et al. (2007). Auditory cortex and anterior cingulate cortex sources of the early evoked gamma-band response: Relationship to task difficulty and mental effort. *Neuropsychologia, 45,* 2294–2306. https://doi.org/10.1016/j.neuropsychologia.2007.02.020.

O'Hanlon, J. F. (1981). Boredom: Practical consequences and a theory. *Acta Psychologica, 49*(1), 53–82. https://doi.org/10.1016/0001-6918(81)90033-0.

Oppenheimer, D. M. (2008). The secret life of fluency. *Trends in Cognitive Sciences, 12*(6), 237–241. https://doi.org/10.1016/j.tics.2008.02.014.

Otto, T., Zijlstra, F. R. H., & Goebel, R. (2014). Neural correlates of mental effort evaluation—involvement of structures related to self-awareness. *Social Cognitive and Affective Neuroscience, 9,* 307–315. https://doi.org/10.1093/scan/nss136.

Pekrun, R., Goetz, T., Daniels, L. M., Stupnisky, R. H., & Perry, R. P. (2010). Boredom in achievement settings: Exploring control-value antecedents and performance outcomes of a neglected emotion. *Journal of Educational Psychology, 102*(3), 531–549. https://doi.org/10.1037/a0019243.

Pronin, E., & Jacobs, E. (2008). Thought speed, mood, and the experience of mental motion. *Perspectives on Psychological Science, 3*(6), 461–485. https://doi.org/10.1111/j.1745-6924.2008.00091.x.

Reber, R., Fazendeiro, T. A., & Winkielman, P. (2002). Processing fluency as the source of experiences at the fringe of consciousness. *Psyche: An Interdisciplinary Journal of Research on Consciousness, 8*(10), 175–188.

Romand, D. (2015). Theodor Waitz's theory of feelings and the rise of affective sciences in the mid-19th century. *History of Psychology, 18*(4), 385–400. https://doi.org/10.1037/a0039797.

Scherer, K. R. (2005). What are emotions? and how can they be measured? *Social Science Information, 44*(4), 695–729. https://doi.org/10.1177/0539018405058216.

Schüll, N. D. (2014). *Addiction by design: Machine gambling in Las Vegas*. Princeton, NJ: Princeton University Press.

Schwarz, N. (2018). Of fluency, beauty, and truth: Inferences from metacognitive experiences. In J. Proust & M. Fortier (Eds.), *Metacognitive diversity: An interdisciplinary approach; metacognitive diversity: An interdisciplinary approach* (pp. 25–46). New York, NY: Oxford University Press.

Stanovich, K. E. (2011). What intelligence test miss. *Inquiry: Critical Thinking Across the Disciplines, 26*(2), 20–20. https://doi.org/10.5840/inquiryctnews201126216.

Stavropoulos, V., Burleigh, C., Beard, C., Gomez, R., & Griffiths, M. D. (2018). Being there: A preliminary study examining the role of presence in internet gaming disorder. *International Journal of Mental Health and Addiction*, 1–11. https://doi.org/10.1007/s11469-018-9891-y.

Teo, T. (2007). Local institutionalization, discontinuity, and German textbooks of psychology, 1816-1854. *Journal of the History of the Behavioral Sciences, 43*(2), 135–157. https://doi.org/10.1002/jhbs.20220.

Ulrich, M., Keller, J., & Grön, G. (2016). Neural signatures of experimentally induced flow experiences identified in a typical fMRI block design with BOLD imaging. *Social Cognitive and Affective Neuroscience, 11*(3), 496–507. https://doi.org/10.1093/scan/nsv133.

U.S. Department of Labor, Bureau of Labor Statistics. (2012). American Time Use Survey. *U.S. Bureau of Labor Statistics*. https://www.bls.gov/tus/home.htm. Accessed February 25, 2019.

Van den Bergh, O., & Vrana, S. R. (1998). Repetition and boredom in a perceptual fluency/attributional model of affective judgements. *Cognition and Emotion, 12*(4), 533–553. https://doi.org/10.1080/026999398379556.

Van Tilburg, W. A. P., & Igou, E. R. (2012). On boredom: Lack of challenge and meaning as distinct boredom experiences. *Motivation and Emotion, 36*(2), 181–194. https://doi.org/10.1007/s11031-011-9234-9.

Vodanovich, S. J. (2003). On the possible benefits of boredom: A neglected area in personality research. *Psychology and Education: An Interdisciplinary Journal, 40,* 28–33.

Westbrook, A., & Braver, T. S. (2015). Cognitive effort: A neuroeconomic approach. *Cognitive, Affective, and Behavioral Neuroscience, 15*(2), 395–415. https://doi.org/10.3758/s13415-015-0334-y.

Whittlesea, B. W. (1993). Illusions of familiarity. *Journal of Experimental Psychology. Learning, Memory, and Cognition, 19*(6), 1235–1253. https://doi.org/10.1037/0278-7393.19.6.1235.

Wilson, T. D., Reinhard, D. A., Westgate, E. C., Gilbert, D. T., Ellerbeck, N., Hahn, C., et al. (2014). Just think: The challenges of the disengaged mind. *Science, 345*(6192), 75–77. https://doi.org/10.1126/science.1250830.

Winkielman, P., Schwarz, N., Fazendeiro, T. A., & Reber, R. (2003). The hedonic marking of processing fluency: Implications for evaluative judgment. In J. Musch & K. C. Klauer (Eds.), *The psychology of evaluation: Affective processes in cognition and emotion* (pp. 189–217). Mahwah, NJ: Lawrence Erlbaum Associates Publishers.

Zajonc, R. B. (1968). Attitudinal effects of mere exposure. *Journal of Personality and Social Psychology, 9*(2), 1–27. https://doi.org/10.1037/h0025848.

Zakay, D. (2014). Psychological time as information: The case of boredom. *Frontiers in Psychology, 5,* 917. https://doi.org/10.3389/fpsyg.2014.00917.

Zuckerman, M. (1979). Attribution of success and failure revisited, or: The motivational bias is alive and well in attribution theory. *Journal of Personality, 47*(2), 245–287. https://doi.org/10.1111/j.1467-6494.1979.tb00202.x.

John Eastwood a Clinical Psychologist, holds an academic appointment at York University in Toronto, Canada, as an Associate Professor of Clinical Psychology, where he trains future psychologists and conducts research on the intersection between cognition and emotion. He has examined how attention is allocated to affective and socially relevant information, the influence of mood and motivation on attention, as well as the affective consequences of attention failures. His current work seeks to better understand the feeling of thinking and how such feelings are an inextricable part of cognition. In particular, he is examining the feeling of boredom associated with the unengaged mind. Recently, he obtained a research grant from the Natural Sciences and Engineering Research Council of Canada to explore the cognitive mechanisms underlying boredom. Among his works on boredom, we should highlight the most quoted: "Does a lack of life meaning cause boredom? Results from psychometric, longitudinal, and experimental analyses" (*Journal of Social and Clinical Psychology*, 2009), "Boredom: An emotional experience distinct from apathy, anhedonia, or depression" (*Journal of Social and Clinical Psychology*, 2011), "The unengaged mind: Defining boredom in terms of attention" (*Perspectives on Psychological Science*, 2012), "Development and validation of the multidimensional state boredom scale" (*Assessment*, 2013), and "Causes of boredom: The person, the situation, or both?" (*Personality and Individual Differences*, 2014).

Dana Gorelik received her Bachelor of Arts Honours in Psychology from York University in 2017. From 2014 to 2017, she was a clinical research assistant at the Opportunities to Understand Childhood Hurt (OUCH) Lab. She worked also as a manager of the Culture and Religion Lab at York University. She is currently a second-year master's student in the clinical psychology program at York University. Her research focuses on developing a scale to measure trait boredom, as well as on investigating the cognitive causes of trait boredom.

Chapter 5
Boredom and Psychoanalysis

María Cecilia Antón and Josefa Ros Velasco

Introduction

From the second half of the twentieth century to the end, the blossoming interest of the mental health professionals on the phenomenon of boredom increased to unimagined levels. Particularly, the psychoanalysts riddled the journals' pages with titles such as those by well-known psychoanalyst Martin Wangh "Boredom in psychoanalytic perspective" (1975), and "Some psychoanalytic observation on boredom" (1979), to name just an example. However, many psychoanalysts were heirs of the father of psychoanalysis, Sigmund Freud. This was also the case of the French psychiatrist and psychoanalyst Jacques Lacan. The present chapter aims to develop the notion of boredom and its relationship with psychoanalysis by taking into account many of its roots in the past century. Particularly, we consider boredom is a symptom of other conditions. Therefore, to work on this concept from a psychoanalytical perspective, we will mainly follow parts of Lacan and Freud's works, who tackled the complex question, and some clinical vignettes.

Boredom is a rich concept to approach from different perspectives: individual, cultural, and historical. At present, boredom is a central piece in the analysis of leisure and the study of communities. That is the reason why we prefer to talk about boredom in its plural form: *boredoms*. We will mention some characteristics of boredom that can be approached from a psychoanalytical point of view in which Freudian and Lacanian theories represent a significant contribution. First, we will talk of the kind of boredom that, being considered as an affection, comes from certain situations we can rescue from a psychoanalytical perspective stated overall by Lacan and Freud. Second, we will focus on boredom experienced during the

M. C. Antón (✉)
National University of Mar del Plata, Buenos Aires, Argentina
e-mail: mariaceceliaanton@gmail.com

J. Ros Velasco
Harvard University, Cambridge, USA

J. Ros Velasco (ed.), *Boredom Is in Your Mind*,
https://doi.org/10.1007/978-3-030-26395-9_5

practice of an activity and its relationship with the flow theory by the Italian psychologist Mihály Csíkszentmihályi (Claremont University, California). We will discuss the importance of being meaningfully engaged when doing something to avoid boredom. Third, we want to address the different possible reactions to boredom, from creative to deviant ones. Fourth, we will delve into one specific philosophical reaction related to introspection and its relationship with psychoanalysis. Fifth, we will elaborate on a clinical case study to see how theory is applied into practice. Finally, we will pay attention to the state of affairs of boredom treatment from a clinical perspective.

Boredom Is an Affection

Jacques Lacan considers, in *Television* (1980), that boredom is one of the soul's passions, following Saint Thomas. He says that passions constitute intimate affections: sadness, happiness, bliss, annoyance (*ennui*, boredom), and bad mood; the last two affections are common among young people. There are modes of boredom; some generate creative acts, and others are linked to extremely unpleasant states and concepts from psychopathology. For this reason, reading this affection in each particular case and in its own context is of interest to address *subjectivity*.

The French psychoanalyst Colette Soler, a commentator of Jacques Lacan, stated in her book *Lacanian affects: The function of affect in Lacan's work* (2015) that it has been Sigmund Freud who said, in his writings "The project for a psychology for neurologists" (1895) and "Repression" (1915), that the concept of quota of affect must be situated along the axis of pleasure–unpleasure. Quota of affect is not repressed (it has thus not disappeared) but is rather displaced: It has become disconnected from its original cause. Additionally, if affect produces changes in the body and disturbs its functioning, does it mean that it comes to the body or from the body? Which is the affecting party and which is the affected one?

In Freud's writings, the treatment of affects raises concerns from the start. In "Repression" (1915), Freud points out that representation (image) and its quota of affect suffer different fates due to the repression of the unbearable. This gives affect a specific nature for it can come to light in a qualitatively colorful affect or mutated, transformed into anguish or suffocated. In "Inhibition, symptoms and anxiety" (1926a), Freud states that to talk about affects, we must leave the realm of psychology and enter the borderland of physiology. Physiology reveals the somatic, organic, and body innervations, which play a central role. Besides, affective states (especially anxiety) have been incorporated in the mind as precipitates of primeval traumatic experiences, and when a similar situation occurs, they are revived like mnemic symbols. Freud links affect to symbols and goes one step further by including them in the pleasure–unpleasure principle and giving them a representative (or qualitative) nature.

Moreover, language is paramount to establish ourselves as human beings and it also affects us deeply in the abovementioned sense. As human beings, we are speakers, subjects attached to language in the sense of how we process mental images, events, experiences, and memories. Therefore, the triad that intervenes in any emotional experience, including boredom, is the subject of the unconscious—the living body—language. With that in mind, the responses to the experience of boredom are diverse, as they depend on each individual in particular. Sometimes the individual *chooses* the way of dealing with boredom, unconsciously and subjectively. This is because the experience of boredom is primarily reactive.

Boredom is a reactive affect in two senses. First, it sets in motion what we call the *unconscious* to make us conscious about something in the context that is not working properly, that is to say, it unconsciously makes us consciously react to the environment—this is something with which psychodynamic theory and Csíkszentmihályi's flow theory agree, as we will see in the next section. Overall, boredom constitutes a matter of levels, of depth. That is also why we allow ourselves to refer to boredom in its plural form, *boredoms*. In *The seminar of Jacques Lacan*, Book V "The formations of the unconscious" (1999), class of January 15, 1958, Jacques Lacan talks about boredom in a specific psychoanalytic practice that could serve as an example for other professional practices. Lacan states (1999, p. 182):

> There is a moment that I am sure you do not think about enough because you live in it, I might say, as in your native air, which is called: boredom. You have perhaps never thought out the degree to which boredom is something that comes to formulate itself in the clearest fashion, that one would like "something other." One may well eat muck every day but not always the same muck. These are sorts of alibis, alibis that are formulated, already symbolized, of what is this essential connection with "something other."

In this passage, Lacan points out that a profession—as well as any other circumstance—becomes a problem when the unconscious regularity involved in it becomes annoying, and criticizes, by the way, particularly the phenomena of the institutionalization of psychoanalysis. He ends the class by introducing the notion of 'the name of the father' and its effects. When a person is bored, he or she seeks to get rid of it by means of desire, astonishment caused by jokes, and the unconscious. Boredom resembles anguish with regard to both being a turning point that allows the subject to take up a stance toward desire or creativity, or to bad things, even though there may be gradations. Thus, secondly, once we are aware of our boredom and its causes, the experience is so unpleasant that we cannot but doing something to change such a context that is causing our boredom and discomfort.

It is also in this sense that some thinkers are suggesting that boredom plays a key role in our individual and social development by pointing out that the driving force of boredom meets an adaptive function. Professor Peter Toohey is the main representative of this new trend as he stated the idea of the driving force of boredom and how it meets an adaptive function in a true Darwinian sense, in his book *Boredom: A lively history* (2011). He was mainly inspired by psychologists Robert Plutchik and Henry Kellerman.

Plutchik and Kellerman claimed, in *Emotion: Theory, research and experience*, that negative emotions of affects like boredom help individuals to cope with survival problems and keep them away from harmful environments and situations.

According to Toohey (2011), we can see boredom as one of that adaptive emotions since it protects us from danger (Plutchik and Kellerman 1980) by highlighting our relationship with the environment and forcing us to develop a strategy to explore new opportunities (see also Todman 2007). As Plutchik and Kellerman, the neurologist Antonio Damasio suggested, in *The feeling of what happens: Body and emotion in the making of consciousness* (1999) and *Looking for Spinoza: Joy, sorrow, and the feeling brain* (2003), that negative emotions directly influence self-regulation by foreseeing the dangers, being an advantage and opportunity for individuals. Boredom may be one of these emotions or affections that might actually have been selected in our evolutionary race due to its role to prevent us from toxic situations and lead the search for new experiences. By the same token, the German philosopher Hans Blumenberg stated, in his posthumous book *Beschreibung des Menschen* [Description of man] (2006), that boredom meets an adaptive role in stimulating the change that keeps our interest. Blumenberg did not hesitate to claim that if we do not suffer from boredom when we are fully adapted, forcing us to be in constant motion, we would be unable to adapt to future changes. This is the reason why, according to him, boredom was selected: to fulfill a cardinal adaptive function and to open the door to future adaptations.

In short, as an affection, boredom might be a symptom or a consequence of one certain environment or circumstance that is different from one person to another. Boredom is a mean to make conscious the unconscious unpleasant experience, that is to say, it is some kind of somatization through which we become aware of what we need to leave behind to move forward. How does it exactly work?

The Sequence of Boredom

It has been in recent years that boredom has become a matter of scientific and clinical interest, being analyzed from its neurological and cognitive conditions (Eastwood et al. 2012; Danckert and Allman 2005). We want to focus now on how boredom does show up during activity and its relationship with the flow theory, according to Csíkszentmihályi, and the psychodynamic principles. To date, it is estimated that boredom arises from a discontinued relationship between the individual and the environment. How does it really happen?

Following the flow theory by Csíkszentmihályi in *Beyond boredom and anxiety* (1975; see also 1990, 1998, 2000), individuals experience boredom when the external stimuli are repetitive and monotonous (understimulation) as well as when they are excessive (hyperstimulation) and do not meet their psychic needs. What happens then is a mismatch between the environment and the individual. An environment that is not able to stimulate us is one that does not provide optimal experiences. This is the situation in which there is not a balance between the level of enjoyment of the experience with the self-perception of control and excitation. Thus, the experiences that represent high-level challenges when individuals are skilled to overcome them result in optimal experience. However, in order to maintain this optimal experience over time, it is necessary to increase the difficulty and the individual's skills when the experience is repeated and repeated not to lose the flow. If the flow is lost, boredom shows up as a psychological state of dissatisfaction, frustration, and negativity that make decrease our neurological state of excitation.

London et al.'s experiments in "Increase of autonomic arousal by boredom" (1972) and those by Berlyne in *Conflict, arousal, and curiosity* (1960) have demonstrated, by measuring individual physiological changes, that when people are bored, the level of cortical excitement falls down and the reticular activating system (RAS) releases to promote an autonomic activation that pushes the bored to look for something else capable of normalizing the excitement cortical levels. That is to say, following Damrad-Frye and Laird, in "The experience of boredom: The role of the self-perception of attention" (1989), when the pattern of external stimulation is very low and boredom shows up, the internal excitement increases to compensate for the environmental weakness resulting in different actions.

Professor of Psychology Josef Revers explained, in his work "Perspectivas antropológicas del aburrimiento" ["Anthropological perspectives of boredom"] (1967, p. 42) that children were the best illustration of that sequence:

> Children [...] are the best to observe the content of boredom. Hardly has the child taken ownership of his body and its members when boredom shows up. As soon as he has fulfilled his vital needs—hunger, thirst, etc.—an urgent need for being occupied is awakened, one that crosses all boundaries.

The experience of boredom seems to be more individualized, recognized, and manifested in children rather than in adults, and this is shown in this short case study. Rodrigo is an 11-year-old teenager, who refuses to do his school assignments. This was the reason why he repeated a year, and his mother turned to a psychologist. Rodrigo said that he was really bored and that he only experienced pleasure from playing computer games. He complained all the time. He was selfless, overweight, slow, and untidy. Shortly, Rodrigo complained about his lack of organization, which was associated with the incipient changes in his body due to puberty. Those physical changes were not accompanied by his psychic maturation. He also suffered from the loss of his loved ones, his father, several years ago. So, all of this happened to him against the backdrop of burden and weariness. Why does a child lose his capacity for astonishment? What could be boring about the school contents, other than the routine which is never accomplished? The answers to those questions will depend on the case and the circumstances.

The common expression 'Mom, I'm bored,' constitutes a call for the presence of Other (the big Other) to promote desire. Overall, the capacity for astonishment and child investigation prevents boredom. And, even though having fun can also become imperative, the term 'bored' provides a glimpse of truth: the capture of the world from impotence or from overadaptation.

The concept of meaningful engagement makes sense in this context. Boredom is not the result of a lack of things or activities to do but of a lack of meaningful things and activities to do: a lack of sense. There is for sure a relationship between boredom and sense, as it constitutes an affect-effect in light of two circumstances: first, when boredom appears as a result of emptiness or lack of sense; second, when it appears as an effect of an excess of sense. In the first case, lack of sense can appear in different gradations, as mentioned before, from the slightest to the deepest. For example, lack of sense can lead to a state of grief, loss of identity and ideals, depression, and melancholy. When boredom is caused by an excess of sense (enjoyment), it is linked to certain injunctions (whether internal or external).

To sum up, boredom is, following from the above, the result of a lack of flow caused by a lack of sense of those non-meaningful activities we engaged, whose main consequence is a lack of mutual adaptation between the individual and the environment. Therefore, this affect usually makes us react to the meaningless situation in the two different stages explained in the first section: first, by making us aware of what is the situation we are rejecting; second, by driving us to some kind of action to get rid of the displeasure state caused by boredom. But, of which kind are these reactions?

Reactions to Boredom

Boredom is experienced by a subject (S) when he or she finds himself or herself in a certain environment (E) that is boring (Parreño Roldán 2013), that is to say, a situation truly hyperstimulating or understimulating to the extent that it loses its sense. Such boredom disappears when something new is introduced in the boring environment (Todman 2003). This has been known as *exogenous boredom* or *situation-dependent boredom* (Martin et al. 2006; see also Mikulas and Vodanovich 1993). The experience of boredom is so powerful that it cannot be ignored. Boredom brings the feeling of discomfort that we need to leave behind. It makes us feel an irritation caused by self-consciousness that becomes unbearable (Blumenberg 2006). When 'the bored' feels that the environment does not meet their needs and expectations (Eastwood et al. 2012), he or she begins being aware that something is not working and his or her boredom becomes reactive (Neu 1998; Todman 2003). Boredom points out the relationship between the individuals and the environment urging them to develop a strategy to explore it and discover novelties that serve to get rid of it (Todman 2007). In this sense, boredom always leads some kind of reaction and consequence (Retana 2011).

Half a century ago, psychoanalyst Otto Fenichel acknowledged, in his paper "On the psychology of boredom" (1951), that the responses to boredom may be truly varied. Individuals not always react to boredom in the same way. In certain circumstances, people respond to boredom disproportionately. At times, the most violent pulsions are followed by an act of creativity. In other cases, the result of boredom is a dangerous or harmful action. Boredom motivates both constructive and destructive, functional and dysfunctional actions (Fisher 1987). It depends entirely on the personal circumstances of the bored and the options offered by the environment (Van Tilburg and Igou 2011). In other words, the consequences of boredom are linked to both the mental and psychic state of the bored and the context in which he or she is immersed. It is possible, in that sense, depending on the context and the subject, for boredom to result in both suicidal tendencies or extra-lucid power.

To cope with boredom, individuals may acquire certain compulsive behaviors or drug abuse problems. There are cases in which sense is produced by drug abuse (e.g., through drug-induced hallucinations) when certain subjects feel empty. Other compulsions or acts can also lead to unpleasure caused by boredom. According to Berlyne (1960), negative consequences of boredom come into place when individuals try to get rid of it but they cannot do it because some other factors impede an alternative reaction. And these factors are related to the individual himself but also to the environment. When boredom is pathological because of the individual's conditions, boredom cannot be put aside even if novelty is introduced throughout the context of the bored. This is because his or her individual RAS fails to lead the reaction phase or just simply because he or she is reluctant to change—for example, some patients state: 'I am like this because I am like my mother or father and I am not going to change;' this way, they justify some of their sufferings, without considering a solution for their problems. When the environment is too restrictive and paternalistic and does not allow the individuals to develop their creativity, boredom may also result in deviant behaviors.

Specialists in mental health include the following psychosocial pathologies resulting from sustained boredom that cannot be avoided because of individual or environmental failures—apart from addiction to drugs: hostile and aggressive behaviors, sex addiction, gambling, irresponsible driving, school deviation, work absenteeism, criminal actions, suicidal tendencies, lack of social affiliation, or irregular food intake, to name a few (see for a complete list Martin et al. 2006; Van Tilburg and Igou 2011; Vodanovich and Watt 1999).

One of the most interesting deviant behaviors resulting from boredom has been considered sexual perversion. From the opposite perspective of desire, boredom (not only by itself) can summon incorrect behaviors. In *The seminar of Jacques Lacan*, Book VII "Ethics in psychoanalysis" (1973), Jacques Lacan states that the work of the Marquis de Sade results in boredom as the response of the *being*, whether reader or writer, at the approach to a center of incandescence or an "absolute zero that is physically unbearable" (p. 243). That repetitive zero reduces the sexual masochist partner to absolutely nothing. In literature, Alphonse Allais, in his short story *The King is naked,* portrays the theme of perversion when the clothes of a female dancer fall off and she is skinned alive by order of the King. After having seen the bloody scarlet flesh, the King does not feel bored anymore.

Surely, literature is one field in which the consequences of boredom are always depicted as deviant behaviors. Beyond perversion, boredom was and will continue to be the subject of literary works in which adultery is the protagonist. Such is the case in the story *The chemist's wife* (1984), by Anton Chekhov, who depicts a bored female character, similar to an unlimited feminine enjoyment, to whom only the passionate love of another man can rescue, as the following lines show (p. 192):

> Everything had long been asleep. The only person not asleep was the young wife of Chernomordik, a qualified distributor who ran the town's pharmacy. She had gone to bed and got up again three times, but could not sleep, and she did not know why. She sat at the open window in her nightdress and looked into the street. She felt bored, depressed, displeased… so displeased that she felt quite inclined to cry — again she did not know why. There seemed to be a lump in her chest that kept rising into her throat.

When facing boredom, love, especially passionate and adulterer love, seems to be one of its remedies (see especially Ros Velasco and Provolt in press; Ros Velasco 2019 to go deeper regarding the place of boredom in literature).

One exception is the temporary lack of sense. It can lead to favorable changes in certain subjects, but it depends always on the individual as we already mentioned. The reactive component of boredom can lead to creativity and innovation in healthy individuals and environments. In this respect, boredom is understood as an axis of thought, progress, and even science. Sociologist Émile Durkheim stated, in *Suicide: A study in sociology* (1997), many forms of original behavior may result from boredom and, following now the words of Walter Benjamin, in *The arcades project* (2002), the starting point of great feats. Leaving behind truly pathological personalities and sociocultural contexts in which the search for novelty is impracticable —for instead, those marked by predictability, in which there is a preplanned response for each demand—the potential of boredom is inherently positive. This is because boredom prevents stillness by giving way to something else. In short, boredom meets benign purposes in healthy contexts and individuals because of its consequences translated into compensatory activities.

Finally, we should note that sometimes we do not react to boredom. For example, when a speech turns monothematic, repetitive, crushing the subjectivity of the listener, the listener has no other option than getting bored. From a philosophical point of view, the German philosopher Martin Heidegger noted, in *Being and time* (2008), that this common situation is experienced, for instead, when people voluntarily expose themselves to a situation such as a high-society meeting or a scientific meeting that is not meaningful for them but superficial and uncompromising. Since the circumstance is meaningless and people's participation in it let them empty, and since people know in advance that the situation was going to be boring and insubstantial, individuals feel that things abandon them to themselves and they abandon them by getting bored.

Then, we can understand the story about this feeling narrated by a woman during an analytic session. The patient never gets out of her house. She stays in her bed sleeping. Even though she has plans, she rules them out due to an excess in a negative sense which prevents her from possible failure and frustrations. This makes her feel sad and increases her feelings of emptiness. In conclusion, an excess of sense (in this case, negative) can cause a lack of significantly pleasant mental images. At times, she ends up abandoning herself by staying in bed. In this case, her boredom is a signal of depression. During the intermediate stage of these psychoanalytic sessions, she broke out of boredom by doing a long-wished activity. These sessions began with appalling anxiety, which was not linked to any conscious thought. This story is useful because it shows a continuous production of negative sense that can lead to inactivity. However, even in this sense, some kind of introspection is taking place.

Boredom and Philosophy

Some authors have stated that boredom may be understood as an opportunity to learn from oneself (Rule 1998), a mechanism of anticipation, a starting point of great works (Butler et al. 2011), and a valuable art (Sloterdijk 2009). Thinkers like Siegfried Kracauer considered, as he did in *The mass ornament* (2005), that to be bored is the only suitable option because boredom provides a kind of guarantee that one is still in control of their own existence. According to Russell in *The conquest of happiness* (1930), we must admit that a certain degree of boredom is essential to living a happy life and is something that should be taught to young people.

Boredom is an experience that triggers anxiety and agitation (Van Tilburg and Igou 2011), and perhaps even something like nervousness (Fenichel 1951). Boredom, detached from the complexity of the mental disease and restrictive environments, leads to innovation. It makes us feel dissatisfied with certain situations because "when we are bored there is something of the context that we are rejecting" (Retana 2011, p. 283) and, thereupon, drives us to seek new opportunities as a reaction. Thus, it is also a symptom that instigates moments of experimentation (Parreño Roldán 2013; Moravia 1960), including a critical element: an expression of deep dissatisfaction (Svendsen 2005). Ultimately, we can safely assume that boredom leads to introspectiveness and cognitive reevaluation (Parreño Roldán 2013). Boredom moves us toward curiosity as well as toward epistemic self-exploration (Van Aart et al. 2010) and positive self-examination (Meyer Spacks 1995). No matter how, boredom is an opportunity to learn about oneself (Rule 1998).

Following Toohey's words (2011, p. 185), based on those of Teresa Belton and Estger Priyadharsini, in the paper "Boredom and schooling: a cross-disciplinary exploration" (2010, p. 588), "boredom can also contain critical reflective potential and can be a powerful stimulus to creativity." They suggest that "a certain amount of boredom, by allowing for contemplation, daydreaming and imagining alternatives, allows a refreshed return to activity" (2010, p. 588). Throughout its experience, we have some chance for reflection and relaxation, that is to say, for going back on ourselves and observe our thoughts. That movement intensifies our self-perception and offers an opportunity to live in slow motion and as if we were one another person (Toohey 2011).

That is the reason why many philosophies and spiritual practices such as Buddhism and Taoism consider boredom as an opportunity for self-learning and illumination and usually wish the good luck by saying 'That you are not born in an interesting time' (Meyer Spacks 1989). And also the old Chinese curses said 'That you are never bored' (Meyer Spacks 1989) and the Turks usually pointed out that the one who is bored is squeezing his or her soul.

Boredom has been a major topic of discussion in the field of philosophy for all these reasons. As regards Martin Heidegger, the philosopher who most reflected on boredom, we want to mention a work by Daniel Lesmes González (2009) titled "Uno se aburre: Heidegger y la filosofía del aburrimiento" ["One is bored: Heidegger and the philosophy of boredom"]. As Lesmes González states concerning *Being and time* (2008), Heidegger proposed abandonment of oneself, a desubjectivation which only boredom can produce; he further defines boredom as complete immersion in the emptiness of modern times, through a transference of ourselves and the entities. During that state of mind, the world becomes indifferent; entities abandon us, and we abandon them.

This twofold concept—being bored and be boring—reaches its highest level in what Heidegger calls *profound boredom*. Boredom ensues and swallows the self. This author points out that being bored dissolves the imaginary-self turning oneself into an indifferent being. Based on a scale of degrees, Heidegger analyzes boredom in three types, especially during the lectures of 1929-1930 at the University of Freiburg—later published in his work *The fundamental concepts of metaphysics* (1995). It is in the third type, when the experience of boredom becomes more and more profound, that the subject becomes no one, i.e., a completely indifferent being. Boredom is one of those affects [Stimmungen], according to the Heideggerian *Gestimmtsein* theory, that, together with others such as fear [Angst], anger [Wut], hope [Hoffnung], happiness [Freude], enthusiasm [Enthusiasmus], and serenity [Heiterkeit], predispose people to one certain existential orientation.

Briefly, affects tell something about the relationship between individuals and the world and predetermine people to one particular experience through the qualities of their ontologic structures, giving shape to our way of thinking and acting (Gumbrecht 2011). Following from the above, we can understand boredom as an essential affect that is an existential orientation: It is a way of being in the world or a way of adopting perspectives toward oneself and the world. According to Heidegger, boredom is able to announce the possibilities of which we were not conscious, which were latent [brachliegen].

Clinical Case

From the psychoanalytic perspective, and based on Sigmund Freud's article "Repression" (1915), a quota of affect or quantum of affect is displaced from the representation to which it is linked through a defense mechanism called repression. This 'quota of affect' separated from its original representation has three different possible destinations. First, it can be suffocated. Second, it can be transformed into anguish. Finally, it can come to light in a qualitatively colorful affect. Thus, through these three possible destinations, the psychic apparatus reduces the psychic tensions according to the pleasure principle. In this way, the psychic apparatus remains in a nirvana state.

Nevertheless, some memories (representations) and their unpleasant affects may appear suddenly as the psychic apparatus is not able to bury them completely. This complex repression theory is illustrated by the following clinical case in which a middle-aged woman who suffers from a vital lack of sense manifested as temporally boredom. Temporary boredom in typical neurosis is very different than deep boredom as lack of sense. For example, another patient who suffered melancholic psychosis said in his therapeutical sessions: 'Why we live if we die later?' In melancholy illustrated in the Dürer's engraving (1514) (Fig. 5.1), with the same name, there is not temporary lack of sense by neurosis.

This clinical case was about a professional woman who had archived all her personal and professional aims. As regards her personal life, she was married and had three kids. She had been married for a long time, and she had a good relationship with her husband. Also, her three school-age children were healthy and happy. Concerning her professional life, she had a well-paid job which she enjoyed doing. However, she felt lonely and bored and decided to consult a psychoanalyst. Throughout therapeutical sessions, she became aware that she was bored with her lifestyle because she had always fulfilled others' demands but not hers. Also, she realized that one satisfying other people's wishes had ignored her own. What is more, she had left them aside for such a long time that she could not think of any. She was not fully motivated at all to set new aims in any aspect of her life.

Based on this state (diagnosis), the psychoanalyst asked the patient in which moments of her life she had felt bored. She linked her current state to three mnemonic images that had left their marks on her. Her boredom had a depressive tinge. Her first weariness memories were associated with a traumatic experience she had had at the age of twelve. She remembered suffering from peritonitis and going through surgery which was complicated by an intrahospital virus. She could still relieve the endless hours she had spent in hospital while trying to recover. Her feelings of boredom and impotence had stayed with her even though time had gone by. Although she had tried hard to release this anguish, she was haunted by it. Thus, she associated these feelings of weariness and impotence with her current depressive state. Her second stream of memories was associated with her dead parents. She recalled their unhappy marriage due to their lack of rapport and long working hours. She had an unpleasant memory of her parent's daily routine full of the workday and home life obligations and responsibilities not finding time to relax or have fun all together. Her third set of associations was linked to experiences of deep, anguish, lack of motivation, and wish for life and her things.

During her childhood, this patient helped her mother in the job and housework. This and other situations made her have certain personal characteristics: excessive responsibilities, exacerbated self-criticism, few friendships, and scaring free time. This clinical case reveals the complexity of the boredom experience as a manifestation linked to a variety of life situations. The relationship among demand, desire, and joy is a key aspect to be considered in each subject. In the former case,

Fig. 5.1 Albrecht Dürer. *Melencolia I*. 1514. Engraving, Plate: 9 7/16 × 7 5/16 in. (24 × 18.5 cm). Collection of The Metropolitan Museum of Art. Public Domain

there is not any controversy about the psychic instances that led the patient to the state of sheer boredom which was mainly caused by complying excessively satisfactorily with other people's demands. In general, a patient feeling conflicted, distressed, or even anguished consults a psychoanalyst to achieve a change of state of mind.

However, the achievement of this aim cannot be always guaranteed. Language is a key to define ourselves as human beings, as we stated earlier in this chapter, and it affects us deeply. As human beings, we are the conjunction of the subject dependent on the language and the physical body. In the tale "The night face up" (1967), by the Argentinean writer Julio Cortázar, the story not only develops around the physical body dimension but it also conveys the pain, fear, and boredom of suffering from insomnia face up at night or in any other occasion. We have always been and we are told in some way by others and Others. While the first refers to equals; the latter is understood as our meaningful ancestors. Hence, the importance of the archeological process during the analytical sessions to look for the patient's buried pieces of the past and to engage him/her in an account of past events, i.e., to encourage the patient to give an account of his or her own past in present time. Both experiences are stages in the psychoanalytical cure mainly as memories adopt their own shape and the past stops being an endless repetition allowing the future to reinvent itself in a different fashion.

The task of the psychoanalyst is to witness and encourage a complex psychic process of elaboration which begins with the image, passes through the sign, and then goes to the mnemic trace and memory. This elaborative process helps to ponder about the origin of certain discomforts, to inquire about them, and to release energy accumulated in them (Antón 2013). In this process, language is needed, in spite of the fact that some scripts will not encode into words and remain unspoken without producing a story or an account. Nevertheless, each story repeats itself and distorts others. Thus, there are as many reasons as to trust and distrust an account at the same time (Gorlier 2008). A patient's account of events is a version that will change according to the ideas and points of view which he/she adopts at a specific point of time. It is possible to change the patient's subjective standpoint thanks to reflection and introspection upon his or her past in the middle of the tyrannical present time that demands an illusionary lucidity.

In psychoanalysis, the inquire and the personal account constitute a method to process the reality of the trauma (extremely shocking events) by elaborating a story or account that helps to relieve the subject. The expression *narrated body and without narrating* refers to the following reflection: At a certain point of time, a narrated body can produce a story whose core are its memories and personal accounts, however, in another occasion that body may not be ready to elaborate a story about personal events because of different reasons such as impotence or the temporary impossibility to translate and symbolize them through language. In this last case, maybe, the only means of expression is acting-out, i.e., an impulsive performance addressed to someone in search of interpretation.

Going back to the topic of boredom and its relationship to the past, some adult subjects recall in the mists of time part of their childhood in analytical sessions. They evoke their repetitive childhood games some of which were always pleasant, while some others were not. If we enquire them about what made them feel happy or bored as children, interesting stories will certainly arise. In general, the childlike ability to inquire and be awed prevents boredom. The expression I am bored denotes a certain truth: It is the perception of the world from the point of view of the impotence or overadaptation (as in the last clinical example about the middle-aged woman). In addition, boredom can be an answer to both the weariness and demands of modern life.

Furthermore, the complete absence of vital desire can manifest itself in profound boredom and lead to suicide as a pure and disastrous expression of the death drive inherent in every human being. The death drive, *Thanatos*, is occasionally separated and divorced from the life drive, *Eros*. To a lesser extent, the lack of desire or enthusiasm in everyday life can manifest itself in different states of mind similar to depression. The Freudian desire, the German word for *Wunch* [desire, wish, aspiration], is a complex concept itself, and its relationship with human beings is singular to each particular subject. According to Lacanian theory, the object of desire is unattainable; it is a metonymic object, and it is considered 'the object cause of desire,' i.e., an object that causes, seduces, encourages, and motivates the movement that is directed toward its search.

It is interesting to analyze the relationships between the subject and his or her desire because he or she will or will not be driven by this captivating force. This desiring drive goes in pursuit of satisfying experiences some of which cannot be achieved completely. This pursuit relieves the tension that can be blocking the inner or outer world by different circumstances such as boredom. That movement that walks in search of satisfactory experiences, without finding them in their totality, but that relieve the tension, that causes pleasure, that is to say, that 'decreases the tension,' is what can be hampered by different circumstances of both the internal and external world.

Boredom counterpoints with anguish. However, they share certain features of doubt and subjective suspension because the general state of boredom is one of stillness, calmness, introspection, drowsiness, discontinuity, and even unconsciousness. In any case, boredom is a way of being in the world. More often than not, boredom is not on its own, but it is accompanied by regrets and inhibitions. Consequently, asking why, when, where, and how a patient feels bored is helpful in the analysis.

The concept of boredom is enriching in its interpretation. If it is understood as an affective manifestation, first it is necessary to comprehend the analysis of the affections by Freud in the texts "Repression" (1915) and "Inhibition, symptom and anguish" (1926a). Also, in the article "Psychoanalysis" (1926b) he states that the impulses are affectively invested representations putting the emphasis in the dynamic character of the affection issue. Some affections, not just some forms of boredom, are intriguing and meaningless for many of us and can become current because they belong to our origin, even our ancestors, and, therefore, are part of our heritage. We can experience affections that do not correspond to us or that we do not get to interpret at all. At this point, boredom would not be significant if we did not know that our passions can be those of past or those of the present time.

Certain statements of the patients may move the analysis deeply. We name things to embrace the infinite. The short story, entitled "We got lost, admit it" (Antón 2013), can be considered as a step before the statement 'I'm bored.' It illustrates the encounter with the *Thing* or existential emptiness which is perceived at first as the unspeakable, the non-portrayed, and the indescribable but, eventually, it becomes consistent, representative, and meaningful through the senses and the word. As these lines show:

> When I got up that morning I found it. It was a horrible, odorous thing which stuck to me. I thought it was at home but when I looked for it, it cunningly vanished. Until I realized it was everywhere: clothes, half empty perfume bottles, books, CDs, photos… however, I could not catch it.
>
> And it came over and over me until it invaded me completely. It was sticky. I could not think beyond its crushing weight or its chocking density. Since then, I can barely swallow the little food I intake. I got lost, I admit it. I cannot get rid of the *Thing*; call as you want, a fulfilled sinister fantasy, an unknown flashback, an insatiable demand, an uncomfortable question, a distressing presence, a giant ameba, an atrocious tarantula, a sinister creature, an obstructive object. Do you know what I mean? It is *that* that I cannot get rid of. It is *that thing* which haunts me, which despairs me, which harasses me.
>
> Call it as you want. One day it simply appeared shapelessly in the backyard of my house. It simply introduced itself following other than the natural laws from this ordinary world, following other logic; maybe the one in my unconsciousness, I do not know. How can I reckon it if it does not belong to my friends or even acquaintances? I know that others have had a similar experience, please tell me if you do know what it is about, we are lost.
>
> I wondered for how long it has been there. I tried to remember. In fact, its arrival was not abrupt; it was opaque, murky and envolving at first. It was an unpleasant sensation like a bitter lemon tea or a chill in a half-clad body until it turned into a sense of helplessness. Little by little, it obstructed me.
>
> Is it part of me? Am I it? Is it an unmanned being that enjoys itself in my body? Do I enjoy the presence of this foreigner? Thinking about this latter possibility relieves me a little. In fact, I am responsible for it. I am not so lost, I admit it.

Conclusion

In essence, we are responsible for our affections. The concept of boredom has different definitions; it is a manifestation of the limits between the symbolic and imaginary registers in an approach to experience reality; also, it can be a way of enjoying the nothingness itself—as in the previous short story. It is associated with human procrastination, and it possesses a jaculatory meaning which gives sense to the expression 'I am bored.' It is key to analyze the affections and types of boredom within a determined subjective context, and especially, within a vast but specific sociocultural universe of values and ideas. Boredom generates affections; it leads us, and it challenges our existence in a particular way.

Affects are not independent of the body. Influences of the language and the unconscious constitute affects. According to Freudian psychoanalysis, affects are not repressed. They are named by means of words and the pleasure–unpleasure principle. Thus, affect is not about energetic *quantity* nor an *amount*, but about the body it affects. We think about boredom from different levels. It can bring about positive or negative action. It is fundamental to know about its effects and ways of development in a particular context of ideals and values. Boredom takes place in a specific and broad sociocultural universe. The reflection about boredom as a sensory experience is a key in modern life. Boredom calls for the challenge of thinking in a particular way of going through our existence.

From the Lacanian psychoanalysis, the concept of boredom has several edges, to mention just a few: It is a form of manifestation of a border zone between the symbolic-imaginary registers in an approach to the experience of the real; it can also constitute a form to experience the enjoyment of nothingness or of the *Thing*; it is associated with human delinquency; it has an ejaculatory that already contributes a sense. It is fundamental to read the effects and forms of boredom within a specific and particular subjective context of values and ideals immersed in a broad and, at the same time, specific sociocultural universe. Boredom generates effects; it drives us. Thus, reflection on boredom as a sensitive experience is central to modern life.

References

Antón, M. C. (2013). *Pesadillas, sonambulismos y bruxismos. Tres fenómenos psicoanálisis*. Buenos Aires: Letra Viva.

Belton, T., & Priyadharsini, E. (2010). Boredom and schooling: A cross-disciplinary exploration. *Cambridge Journal of Education, 37*(4), 579–595. https://doi.org/10.1080/03057640701706227.

Benjamin, W. (2002). *The arcades project*. Cambridge, MA: Harvard University Press.

Berlyne, D. E. (1960). *Conflict, arousal and curiosity*. New York, NY: McGraw-Hill.

Blumenberg, H. (2006). *Beschreibung des Menschen*. Frankfurt: Suhrkamp.

Butler, N., Olaison, L., Sliwa, M., Sørensen, B. M., & Spoelstra, S. (2011). Work, play and boredom. *Ephemera, 11*(4), 329–335.

Chekhov, A. (1984). *Tales of Chekhov*. New York, NY: Ecco.

Cortázar, J. (1967, April 22). The night up face. *The New Yorker*, p. 49.

Csíkszentmihályi, M. (1975). *Beyond boredom and anxiety*. San Francisco, CA: Jossey Bass.

Csíkszentmihályi, M. (1990). *Flow: The psychology of optimal experience*. New York: Harper & Row.

Csíkszentmihályi, M. (1998). *Finding flow: The psychology of engagement with everyday life*. New York, NY: Basic Books.

Csíkszentmihályi, M. (2000). Boredom. In A. E. Kazdin (Ed.), *Encyclopedia of psychology* (Vol. 1, pp. 442–444). New York, NY: Oxford University Press.

Damasio, A. R. (1999). *The feeling of what happens: Body and emotion in the making of consciousness*. New York: Harcourt Brace & Co.

Damasio, A. R. (2003). *Looking for Spinoza: Joy, sorrow, and the feeling brain*. North Eugene, OR: Harvest.

Damrad-Frye, R., & Laird, J. D. (1989). The experience of boredom: The role of the self-perception of attention. *Journal of Personality and Social Psychology, 57*(2), 315–320. https://doi.org/10.1037/0022-3514.57.2.315.

Danckert, J. A., & Allman, A. A. A. (2005). Time flies when you're having fun: Temporal estimation and the experience of boredom. *Brain and Cognition, 59*(3), 236–245. https://doi.org/10.1016/j.bandc.2005.07.002.

Durkheim, É. (1997). *Suicide. A study in sociology*. Florence, MA: Free Press.

Eastwood, J. D., Frischen, A., Fenske, M. J., & Smilek, D. (2012). The unengaged mind. *Perspectives on Psychological Science, 7*(5), 482–495. https://doi.org/10.1177/1745691612456044.

Fenichel, O. (1951). On the psychology of boredom. In D. Rapaport (Ed.), *Organization and pathology of thought: Selected sources* (pp. 349–361). New York, NY: Columbia University Press.

Fisher, C. D. (1987). *Boredom: Construct, causes and consequences*. Texas, TX: A&M University, College Station, Department of Management.

Freud, S. (1895). The project for a psychology for neurologists. *Complete works* (Vol. 1, pp. 323–446). Amorrortu: Buenos Aires.

Freud, S. (1915). Repression. *Complete works* (Vol. 16, pp. 262–276). Amorrortu: Buenos Aires.

Freud, S. (1926a). Inhibition, symptom and anguish. *Complete works* (Vol. 20, pp. 71–165). Amorrortu: Buenos Aires.

Freud, S. (1926b). Psychoanalysis. *Complete works* (Vol. 20, pp. 245–246). Amorrotu: Buenos Aires.

Gorlier, J. (2008). ¿Confiar en el relato? Narración, comunidad, disidencia. *Textos y fragmentos* (pp. 34–43). Mar del Plata, Argentina: Universidad Nacional de Mar del Plata.

Gumbrecht, H. U. (2011). *Stimmungen lesen: über eine verdeckte Wirklichkeit der Literatur*. Munich: Carl Hanser.

Heidegger, M. (1995). *The fundamental concepts of metaphysics*. Indianapolis, IN: Indiana University Press.

Heidegger, M. (2008). *Being and time*. New York, NY: Harper Perennial.

Kracauer, S. (2005). *The mass Ornament: Weimar Essays*. Cambridge, MA: Harvard University Press.

Lacan, J. (1999). *The Seminar, Book 5, The formations of the unconscious*. Buenos Aires: Paidós.

Lacan, J. (1973). *The Seminar, Book 7, Ethics in psychoanalysis*. Buenos Aires: Paidós.

Lacan, J. (1980). *Television: A challenge to the psychoanalytic establishment*. New York, NY: W. W. Norton & Company.

Lesmes, D. (2009). Uno se aburre: Heidegger y la filosofía del tedio. *Bajo Palabra. Revista de Filosofía, 4,* 167–172.

London, H., Schubert, D. S. P., & Washburn, D. (1972). Increase of autonomic arousal by boredom. *Journal of Abnormal Psychology, 80*(1), 29–36. https://doi.org/10.1037/h0033311.

Martin, M., Sadlo, G., & Stew, G. (2006). The phenomenon of boredom. *Qualitative Research in Psychology, 3,* 193–211. https://doi.org/10.1191/1478088706qrp066oa.

Meyer Spacks, P. (1989). The necessity of boredom. *Virginia Quarterly Review, 65*(4), 581–599.

Meyer Spacks, P. (1995). *Boredom. The literary history of a state of mind*. Chicago, IL: The University of Chicago Press.

Mikulas, W. L., & Vodanovich, S. J. (1993). The essence of boredom. *The Psychological Record, 43*(1), 3–12.

Moravia, A. (1960). *La noia*. Milan: Bompiani.

Neu, J. (1998). Boring from within: Endogenous versus reactive boredom. In W. F. Flack & J. D. Laird (Eds.), *Emotions in psychopathology: Theory and research* (pp. 158–170). New York, NY: Oxford University Press.

Parreño Roldán, C. (2013). Aburrimiento y espacio: Experiencia, modernidad e historia. *Revista de la Escuela de Arquitectura de la Universidad de Costa Rica, 2*(3), 1–15.

Plutchik, R., & Kellerman, H. (1980). *Emotion: Theory, research, and experience* (Vol. 1)., Theories of emotion New York, NY: Academic.

Retana, C. (2011). Consideraciones acerca del aburrimiento como emoción moral. *Káñina, Revista de Artes y Letras, Universidad de Costa Rica, 35*(2), 179–190.

Revers, W. J. (1967). Perspectivas antropológicas del aburrimiento. CONVIVIUM, *23,* 38–47.

Ros Velasco, J. (2019). Ladies and gents spaces in romantic literature: The expression of boredom. *Negotiating spaces: Positions of race, gender, and sexuality across the arts*. North Calorina, NC: Duke University.

Ros Velasco, J., & Provolt, N. (in press). Upper-class female boredom in marriage in the nineteenth century western literature as a manifestation of socio-cultural pressures. In *The culture of boredom*. Boston, MA: BRILL.

Rule, W. R. (1998). Unsqueezing the soul: Expanding choices by reframing and redirecting boredom. *Journal of Contemporary Psychotherapy, 28*(3), 327–336.

Russell, B. (1930). *The conquest of happiness*. London, UK: Allen & Unwin.

Sloterdijk, P. (2009). Inspiration. *Ephemera, 9*(3), 242–251.

Soler, C. (2015). *Lacanian Affects: The function of affect in Lacan's work*. London, UK/New York, NY: Routledge.

Svendsen, L. (2005). *A philosophy of boredom*. London, UK: Reaktion Books.

Todman, M. (2003). Boredom and psychotic disorders: Cognitive and motivational issues. *Psychiatry, 66*(2), 146–167. https://doi.org/10.1521/psyc.66.2.

Todman, M. (2007). Psychopathology and boredom: A neglected association. In K. A. Fanti (Ed.), *Psychological science: Research, theory and future directions* (pp. 1–12). Athens: Atiner Press.

Toohey, P. (2011). *Boredom. A lively history*. New Haven, CT: Yale University Press.

Van Aart, J., Bartneck, C., Hu, J., Rauterberg, M., & Salem, B. (2010). How to behave as Alice in Wonderland–about boredom and curiosity. *Entertainment Computing, 1*, 125–137. https://doi.org/10.1016/j.entcom.2010.09.003.

Van Tilburg, W. A. P., & Igou, E. R. (2011). On boredom: Lack of challenge and meaning as distinct boredom experiences. *Motivation and Emotion, 36*(2), 181–194. https://doi.org/10.1007/s11031-011-9234-9.

Vodanovich, S. J., & Watt, J. D. (1999). The relationship between time structure and boredom proneness: An investigation within two cultures. *The Journal of Social Psychology, 139*(2), 143–152. https://doi.org/10.1080/00224549909598368.

Wangh, M. (1975). Boredom in psychoanalytic perspective. *Sociological Research, 42*, 538–550.

Wangh, M. (1979). Some psychoanalytic observations on boredom. *International Journal of Psycho-Analysis, 60*, 515–526.

María Cecilia Antón holds MA in Psychoanalysis and Ph.D. in Psychology (National University of Mar del Plata 1992). She is Researcher and Professor at the School of Psychology at National University of Mar del Plata; Coordinator of the Teaching and Research Committee of the General Pueyrredón's Health Secretary (Buenos Aires, Argentina); Ex-Resident and Chief Resident of Psychology at the General Hospital Acute Inter-zonal in Mar del Plata; and Psychology Specialist in maternal and child health at the Center for Primary Health Care in Mar del Plata. She is the author of scientific articles and books such as *Pesadillas, sonambulismos y bruxismos. Tres fenómenos en los márgenes del psicoanálisis* (Letra Viva, 2013), and *Bruxismos dentarios. Perturbaciones del dormir y Psicoanálisis. Fenómenos en el cuerpo y la clínica* (EAE, 2017). She is also the author of the study "Boredom" (*Perspectives in Psychology*, 2012).

Dr. Josefa Ros Velasco is Associate and Teaching Assistant in the Department of Romance Languages and Literatures at Harvard University and Real Colegio Complutense at Harvard Postdoctoral Fellow. She is conducting multidisciplinary research on the evolution of the understanding of boredom as a mental pathology. As part of this approach, she is examining how the comprehension of boredom in terms of mental disease has gradually formed historically by paying attention to philosophical, theological, and literary narratives. Dr. Ros Velasco holds a Ph. D. in Philosophy with International Mention at the Excellent Program of Doctorate in Philosophy at the Complutense University of Madrid (UCM, Spain), funded by the Spanish Ministry of Culture and Education. Her Dissertation was entitled *Boredom as a selective pressure in Hans Blumenberg*, with which she got the Extraordinary Doctorate Award (2016–2017), MA in Contemporary Thinking, and MA in Teachers Training. She was visiting researcher at the *Internationales Zentrum für Kultur- und Technikforschung* at Stuttgart Universität (IZKT, Germany) as a DAAD (Deutscher Akademischer Austauschdienst) scholar, and at the Deutsches

Literatur-Archiv Marbach (DLA, Germany) as a DLA fellow. She is a member of the Research Groups *Saavedra Fajardo Library for Hispanic Political Thought* at the UCM; *History and Video Games* at the University of Murcia; and *History and Philosophy of Emotions* at CCHS-CSIC. She is the editor and the author of academic papers such as "Hans Blumenberg's philosophical anthropology of boredom" (Karl Alber, 2019), "Boredom: humanising or dehumanising treatment" (Vernon, 2018); or "Boredom: A comprehensive study of the state of affairs" (*Thémata*, 2017). She is currently working on her next books: *La enfermedad del aburrimiento. El camino de la medicalización y sus alternativas* (2020), *The culture of boredom* (Brill, 2019), and *The faces of depression in literature* (Peter Lang, 2019).

Chapter 6
The Transformative Potential of Boredom

William McDonald

Introduction

There is a burgeoning literature on boredom, particularly in psychology (e.g., Vogel-Walcutt et al. 2012; Fahlman et al. 2013; Vodanovich and Watt 2016; Elpidorou 2018). Its main focus is on defining, categorizing, measuring, and identifying the causes of two phenomena: (1) state boredom, which the literature takes to be the mental state found in particular psychological occurrences or events; and (2) trait boredom, which the literature takes to be a proneness to falling into state boredom.[1] The psychological literature on boredom also examines state boredom in particular settings, such as education (Weinerman and Kenner 2016; Goetz et al. 2010), the workplace (Cummings 2016), prisons (Grassian 2006) and organisations (Johnsen 2016), or of particular age groups, such as adolescents (Hunter and Csíkszentmihályi 2002) and retirees (Weinstein et al. 1995), and in problem internet use (Skues et al. 2016). Some of the psychological literature is devoted to finding neurophysiological or psychophysiological correlates of experiences of boredom (e.g., Posner et al. 2005; Pattyn et al. 2008; Merrifield and Danckert 2014; Elpidorou 2018), while some tries to identify psychopathological correlates of boredom proneness (e.g., Posner et al. 2005; Eastwood et al. 2007, 2012; Sansone and Thoman 2005).

Most of the psychological literature uses quantitative methods, including the Boredom Proneness Scale, the Boredom Susceptibility subscale of the Sensation Seeking Scale, the Boredom Coping Scale, the Leisure Boredom Scale, the Free

[1]On the distinction between state boredom and trait boredom, see Elpidorou (2018, pp. 457–468). On the measurement of state boredom, see, for example, Fahlman et al. (2013). On trait boredom, or boredom proneness, see Skues et al. (2016). For psychological definitions of boredom, see Eastwood et al. (2012) and Vogel-Walcutt et al. (2012).

W. McDonald (✉)
United Arab Emirates University, Al Ain, United Arab Emirates
e-mail: wmcdonal@uaeu.ac.ae

J. Ros Velasco (ed.), *Boredom Is in Your Mind*,
https://doi.org/10.1007/978-3-030-26395-9_6

Time Boredom Scale, the Sexual Boredom Scale, the Multidimensional State Boredom Scale, the State Boredom Measure, the Boredom Experience Scale, and the Academic Boredom Scale (Vodanovich and Watt 2016, p. 194). However, some of the psychological literature advocates or uses qualitative methods (e.g., Martin et al. 2006; Elpidorou 2018).

While much of the psychological literature presupposes boredom to be a negative emotion, the measurement and understanding of which is a prerequisite to treating it or ameliorating its effects, a small proportion of the literature regards boredom as having positive potential, for motivating creativity or informing and regulating behavior (e.g., Bench and Lench 2013; Hunter et al. 2016; Johnsen 2016; Elpidorou 2018).

Recent philosophical literature on boredom, on the other hand, has been relatively sparse.[2] However, some of the older philosophical literature on boredom is worth revisiting since it stands in stark contrast to the recent psychological literature and has some neglected insights to offer. In particular, I want to revisit the work on boredom of Søren Kierkegaard and Martin Heidegger. They approach the phenomenon of boredom using radically different methods and seem to come to very different conclusions about boredom than recent psychology. Moreover, they both construe boredom as an important mood or existential 'attunement,' which has the potential to transform us in the task of becoming (authentic) selves.

Definitions

There is surprisingly little agreement in the psychological literature on a definition of state boredom, upon which definitions of trait boredom are logically dependent (Elpidorou 2018, pp. 456–457). There are numerous working definitions, though some of them include elements that seem to contradict elements in other working definitions.[3] Most of the studies proceed without definition, either leaving its identification to the self-reporting of subjects or to the parameters laid down in the boredom measurement scales. The literature on boredom measurement scales typically refers to boredom as a 'construct'—that is, an attribute that can only be measured indirectly (e.g., Vodanovich and Watt 2016, p. 195; Eastwood et al. 2012, p. 488; Vogel-Walcutt et al. 2012, p. 89; Goetz et al. 2010, p. 45; Johnsen 2016, p. 1405; Merrifield and Danckert 2014, p. 482; Boden 2009, p. 205). Many of the definitions of boredom in the psychological literature emphasize perceived

[2]Exceptions are O'Brien (2014); Calhoun (2011); Dalle Pezze and Salzani (2009); Svendsen (2005) and Frankfurt (1992). Although Elpidorou is a philosopher and his article is published in a cognitive science journal, I count Elpidorou (2018) as part of the psychological literature since it develops its theory of boredom primarily on the basis of a review of the psychological literature.

[3]For example, some studies point to low arousal as a defining feature of boredom while others regard it as a high arousal state (Vodanovich and Watt 2016, p. 195). Elpidorou (2018) has a plausible explanation for this discrepancy, to which we will return.

monotony and repetition as central, while others mention difficulties with focusing attention (Vodanovich and Watt 2016, p. 195). Some definitions highlight the inability to structure free time adequately and the consequent feeling of time dragging (2016, p. 195). Other definitions include lack of challenge in the environment, a sense of meaninglessness, and a state of low arousal combined with negative feelings (2016, p. 195).

One widely cited definition is that of Eastwood et al., which claims boredom is "universally conceptualized as 'the aversive experience of wanting, but being unable, to engage in satisfying activity'" (2012, p. 482). This definition is flawed since it is too inclusive. It seems more appropriate as a definition of frustration, of which boredom is at most a special subclass.[4] Nor, as we will see, does Eastwood's definition fit neatly with the way boredom is understood by Kierkegaard and Heidegger. In fact, Heidegger regards the attempt to explain boredom in terms of its psychological provenance as "a blind alley" (Heidegger 1995, p. 183) since such an attempt results in objectifying the phenomenon instead of enabling it to play a fundamental role in becoming an authentic self (*Dasein*).

Heidegger and Kierkegaard do not offer alternative definitions of boredom, although both offer some characterizations. Both thinkers explore boredom, not as an isolated psychological phenomenon, but as an entry point for the project of becoming a self. For Kierkegaard boredom is a mood [Stemning], whose dialectical antithesis, *the interesting*, lies in a *confinium* [border region] between the aesthetic and ethical spheres of existence (Kierkegaard 1954, p. 92). As such it has the potential to help an individual transition to a higher existential stage. For Heidegger, boredom is a mood [Stimmung][5] with the potential to be a fundamental attunement [Grundstimmung] for *Dasein* [being-there]—his term for authentic human being-in-the-world. He identifies four different types of boredom: (1) superficial or everyday boredom: being bored *by* a determinate intentional object (Heidegger 1995, pp. 78–105); (2) deeper boredom: being bored *with* an extended situation, without being bored by any of its constituent objects (1995, pp. 106–131); (3) profound boredom: being indifferent to everything, without being bored by anything in particular or with any specific extended situation (expressed impersonally as "it is boring for one" [es ist einem langweilig]) (1995, pp. 132–159); and (4) contemporary boredom: a particular form of profound boredom that is socially and technologically induced in modernity, which acts as an impediment to

[4]Even Eastwood's expanded definition fails to distinguish boredom from frustration: "Specifically, we propose that boredom be defined in terms of attention. That is, boredom is the aversive state that occurs when we (a) are not able to successfully engage attention with internal (e.g., thoughts or feelings) or external (e.g., environmental stimuli) information required for participating in satisfying activity (b) are focused on the fact that we are not able to engage attention and participate in satisfying activity, and (c) attribute the cause of our aversive state to the environment" (Eastwood et al. 2012, p. 482).

[5]Note that the Danish *Stemning* and the German *Stimmung* share the same etymology and are related to the words for "voice," "vote," and "attune" (Nielsen 1966, p. 381).

becoming attuned to profound boredom (1995, pp. 160–167).[6] Heidegger further analyzes boredom in all its forms as having two structural dimensions: (1) being held in limbo and (2) being left empty; furthermore, these two dimensions have "an intrinsic unity" or "an original unity" (Heidegger 1995, pp. 107, 161). These two dimensions have different meanings in each of the types of boredom. However, it is not enough to know what they are in their surface meaning to come to an adequate understanding of boredom as a fundamental attunement for *Dasein*.

Instead of defining boredom, Kierkegaard and Heidegger seek to induct the reader or listener into an understanding of boredom as it relates to becoming a self. This understanding is not simply psychological. Although Heidegger produces a structural analysis of boredom, he warns against using it as a ready-made definition, since that would only serve to objectify boredom. Rather, Heidegger wants to awaken his audience to the possibility of becoming *attuned* to profound boredom as their fundamental way of being in the world. Kierkegaard wants to do something similar: to awaken in his reader, who is likely immersed in the aesthetic sphere of existence governed by the pursuit of the interesting, the potential for becoming a self.

Kierkegaard and Heidegger differ from recent psychology not only in their definitions of boredom but also in their aims in analyzing or characterizing it and in their methods for coming to understand it and represent it.

Aims

Psychology aims at an objective, scientific understanding of the experience of boredom conceived as an episodic psychological state and as a proneness to fall into this state. It seeks this aim primarily for the sake of assessing boredom (e.g., Vogel-Walcutt et al. 2012; Vodanovich and Watt 2016; Goetz et al. 2010; Boden 2009, p. 205). In order to achieve this aim, psychology seeks to identify the causes of boredom, its behavioral and psychophysiological correlates, possible pathologies, its cognitive and volitional nature and its relationship to other mental states or traits. Because most of the literature presupposes that boredom is an aversive state, it aims to alleviate the suffering boredom entails, by means of therapy, diversion or removal of its causes.

Kierkegaard, by contrast, aims to awaken his reader to an understanding of boredom so that she might use it in her task of becoming a self. While Kierkegaard recognizes the aversion people commonly feel toward boredom and illustrates some of the means by which they seek to avoid it, he also aims to show how these means of avoidance can serve to stop the individual from developing as a self. His writing is an indirect communication of boredom's potential for self-transformation.

[6]Note that Heidegger claims that these forms of boredom are not necessarily discrete: "the forms of boredom are themselves fluid: there are manifold intermediate forms in accordance with the depth from which the boredom arises, more accurately: according to the depth which man grants his own Dasein" (Heidegger 1995, p. 157).

Indirect communication is crucial to his aim, as it enables the reader to appropriate insights with her own subjective passion and to reduplicate them in her own life.

Heidegger has a similar aim to Kierkegaard: to awaken his audience to what is involved in becoming an authentic self. However, whereas Kierkegaard ultimately assigns a central role to God in the task of becoming a self, Heidegger aims at a secular understanding of that task. His aim is to awaken his reader/listener to the task of attuning herself fundamentally to profound boredom in order to become an authentic self in the contemporary world. Heidegger, like Kierkegaard, recognizes that some means of avoiding boredom are impediments to becoming *Dasein*—which he conceives as the being that asks the question of (the meaning of) being, both of beings in general and of its own being in particular (1962, pp. 26–27).

Methods

Psychology uses quantitative methods to investigate boredom, including statistical analysis of questionnaires and self-reports (Vodanovich and Watt 2016), factor analysis and multidimensional scaling (Posner et al. 2005, p. 720), laboratory measurements of galvanic skin response (Cummings 2016, p. 292; Merrifield and Danckert 2014), neuroimaging of brain activity (Posner et al. 2005, p. 726), facial electromyographic measurements (Posner et al. 2005, p. 720), correlations of behavior with boredom proneness (Skues et al. 2016; Danckert and Allman 2005), and correlation of boredom with other emotions (Goetz et al. 2010). It also uses qualitative methods, such as literature reviews, sample narrative accounts (Vodanovich and Watt 2016; Elpidorou 2018; Martin et al. 2006), or written responses to open-ended questions, which are then subjected to "grounded theory analysis" (Fahlman et al. 2013, p. 71), as well as other combinations of theory and empirical inquiry (Bench and Lench 2013). Psychology also seeks to study boredom experimentally in the laboratory under controlled conditions. To this end, it tries to induce boredom by forcing subjects to undertake repetitive, meaningless tasks or to watch monotonous, meaningless videos (e.g., Fahlman et al. 2013; Merrifield and Danckert 2014).[7]

Kierkegaard's method for investigating boredom is entirely different. He develops an informal method he refers to as "experimenting [experimenterende] psychology" (see McDonald 2019 for an extended analysis). It is an alternative to the rational, empirical, and transcendental psychologies of the eighteenth and

[7]Note that there are methodological problems with inducing boredom in subjects by prescribing repetitive, monotonous and meaningless tasks since this limits the types of boredom to Heidegger's superficial boredom, or being bored *by*. It is not necessarily legitimate to generalize results from this type of boredom to other types. There are also potential methodological problems for those studies that correlate boredom with alexithymia, the inability to correctly identify one's own emotional states, if they require subjects to be able to identify themselves correctly as being bored.

nineteenth centuries. It is also an alternative to the experimental psychology developed later by Wilhelm Wundt, Alfred Lehmann, and others, which underpins the methodology of much of the recent psychological literature on boredom.

Kierkegaard's experimenting psychology seeks to preserve the subjective experience of psychological phenomena, while also pursuing the scientific ideals of objectivity and universal validity. To this end, he utilizes the principle of *unum noris omnes* [if you know one you know all]. He thinks that if you know yourself (or anyone) deeply enough, it is possible to apply that knowledge universally. But this knowledge is not based on simple introspection, which Kierkegaard, following Kant, thinks is flawed as a method for psychological science (Kitcher 1990, p. 11). Instead, Kierkegaard seeks self-knowledge by means of critical recollection and (self)-observation over time, rather than by introspection—where the latter is understood as real-time self-observation of mental events. (Self)-observation and recollection have to be followed up with "an original thinking through of that which has been observed" (Nordentoft 1978, p. 1). This thinking through includes verifying the observations in oneself, either by recollection or repetition of the phenomena. It must also be dialectical since mental phenomena are dynamic and can develop in response to one's past, present, and future, as well as one's own internal contradictions or tensions. In order to follow possible trajectories, the observer needs dialectical skill and imagination. Observations can be falsified by finding practical contradictions between what the observer says and how the observer acts in everyday life (Kierkegaard 1992, p. 304). Observations can also be falsified by seeing that they are conducted in an inappropriate mood (Kierkegaard 1980a, 14n). The psychological observer needs to take into account that she is always already in a mood, or attuned in a certain way, which may or may not be appropriate to the phenomenon under investigation. This is particularly important for investigations that require empathy.

Kierkegaard's method is grounded in his understanding that mental phenomena do not occur in isolation. Not only are there collateral mental events, but these occur in the context of a person's life.[8] Moreover, Kierkegaard thinks that a human being has the potential to become a self, which is a task, not something that just happens. The task requires self-reflection and critical responsiveness to its potential constituents. The self is a process of self-relating, which requires synthesis and grounding of its relata. This process occurs in freedom, by resolute acts of free choice (Kierkegaard 1980b, pp. 13–14).

Kierkegaard uses a method of indirect communication in order to awaken the reader to her possibilities as a self. He uses pseudonyms and other bracketing devices, such as epigraphs, forewords, prefaces, postscripts, interludes, and parallel series of texts, to avoid imposing authorial authority. Kierkegaard uses paradox, different narrative voices, figures from literature, folklore, history and religion,

[8]Kierkegaard derives the notion of collateral mental events from his teacher F. C. Sibbern, who also thought that psychology should be understood in the context of a person's existence, which develops dialectically. See Malantschuk (1980, pp. 162–176) and Koch (2016, p. 234).

genres ranging from the novel to the essay to the devotional homily, and disciplinary perspectives including philosophy, theology, psychology, and literary criticism. "Such works are mirrors," he quotes Lichtenberg as saying, "when an ape looks in, no apostle can look out" (1988, p. 8). The task of becoming a self can only be achieved by the individual herself, so Kierkegaard's method of indirect communication is designed to prevent rote appropriation, to provoke critical self-reflection, to induce appropriate moods and passions, and to awaken the reader to possibilities—including the possibility of becoming herself.

Kierkegaard presents existential possibilities primarily in the form of characters, pseudonyms, narrative voices, and 'imaginary constructions' [Experimenter]. These represent his famous 'stages' or 'spheres' of existence: the aesthetic, the ethical, and the religious.[9] He also presents various points of transition between existential stages. One of these is 'the interesting,' which is the dialectical opposite of boredom.[10] The interesting lies on the border between the aesthetic and ethical spheres of life. It therefore offers the possibility of transition or transformation for the person seeking to become a self. Boredom is perceived as a limit for the aesthete, who is primarily driven by desire for what is interesting. The aesthete can either get stuck demonically in pursuit of the interesting (McDonald 2009) or can overcome the dialectic of boring/interesting by choosing the ethical. If he chooses the ethical, he chooses *himself,* by taking responsibility for his life, by striving to choose the good, by embracing his self-continuity as someone with a history, and by eschewing decisions based solely on desire.

The ultimate test for whether Kierkegaard's presentation captures the truth of boredom and its role in the task of becoming a self is for the reader to try it out in her own life through the process of what Kierkegaard calls *reduplication* (on this concept, see Kaftanski 2015).

Heidegger uses an historical, hermeneutic method to awaken his audience to the call of being, which is implicit in boredom as a fundamental attunement. He draws on the resources of the history of western philosophy to raise the question of how to ask metaphysical questions—and to show how the tradition can go astray. This is an oblique entry to the question of how we are attuned. It is indirect in a different way to Kierkegaard's indirect communication. It circles the question of metaphysics, probing from different angles. This is not a vicious circle, but the beginning of a hermeneutic circle, in which this probing from various angles helps determine the centre of the circle (Heidegger 1995, p. 180).

Like Kierkegaard, Heidegger thinks that existential questions need to be asked from within the appropriate mood/attunement. Heidegger also thinks that a characteristic of moods is that they color the way we experience every entity while the mood lasts. Moods thereby awaken us to the idea of beings-as-a-whole, but in a

---

[9]Note that these are far from exhaustive of Kierkegaard's existential stages and are not necessarily as discrete from one another as they are often presented.

[10]The interesting "is properly the category of the turning point" (Kierkegaard 1954, p. 92).

non-conceptual way that prepares the ground for our metaphysical or transcendental comprehension of the entirety of being (Lewis 2017, p. 50).

Heidegger's lecture series *The fundamental concepts of metaphysics: World, finitude, solitude* is divided into two parts. In the first part, he tries to awaken an attunement to things as a whole on the basis of the mood of boredom, and in the second part, he uses a comparative method to develop our understanding of our place in nature [physis], by comparing human being in the world to the being of stones (the inorganic) and animals (the organic). The two parts of the lecture series are preceded by a "Preliminary Appraisal," which delves into the history of metaphysics, including the etymology of the term and its subsequent reception and translation. The word "metaphysics" is first used of those works of Aristotle that come after or go beyond [meta] his *Physics*. But Heidegger points to another meaning of *meta*: to turn "away from something toward something else" (1995, p. 39). He wants to revive this now forgotten meaning of *meta* to awaken his audience to the possibility of turning away from received opinion about metaphysics and the question of being toward something else. That something else is themselves as *Dasein*, as that being which asks the question of the meaning of being.

The methods of hermeneutic circling and comparative examination are not the only paths to the question of being. These paths share the characteristic of starting with the familiar and gradually defamiliarizing us from our everyday understanding, as a propaedeutic to disclosing what comes ever more clearly into view (Heidegger 1995, p. 178). Everyday understanding is an impediment to the discovery of truth, which Heidegger ultimately takes to be a matter of being revealing itself to us (1962, pp. 261, 267–270). However, for being to reveal itself, the recipient must be prepared: *Dasein* must be "cleared"; that is, "*as* Being-in-the-world," we must ourselves *be* the clearing (1962, p. 171). Heidegger thinks the way to be cleared is to listen to the call of conscience, which "has the character of an *appeal* to *Dasein* by calling it to its ownmost potentiality-for-Being-its-Self" (Heidegger 1962, p. 314). Once cleared and open to the call of being, we can use our fundamental attunement of boredom to hear that call, and thereby become ourselves as *Dasein*.

Boredom in Recent Psychology

The psychological literature does not converge on an agreed set of facts about what boredom is, what its causes are, how to treat it, or even how to value it. Some of the investigations into its nature, however, go some way toward explaining this lack of convergence.

Much of the literature presupposes that boredom is a basic emotion. That is, it assumes that boredom arises from "a discrete and independent neural system" (Posner et al. 2005, p. 715) and is activated "within unique neural pathways of the central nervous system" (2005, p. 716). Research into basic emotions originated with Darwin, was developed by William James, and has been developed more recently by Paul Ekman and others. The theory has been built on the idea that basic emotions have evolved to enable human beings to react automatically in universally shared situations (Ekman and Cordaro 2011). If this is the case, then we would expect to find evidence in animal studies, studies of human development, and in correlations with typical physiological expressions of these basic emotions. But in each of these areas, the research does not unequivocally support the theory of basic emotions. Even Ekman concedes that basic emotions need not have evolutionary origins but may include socially constructed emotions (see, e.g., Ekman and Cordaro 2011; for evidence that boredom is a basic emotion, see Cowen and Keltner 2017). Nor does recent research support the idea that each basic emotion is strictly correlated with a facial expression or other peripheral physiological responses (Ekman 1993; Elpidorou 2018, p. 466). Animal studies require the attribution of emotions to animals based on their behavior, without adequate evidence that behavior is necessary or sufficient as an expression of affect (Posner et al. 2005, p. 717). There are similar limitations to the study of basic emotions in human infants, and it is difficult to rule out the possibility that the results are due to interpretations or projections by the researchers based on their theoretical presuppositions (2005, p. 718).

The construal of boredom as a basic emotion has been challenged by the circumplex model of affect, which asserts that "all affective states arise from cognitive interpretations of core neural sensations that are the product of *two* independent neurophysiological systems" (Posner et al. 2005, p. 715, my emphasis). This model is supported by the neurophysiological evidence (2005, pp. 721–723). It also accounts for the fact that we typically experience emotions as ambiguous and lacking discrete boundaries (2005, p. 719). Many studies using multidimensional scaling and factor analysis of self-reports have resulted in two-dimensional models of affective experience. Although they use various labels for these two dimensions, they attempt to capture similar meanings. Posner calls them "the valence and arousal systems" (2005, p. 719)—in other words, the positive or negative value of the affect (valence) and the amount of tension or energy it carries (arousal). These two dimensions can be mapped to the interaction between neurophysiological structures, principally the neo-cortex for cognitions and subcortical structures for valence and arousal. All affective experience, including boredom, can be construed as our cognitive interpretation of the interaction of these two independent systems (2005, p. 719).

The dynamic nature of affective experience and its dependence on the interaction between two different neural systems, on the circumplex model, help to explain the range of characteristics various studies attribute to boredom. State boredom would typically be mapped onto the low arousal, low valence ends of the two dimensions, placing it in the vicinity of depression and sadness (2005, Fig. 1, p. 716). At the same degree of arousal, but with positive valence, we find calmness. Various studies demonstrate that mindfulness is an antidote to boredom (e.g., LePera 2011; Lee and Zelman 2019); one of the effects of practising mindfulness is calmness. Mindfulness is a method of focusing on our thoughts in the present moment without judgment, unlike feeling bored, in which we make at least the implicit judgment that it has a negative value.

Boredom proneness might be linked to temperament, conceived as a relatively stable psychological profile stretching from infancy to adulthood. Temperaments can be mapped according to their emotional valence. The circumplex model might also explain the link between boredom and various forms of psychopathology, including mood disorders. Children have limited ability to differentiate emotions and tend to express their affective states in terms of valence alone while ignoring the arousal dimension (Posner et al. 2005, p. 729). Only as they mature do they learn to master the cognitive skill of conceptualizing their emotions, by learning to interpret and label their experiences of the affective circumplex. The adult capacity to give more nuanced descriptions for feelings may lead to more varied symptoms of comorbidity, without the underlying neurophysiology having changed. This may help explain why children with temperaments skewed toward negative valence, often expressed as feeling bored, have increased risk of developing mood and other affective disorders (2005, pp. 727, 729).

Although many studies construe boredom as a low arousal state (e.g., Vogel-Walcutt et al. 2012; Vodanovich and Watt 2016), some construe it as a high arousal state (e.g., Bench and Lench 2013; O'Brien 2014), and others construe it as both (Eastwood et al. 2012; Fahlman et al. 2013; Van Tilburg and Igou 2017). The circumplex model might explain this in terms of the ambiguity and complexity arising from the dynamic interaction between the different neurological systems. Elpidorou has a different explanation. He conceives of boredom as a functional emotion, which plays an important role in informing and regulating our behavior. It informs us that the activities or situations we find ourselves in are unsatisfactory and motivates us to find something more meaningful or attractive. Boredom also has the important existential function of promoting "the restoration of the perception that one's activities are meaningful and congruent with one's overall projects" (2018, p. 455). Boredom often feels like a low arousal state, when time drags and one feels lethargic. But boredom is also often associated with high arousal states, such as anxiety, frustration, restlessness, and irritability. Even the physiological evidence is not definitive since it has linked boredom with both low and high arousal (Elpidorou 2018). But a plausible explanation of the apparently contradictory evidence, apart from the possible ambiguity and imprecision of self-reports upon which many of the studies rely, is that boredom can be both a low arousal state and a high arousal state at different times or at different stages. An individual might find herself bored by lack of external stimulation, and consequently in a state of low physiological arousal, but this might motivate her to try to overcome the boredom by seeking endogenous sources of stimulation, which will increase her arousal (Sansone and Thoman 2005; Eastwood et al. 2012; Elpidorou 2018).

Boredom in Kierkegaard

The fullest explicit account of boredom in Kierkegaard's *oeuvre* is to be found in the essay "The rotation method" in the first volume of *Either/Or*. The essay is presented as the work of the aesthete, A, and must be understood in the context of *Either/Or* as a whole and as part of Kierkegaard's wider authorship.

The argument of "The rotation method" is based on two principles: that "all human beings [*Mennesker*] are bores" and "boredom is the root of all evil" (Kierkegaard 1959, p. 281, translation modified). The aesthete takes these to be negative principles of motion: "not merely repellent, but infinitely forbidding" (Kierkegaard 1959, p. 281). This tells us something about the values of the aesthete and also introduces the concept of motion. Motion is a central concern for Kierkegaard, explored at greatest length in his book *Repetition*. His concern is not with physical motion but with the spiritual change involved in becoming a self. He is also concerned with the question of how we can preserve personal identity through a process of radical change. The notions of transition [Overgang] and repetition [Gjentagelse] are crucial. Transition is the movement or change of a substance from one state to another. Kierkegaard finds the key to understanding transition in Aristotle's notion of *kinesis*, conceived as movement or change by actualizing possibility. This is also the key to freedom: imagining a possibility, then choosing to realize it. Repetition, too, brings something new into existence, while at the same time preserving something from the past: "The dialectic of repetition is easy, for that which is repeated has been—otherwise it could not be repeated—but the very fact that it has been made the repetition into something new" (Kierkegaard 1983, p. 149).

Kierkegaard contrasts the 'modern' notion of repetition with the Greek concept of recollection:

> Just as [the Greeks] taught that all knowing is a recollection, modern philosophy will teach that all life is a repetition [...] Recollection and repetition are the same movement, except in opposite directions, for what is recollected has been, is repeated backward, whereas genuine repetition is recollected forward. (1983, p. 131).

Movement, transition and repetition are all temporal notions, which involve moving from past, through present, to the future. Boredom provides an immediate, negative experience of one's temporality, in which time drags or stagnates—sometimes caused by the meaningless repetition of the same thing in the same way. As A puts it, "Everyone who feels bored cries out for change" (Kierkegaard 1959, p. 287).

A tries to escape boredom by manipulating his moods and by limiting and controlling his experiences. To this end, he develops his "rotation method," which relies on the paradoxical idea that "the more you limit yourself, the more fertile you become in invention" (Kierkegaard 1959, p. 288). He also discovers that he can manipulate the way he feels by means of "*remembering* and *forgetting*" for it is between these two currents that "life in its entirety moves" (1959, p. 287). The art of forgetting is dependent on the art of remembering, and both depend on how one experiences reality in the first place. Poetic remembering "is really only another expression for forgetting. In a poetic memory, the experience has undergone a transformation, by which it has lost all its painful aspects" (1959, p. 289). A finds that he needs to temper his experiences so that they are not too intense, as intensity "will make it impossible either to remember or to forget" (1959, p. 289). Instead, he tries to inject a pause into his current experience, in which he observes it with a view to remembering it. He also abandons hope from his repertoire of emotions, because "hope precludes self-limitation" (1959, p. 288). He thereby limits his temporal experience to an artificial present or series of fleeting moments.

The aesthete recommends that one guard against friendship and never marries because both compromise individual freedom. Freedom is the aesthete's goal, but he conceives it primarily as freedom from boredom and freedom to satisfy one's desires. He implicitly conceives it, also, as freedom from vulnerability and suffering. Another method he uses to manipulate his moods, besides poetic remembering and forgetting, is to insert something arbitrary or accidental into routine situations. He recommends going "to see the middle of a play" or to "read the third part of a book" so that your enjoyment is independent of what the author has planned for you (1959, p. 295). "One should [...] always have an eye open for the accidental", and strive to "transform something accidental into the absolute" (1959, p. 296). This will give endless opportunity to transform the boring into the amusing.

While A is witty, insightful, ironic, and amusing, his account of boredom is framed foremost by the second volume of *Either/Or*, which consists of a series of letters to A by his friend Judge William, the ethicist. William implores A to choose himself in his absolute validity (Kierkegaard 1972, p. 218), rather than to remain stuck in the pseudo-freedom of his aesthetic lifestyle, where he pursues only what is interesting in his flight from boredom. In this respect, A engages in what might now be described as diversional therapy. He does not address the underlying causes of his despair but seeks only immediate relief from the symptom of boredom. To choose himself, he needs to embrace his continuity as an historical being persisting through time, rather than to forget. He also needs to choose himself as a concrete individual, who is "a social, civil self" (1972, p. 267).

Kierkegaard's *oeuvre* includes two major types of transition: those that occur through immanent changes and those that transcend immanence by means of a leap or radical break. Strictly speaking, immanent changes do not amount to an existential transition (Kierkegaard 1992, p. 295). The sorts of changes the aesthete makes in order to avoid boredom are immanent, leaving him stuck in his circumscribed way of life. Leaps, or discontinuous changes that enable the transcendence of an existence sphere, have to be dialectical, qualitative, or pathos-laden transitions (Schreiber 2015, p. 187). Merely dialectical transitions, however, are confined to the sphere of thought and do not apply directly to existence. It is only a passionate interest that can motivate an existential leap. Such qualitative transition involves "a leap from non-existence into existence" (2015, p. 188) by actualizing a possible mode of being, without altering one's essence. A self can only come into existence from non-existence when its possibility is grasped as a task and realized with passion through an act of freedom. These pathos-laden leaps are motivated by a person's "infinite interest in his own existence" (2015, p. 189) but are ultimately a matter of exercising the will.

It is not enough merely to choose another mode of existence with passion to become a self. One also has to choose *oneself*, that is, choose who one is *essentially*. This already exists within the human being as "dreaming spirit" (Kierkegaard 1980a, pp. 41ff) but needs to be awoken—and chosen. Only at the moment [Øieblikket], in which time and eternity intersect, can one can choose one's essential self (for an analysis of this concept in Kierkegaard, see McDonald 2014). Eternity here is conceived as the domain of unchanging truth, which is also the domain of essences; time is where events occur, including choices to actualize possible modes of existence. To get on the path to selfhood, one needs to choose a mode of existence that intersects with one's essence. To do otherwise is to fail to become a self or who you (essentially) are. Once one has chosen oneself, in the moment of vision, one has the task of repetition: to take oneself again and again, with passion, to make oneself anew.[11]

The aesthete, then, has the potential to become a self because he has an essence and an interest in his own existence. His negative motivation by boredom and his positive motivation by a desire for the interesting provide him with sufficient energy to make an existential leap. However, his rotation method amounts only to immanent change, to protect the existence he is comfortable with. He constructs a fantasy world, in which he manipulates his own feelings by poeticizing his experience and by artfully remembering and forgetting. His only leap in the end is back into himself, demonically, instead of into a higher mode of existence such as the ethical life. He fails to grasp the potential for repetition by instead falling into a kind of recollection, where he lives his life backwards.

Boredom in Heidegger

Heidegger presents the existential dimension of boredom indirectly, in the context of his fundamental ontology. He first wants to defamiliarize his reader/listener from the world and herself so that world and self may be approached afresh, as an original experience. He uses the term 'Dasein' (literally 'being there') to indicate the being who asks the question of the meaning of being (1962, pp. 27, 65), and he aims to enable the listener to become *Dasein* rather than to remain in her everyday self-conception. In *Being and time,* Heidegger takes *Dasein* to be characterized by being-in-the-world, being-with-others and being-oneself, being-*there*—to which *Dasein* is brought by "the primordial disclosure belonging to moods" (1962, p. 173)—and care as the being of *Dasein* (Heidegger 1962, pp. 65–263), before introducing his analysis of *Dasein* and temporality, which takes the reader through the ideas of become an authentic *Dasein* by being-towards-death and being-a-whole (1962, pp. 274–382).

To become *Dasein,* we need to ask the question of being in general and not piecemeal of individual entities. Moods are a way to experience being in general since a mood colors our experience of everything. Moods such as grief, good humor, anxiety, or melancholy do not alter the things in the world, nor are they

[11]Kierkegaard's pseudonym Constantin Constantius congratulates the Danish language on its word for repetition, *Gjentagelse*, which literally means a "taking again" (Kierkegaard 1983, p. 149).

simply projections of a subject onto objects. Rather, moods are ways of being *attuned* to being-in-the-world (Heidegger 1995, pp. 66–69).

Boredom is an appropriate mood with which to begin an inquiry into the meaning of being, since it is familiar, known to everyone and non-conceptual—and therefore available independently of education or culture.[12] Heidegger, therefore, starts to awaken his listener by considering superficial, everyday boredom. We experience this type of boredom when we are bored *by* some particular thing or circumstance, such as a book or waiting for a train (Heidegger 1995, pp. 85ff, 93–94). This sort of boredom has a determinate intentional object so does not yet color our experience of everything. Nevertheless, it is a means of awakening attunement, which is "a grasping of Da-sein as Da-sein" (1995, p. 66). "Attunements are the fundamental ways in which we *find* ourselves *disposed* [...] Attunements are the '*how*' [Wie] according to which one is in such and such a way" (1995, p. 84).

When we are bored by a particular object, the boringness belongs to the object but is also related to the subject (1995, p. 84). The book is wearisome, holding us in limbo, and is also tedious, leaving us feeling empty. That which bores us is not "the outer cause" of boredom as "the inner effect" (1995, p. 87). Heidegger wants to nudge the listener toward regarding boredom as an attunement of *Dasein* to its being-in-the-world: "boredom [...] is a hybrid, partly objective, partly subjective" (1995, p. 88).

When we are bored, we want to kill time or make it pass quickly because it drags (Heidegger 1995, p. 93). This might make us think that being bored "is a peculiar *being affected in a paralysing way by time as it drags and by time in general*" (Heidegger 1995, p. 98). But this seems to attribute to time itself the power to oppress us. However, the lesson to be learned is that to realize ourselves as *Dasein*, we need to become attuned to our own temporality. The temporality of *Dasein*, like the boring book, is a hybrid.

In addition to being held in limbo by time as it drags, boredom leaves us feeling empty. Heidegger analyzes the notion of being left empty in terms of finding nothing at hand that offers us anything (1995, p. 103). These are the totality of things in our reach. But, again, it is not the things as such that offer us nothing. These things, too, are hybrid. It is the way in which they are connected to our being-in-the-world that leaves us feeling empty. Being left empty involves a withdrawal of beings, while being held in limbo provides a corresponding revelation, "in which what is withdrawn is also announced" (Withy 2013, p. 166). When I find a book boring, the book refuses to engage me, but in so doing it potentially reveals that books usually engage me. We need to be attuned in order to notice the potential.

Heidegger thinks that being held in limbo and being left empty are structural dimensions of boredom, which have an intrinsic unity. This unity arises from "the

[12]Note that Heidegger does not claim that boredom is the only possible mood with which to start this inquiry. In *Being and time,* he focuses on the mood of anxiety instead.

whole structure of being bored" (1995, p. 107). If we use this supposition as a methodological guide, in trying to find this intrinsic unity, we should be led to "a *more profound* boredom" (1995, p. 107).

Heidegger now circles around the phenomenon of boredom again. This time he adverts to a different example, in which boredom does not have a determinate intentional object. Imagine you spend an evening at a party, in which you find "*nothing that is boring*" (1995, p. 114). But in retrospect, you discover that you were bored *with* the whole event, without having been bored *by* any particular things or occurrences. The problem in this situation is that we just "go with the flow," and thereby cut ourselves off from "our *own having-been* and our *own future*" (1995, p. 124), thereby rendering the whole evening as "standing time," which "is *we ourselves*" (1995, p. 125). This "standing 'now'" provides the intrinsic unity of the two structural moments of boredom since it simultaneously leaves us empty and holds us in limbo (1995, p. 126). We drifted through the evening or engaged only at a superficial level of diversion, like Kierkegaard's aesthete. But this deeper form of boredom opens us to the possibility of recognizing that it "*springs from the temporality of Dasein*" (1995, p. 127).

However, there are yet deeper forms of boredom. Heidegger circles again. This time he introduces us to *profound boredom*, which he takes to be "a fundamental attunement of contemporary Dasein" (1995, p. 132). Profound boredom is characterized by the impersonal expression "it is boring for one." The dimension of being left empty is construed in terms of "beings' telling refusal of themselves as a whole" (1995, p. 137), while the dimension of being held in limbo is construed as a "*pointing to the possibilities left unexploited* which lies in such a refusal itself" (1995, p. 141). The telling refusal of beings is also hybrid and implicates *Dasein* in being indifferent to everything including itself. This indifference means that nothing in the world is seen in terms of possibility. Yet it is precisely possibility that makes *Dasein* possible. The withdrawal or refusal of things as a whole potentially announces all the unexploited possibilities. Therefore, profound boredom can disclose (albeit negatively) the very possibility of becoming *Dasein* (1995, pp. 140–144).

Heidegger discusses one more level of boredom, the historically specific form found in modernity. It may be a variant of profound boredom, rather than an entirely distinct type (Withy 2013, p. 166). Heidegger refers to the dialectic of withdrawal and announcement in the two dimensions of boredom as an "oscillation" because "we do not leave the withdrawn entities behind [but] remain tethered to them" (Withy 2013, p. 167). When entities withdraw, being as a whole is potentially revealed and this is essential to our becoming *Dasein*. The problem with contemporary boredom is that it prevents this oscillation. In contemporary boredom, the withdrawal takes the form of "the *very absence of any essential oppressiveness in our Dasein as a whole*" (Heidegger 1995, p. 163). We feel so secure and complacent that we lose our curiosity and wonder about the meaning of being. There is no call to our being corresponding to the absence of essential oppressiveness. We no longer oscillate in the ontological difference between being and entities but relate to beings as mere entities. Heidegger refers to this as the "forgetting" of being (e.g., Heidegger 1962, pp. 338–339).[13] This amounts to a failure to realize the revelatory potential of profound boredom (Withy 2013, p. 168). While superficial boredom is a mood, attunement to profound boredom is a means of opening ourselves to being.

Profound boredom indicates a lack of care or concern about the world and ourselves. We lack the necessary pathos to motivate engagement with the world or to realize our being-in-the-world. Insofar as we lack engagement we approximate the inert objectivity of stones. Heidegger also contrasts us with animals, which he characterizes as being "poor in world" (1995, p. 268). Human beings are supposed to be characterized by the capacity for "world-forming" (1995, p. 274). We need to become *attuned* to our profound boredom so that through the oscillation between the withdrawal of beings and the revelation of being-as-a-whole, which attunement enables, we can, in a moment of vision [Augenblick],[14] become *Dasein*, to form our world with care.[15] The moment of vision is the pivot from withdrawal to revelation, the fullness of time in which we awaken to our potential as *Dasein*.

Conclusion

The psychological literature has given us the insight that boredom is not a basic emotion but occupies an approximate and changeable location in an affective circumplex. It is a functional emotion, which informs and regulates our behavior, motivating us to find something more meaningful or satisfactory—especially activities that fit our overall projects.

Kierkegaard and Heidegger complement these findings, rather than contradict them. Neither gives a precise definition of boredom as a psychological state or trait, but like the self-report studies in the psychological literature, they rely, at least initially, on an intuitive understanding of boredom as an experience with which everyone is familiar. They then take that familiar experience as a starting point for awakening the reader to her potential for becoming an authentic self. The task of becoming a self is conceived as our primary overall project.

Heidegger goes further in deepening the notion of boredom itself. He defamiliarizes the reader from the superficial, intuitive understanding of the phenomenon, but in a way that opens the reader to the possibility of discovering something about herself and her being-in-the-world. In arriving at the notion of profound boredom,

---

[13]This passage is reminiscent of the aesthete's discussion of the art of forgetting in *Either/Or*.

[14]For a comparison of Kierkegaard's notion of the moment [Øieblik] with Heidegger's notion of moment of vision [*Augenblick*], and their common derivation from the Christian notion of the fullness of time, see (Carlisle 2015, pp. 37, 49–52).

[15]Note that a predecessor concept to boredom is *acedia*, a word that derives from the Greek for not-caring. Harry Frankfurt (1992), approaching the concept of boredom from a very different philosophical perspective from Kierkegaard and Heidegger, also finds a potential within boredom to inform us about what we should care about, especially in terms of our 'final ends.'

however, in which one becomes indifferent to everything, he perhaps conflates boredom with apathy. This is not so different from Kierkegaard's aesthete, who transforms boredom by means of ironic indifference, self-limitation, and arbitrariness, thereby rendering himself demonically bored (see McDonald 2009) and unable to transition to another existential stage by means of the appropriate passion. Yet both Kierkegaard's and Heidegger's transformations of superficial boredom are congruent with the affective circumplex model of boredom.

The greatest difference between the psychological literature and Kierkegaard and Heidegger is in their respective aims and frames of reference. Psychology aims only to describe, assess, and treat a psychological state or trait, while Kierkegaard and Heidegger are concerned to situate boredom in the framework of the individual's task of becoming a self. While psychology allows the possibility that boredom can inform and motivate our behavior, the philosophers open up a prospect for how boredom can transform our whole way of being-in-the-world.

References

Bench, S. W., & Lench, H. C. (2013). On the function of boredom. *Behavioral Sciences, 3,* 459–472. https://doi.org/10.3390/bs3030459.

Boden, J. (2009). The devil inside: Boredom proneness and impulsive behaviour. In B. Dalle Pezze & C. Salzani (Eds.), *Essays on boredom and modernity* (pp. 203–226). Amsterdam/New York, NY: Rodopi.

Calhoun, C. (2011). Living with boredom. *Sophia, 50,* 269–279. https://doi.org/10.1007/s11841-011-0239-3.

Carlisle, C. (2015). A tale of two footnotes: Heidegger and the question of Kierkegaard. In D. McManus (Ed.), *Heidegger, authenticity and the self. Themes from division two of Being and time* (pp. 37–55). London, UK/New York, NY: Routledge.

Cowen, A. S., & Keltner, D. (Eds). (2017). *Self-report captures 27 distinct categories of emotion bridged by continuous gradients.Proceedings of the National Academy of Sciences of the United States of America.* https://doi.org/10.1073/pnas.1702247114.

Cummings, M. L. (2016). Boredom in the workplace: A new look at an old problem. *Human Factors, 58*(2), 279–300. https://doi.org/10.1177/0018720815609503.

Dalle Pezze, B., & Salzani, C. (2009). *Essays on boredom and modernity.* Amsterdam/New York, NY: Rodopi.

Danckert, J. A., & Allman, A. A. A. (2005). Time flies when you're having fun: Temporal estimation and the experience of boredom. *Brain and Cognition, 59,* 236–245. https://doi.org/10.1016/j.bandc.2005.07.002.

Eastwood, J. D., Cavaliere, C., Fahlman, S. A., & Eastwood, A. E. (2007). A desire for desires: Boredom and its relation to alexithymia. *Personality and Individual Differences, 42,* 1035–1045. https://doi.org/10.1016/j.paid.2006.08.027.

Eastwood, J. D., Frischen, A., Fenske, M. J., & Smilek, D. (2012). The unengaged mind: Defining boredom in terms of attention. *Perspectives on Psychological Science, 7*(5), 482–495. https://doi.org/10.1177/1745691612456044.

Ekman, P. (1993). Facial expression and emotion. *American Psychologist, 48,* 384–392. https://doi.org/10.1037/0003-066x.48.4.384.

Ekman, P., & Cordaro, D. (2011). What is meant by calling emotions basic? *Emotion Review, 3*(4), 364–370. https://doi.org/10.1177/1754073911410740.

Elpidorou, A. (2018). The bored mind is a guiding mind: toward a regulatory theory of boredom. *Phenomenology and the Cognitive Sciences, 17,* 455–484. https://doi.org/10.1007/s11097-017-9515-1.

Fahlman, S. A., Mercer-Lynn, K. B., Flora, D. B., & Eastwood, J. D. (2013). Development and validation of the multidimensional State Boredom Scale. *Assessment, 20*(1), 68–85. https://doi.org/10.1177/1073191111421303.

Frankfurt, H. (1992). On the usefulness of final ends. *The Jerusalem Philosophical Quarterly: Iyyun,* 3–19.

Goetz, T., Cronjaeger, H., Frenzel, A. C., Lüdtke, O., & Hall, N. C. (2010). Academic self-concept and emotion relations: Domain specificity and age effects. *Contemporary Educational Psychology, 35,* 44–58. https://doi.org/10.1016/j.cedpsych.2009.10.001.

Grassian, S. (2006). Psychiatric effects of solitary confinement. *Washington University Journal of Law and Policy, 22,* 325–383.

Heidegger, M. (1962). *Being and time*. New York, NY: Harper & Row.

Heidegger, M. (1995). *The fundamental concepts of metaphysics: World, finitude, solitude*. Bloomington, IN/Indianapolis, IN: Indiana University Press.

Hunter, J. B., & Csíkszentmihályi, M. (2002). The positive psychology of interested adolescents. *Journal of Youth and Adolescence, 32*(1), 27–35. https://doi.org/10.1023/a:1021028306392.

Hunter, J. A., Abraham, E. H., Hunter, A. G., Goldberg, L. C., & Eastwood, J. D. (2016). Personality and boredom proneness in the prediction of creativity and curiosity. *Thinking Skills and Creativity, 22,* 48–57. https://doi.org/10.1016/j.tsc.2016.08.002.

Johnsen, R. (2016). Boredom and organization studies. *Organisation Studies, 37*(10), 1403–1415. https://doi.org/10.1177/0170840616640849.

Kaftanski, W. (2015). Redoubling/Reduplication. In S. M. Emmanuel, W. McDonald, & J. Stewart (Eds.), *Kierkegaard's concepts. Tome V: Objectivity to sacrifice* (pp. 205–211). New York, NY/Abingdon, VA: Routledge.

Kierkegaard, S. (1954). *Fear and trembling & the sickness unto death*. Princeton, NJ: Princeton University Press.

Kierkegaard, S. (1959). *Either/Or* (Vol. I). Princeton, NJ: Princeton University Press.

Kierkegaard, S. (1972). *Either/Or* (Vol. II). Princeton, NJ: Princeton University Press.

Kierkegaard, S. (1980a). *The concept of anxiety*. Princeton, NJ: Princeton University Press.

Kierkegaard, S. (1980b). *The sickness unto death*. Princeton, NJ: Princeton University Press.

Kierkegaard, S. (1983). *Fear and trembling / Repetition*. Princeton, NJ: Princeton University Press.

Kierkegaard, S. (1988). *Stages on life's way*. Princeton, NJ: Princeton University Press.

Kierkegaard, S. (1992). *Concluding unscientific postscript to philosophical fragments*. Princeton, NY: Princeton University Press.

Kitcher, P. (1990). *Kant's transcendental psychology*. New York, NY/Oxford, UK: Oxford University Press.

Koch, C. H. (2016). Frederik Christian Sibbern: 'The lovable, remarkable thinker, Councilor Sibbern' and 'the political Simple-Peter Sibbern'. In J. Stewart (Ed.), *Kierkegaard and his Danish contemporaries. Tome I: Philosophy, politics and social theory* (pp. 229–260). New York, NY/Abingdon, VA: Routledge.

Lee, F. K. S., & Zelman, D. C. (2019). Boredom proneness as a predictor of depression, anxiety and stress: The moderating effects of dispositional mindfulness. *Personality and Individual Differences, 146,* 68–75. https://doi.org/10.1016/j.paid.2019.04.001.

LePera, N. (2011). Relationships between boredom proneness, mindfulness, anxiety, depression, and substance use. *New School Psychology Bulletin, 8,* 15–25.

Lewis, M. (2017). The relation between transcendental philosophy and empirical science in Heidegger's *Fundamental concepts of metaphysics. Cosmos and History: The Journal of Natural and Social Philosophy, 13*(1), 47–72.

Malantschuk, G. (1980). *Frihed og ekistens. Studier i Søren Kierkegaards tænkning*, Copenhagen: C.A. Reitzel.

Martin, M., Sadlo, G., & Stew, G. (2006). The phenomenon of boredom. *Qualitative Research in Psychology, 3,* 193–211. https://doi.org/10.1191/1478088706qrp066oa.
McDonald, W. (2009). Kierkegaard's demonic boredom. In B. Dalle Pezze & C. Salzani (Eds.), *Essays on boredom and modernity* (pp. 61–84). Amsterdam/New York, NY: Rodopi.
McDonald, W. (2014). Moment. In S. M. Emmanuel, W. McDonald, & J. Stewart (Eds.), *Kierkegaard's concepts, Tome IV: Individual to novel* (pp. 173–179). New York, NY/Abingdon, VA: Routledge.
McDonald, W. (2019). Kierkegaard's experimenting psychology. In A. Buben, E. Helms, & P. Stokes (Eds.), *The Kierkegaardian mind* (pp. 39–51). New York, NY/Abingdon, VA: Routledge.
Merrifield, C., & Danckert, J. (2014). Characterizing the psychophysiological signature of boredom. *Experimental Brain Research, 232,* 481–491. https://doi.org/10.1007/s00221-013-3755-2.
Nielsen, N. Å. (1966). *Dansk etymologisk Ordbog*. Copenhagen: Gyldendal.
Nordentoft, K. (1978). *Kierkegaard's psychology*. Pittsburgh, PA: Duquesne University Press.
O'Brien, W. (2014). Boredom. *Analysis, 74*(2), 236–244. https://doi.org/10.1093/analys/anu041.
Pattyn, N., Neyt, X., Hedenrickx, D., & Soetens, E. (2008). Psychophysiological investigation of vigilance decrement: Boredom or cognitive fatigue? *Physiology & Behavior, 93*(1–2), 369–378. https://doi.org/10.1016/j.physbeh.2007.09.016.
Posner, J., Russell, J. A., & Peterson, B. S. (2005). The circumplex model of affect: An integrative approach to affective neuroscience, cognitive development, and psychopathology. *Development and Psychopathology, 17,* 715–734. https://doi.org/10.1017/S0954579405050340.
Sansone, C., & Thoman, D. B. (2005). Interest as the missing motivator in self-regulation. *European Psychologist, 10*(3), 175–186. https://doi.org/10.1027/1016-9040.10.3.175.
Schreiber, G. (2015). Transition. In S. M. Emmanuel, W. McDonald, & J. Stewart (Eds.), *Kierkegaard's concepts, Tome VI: Salvation to writing* (pp. 185–191). New York, NY/Abingdon, VA: Routledge.
Skues, J., Williams, B., Oldmeadow, J., & Wise, L. (2016). The effects of boredom, loneliness, and distress tolerance on problem internet use among university students. *International Journal of Mental Health Addiction, 14,* 167–180. https://doi.org/10.1007/s11469-015-9568-8.
Svendsen, L. (2005). *A philosophy of boredom*. London, UK: Reaktion Books.
Van Tilburg, W. A. P., & Igou, E. R. (2017). Boredom begs to differ: Differentiation from other gegative emotions. *Emotion, 17*(2), 309–322. https://doi.org/10.1037/emo0000233.
Vodanovich, S. J., & Watt, J. D. (2016). Self-report measures of boredom: An updated review of the literature. *The Journal of Psychology, 150*(2), 194–226. https://doi.org/10.1080/00223980.2015.1074531.
Vogel-Walcutt, J. J., Fiorella, L., Carper, T., & Schatz, S. (2012). The definition, assessment, and mitigation of state boredom within educational settings: A comprehensive review. *Educational Psychology Review, 24,* 89–111. https://doi.org/10.1007/s10648-011-9182-7.
Weinerman, J., & Kenner, C. (2016). Boredom: That which shall not be named. *Journal of Developmental Education, 40*(1), 18–23.
Weinstein, L., Xie, X., & Cleanthous, C. C. (1995). Purpose in life, boredom, and volunteerism in a group of retirees. *Psychological Reports, 76*(2), 482–482. https://doi.org/10.2466/pr0.1995.76.2.482.
Withy, K. (2013). The strategic unity of Heidegger's *The fundamental concepts of metaphysics*. *Southern Journal of Philosophy, 51*(2), 161–178. https://doi.org/10.1111/sjp.12012.

William McDonald is Chair of the Philosophy Department at the UAE University. He has a Ph.D. in Philosophy from the University of Sydney (1990), MA in Education (University of New England, 1982) and BA in Arts with Honors (University of New England, 1980). He has worked at the University of Sydney, the University of New England, the American University of Central

Asia, and the United Arab Emirates University. He has received research fellowships at the University of Copenhagen, St Olaf College Minnesota, the Slovak Academy of Sciences, Monash University and the University of Hertfordshire. Dr. McDonald has research expertise in the history of philosophy, comparative philosophy of religion, philosophical psychology and aesthetics. He is an internationally recognized Kierkegaard scholar, who made the first translation into English of Kierkegaard's Prefaces and has written many standard reference works on Kierkegaard. He is the author of many standard reference articles (h-index 5) on the work of Søren Kierkegaard, including those in the *Stanford encyclopedia of philosophy,* the *Internet encyclopedia of philosophy* and the *Literary encyclopedia.* He is also co-editor, with Jon Stewart and Steven Emmanuel, of the six-tome work, *Kierkegaard's concepts* (Routledge, 2013–2015). He has published extensively on topics in the history of philosophical psychology, including 'Kierkegaard's demonic boredom', in Carlo Salzani & Barbara Dalle Pezze (eds.), *Essays on boredom and modernity* (Rodopi, 2009).

Chapter 7
Heidegger on Creativity: From Boredom to Re-engagement with the World

Erik Ringmar

Experimental psychologists have discussed whether boredom can help us become more creative. At first blush, this would seem to be rather unlikely. When we are bored, we are disengaged; we cannot be bothered and nothing seems worthwhile; we have no interest in the world around us. Such a condition, surely, is not conducive to creativity (Haager et al. 2018). Yet some psychologists disagree (Gasper and Middlewood 2014). Boredom, they explain, breaks down entrenched routines and thought-patterns and provides us with an opportunity to think again and anew. Respondents in "approach-oriented states" such as boredom engage in more "associative thought" than those in "avoidance-oriented affective states." This is how boredom comes to encourage "the quest for meaning and exploration" (Gasper and Middlewood 2014, pp. 53–55).

How we come down on this issue depends on what we take boredom to be. This is where the case made by experimental psychologists looks weak. Whether they are defending the creativity-thesis or rejecting it, they all have a shallow understanding of what boredom is and how it works. In their rush to quantify and to measure, they have not paid sufficient attention to the way boredom *feels*. Boredom is not a thing after all, but rather one of the many ways in which we may find ourselves in the world. How one finds oneself in the world is difficult to measure. What we need is a far better grasp of the phenomenology involved. And if this is the task, whom better to rely on than Martin Heidegger? Heidegger discussed boredom at some considerable length in a series of lectures given in Freiburg in the winter of 1929/1930 and subsequently published as *Fundamental concepts of metaphysics* (2001, pp. 78–167). In these lectures, he discussed creativity too, or rather what he referred to as "authenticity." Although authenticity is not the same thing as creativity, a connection between the two concepts is not difficult to

E. Ringmar (✉)
Ibn Haldun University, Istanbul, Turkey
e-mail: Erik.ringmar@ihu.edu.tr

J. Ros Velasco (ed.), *Boredom Is in Your Mind*,
https://doi.org/10.1007/978-3-030-26395-9_7

establish. To live an authentic life is to live a creative life, a life which we have made for ourselves and which is lived on our own terms.

But Heidegger was a conservative thinker who took a dim view of individualism, and he was skeptical regarding romantic notions of self-assertion (Davis 2007; Ringmar 2017). As human beings, he pointed out, we always find ourselves in situations that others have created and over which we have little or no power. We are 'thrown' into the world and always live together with, and in relation to, other people. We are always hanging out with *das Man*, as it were, and we always do, say and think what this Mr. Everyman does, says, and thinks (Heidegger 1962, pp. 163–168). The problem for Heidegger is how an authentic life is possible under such conditions. Clearly, it cannot simply be a matter of breaking free of social constraints since any conception of freedom itself will be historically, culturally, and socially determined. Yet Heidegger did believe that there may be moments when we have the opportunity to reassess our lives. These are extreme moments when the world temporarily stops making sense. Heidegger found one such moment in anxiety, and he discussed that in *Being and time* (1962, pp. 228–235). The other such moment is boredom, and that is what he discusses in *Fundamental concepts of metaphysics*.

As always, however, Heidegger makes no concessions to established terminology, and he has little respect for empirical science (2001, pp. 88–92). This means that any engagement between his work and that of experimental psychologists requires what we could think of as an act of translation. In this chapter, we will contribute to this task by looking for an independent set of terms by which a translation can take place. While invoking Heidegger, we will try our best not to be entranced by his language. Boredom, we will say, is the affective state in which we find ourselves once our attention no longer is entrained. It is when the attention flags that we get bored. Once this has happened, the question is how to re-engage with the world. Creativity, from this point of view, is a matter of the terms on which such re-engagement takes place. Eventually, we want to tell a new, more authentic, story about our plans, our lives, and ourselves.

Two Forms of Entrainment

As long as we pay attention to something we are not bored (James 1884; Ringmar 2016a). From the Latin *ad-* meaning 'to' and *tendere* meaning 'to stretch,' to attend to something is 'to give heed to' or 'to direct one's mind or energies toward' something. Yet as we know, paying proper attention to something is difficult under the best of circumstances and often we cannot do it for more than a few seconds at a time. Paying attention is far easier if we are presented with some form of a *Gestalt*; that is, a pattern, a figure, or a structure of some kind. First, our attention is captured by the overall pattern of the *Gestalt*, then our attention is maintained as its individual components gradually come to be revealed. We pay attention since we want to see, hear, or feel what is about to happen. The technical term is 'entrainment'

(Krueger 2014). We are entrained as our attention is captured, held, and carried along by the *Gestalt.* Boredom, from this point of view, occurs when entrainment fails. There is suddenly nothing that captures our attention, holds it and carries it along. We are bored since there is nothing to which we can pay attention.

There are basically two ways in which our attention can be entrained. We pay attention with our minds but also with our bodies. More than anything, our minds are entrained by means of narrative structures. We are entrained as we follow a story and interpret the events and persons which it contains. We pay attention since we want to know how the book, the play, or the movie will end. But there are also narrative-like structures—such as music—which function in a similar fashion. Music too has a plot of sorts—musical themes are introduced and developed—and we keep on listening since we want to know where the music will take us. Narratives, and quasi-narratives such as music, are human creations. By means of the structure of the plot, the world comes to be organized in a certain fashion. Or perhaps we could say that the narratives allow us to create our own world, a virtual reality which we join as a consequence of our entrainment.

But we are also entrained by the world in an immediate, and unmediated, fashion. By means of our bodies, we pay direct attention to the situations in which we find ourselves. Literally, thousands of minuscule pieces of information have to be gathered and processed in order for us to even be able to walk across the floor. Here too *Gestalts* are important. Our bodies react to smells, to light, and to a vertical orientation, and they love to give into the temptations of rhythms. It is a matter of the shapes and surfaces of things, the position of our bodies in space, body coordination and the interaction between our body and the bodies of others. This information is usually not explicitly recognized by consciousness, and instead, our bodies find their place in the world by themselves. It all happens behind our backs, as it were.

Habits are crucial in explaining such automatic behavior. As a result of the habits we have developed, we rarely have to think about what we are doing. Instead, when a certain situation arises, we simply act. It is as though a situation was calling out to us, and we respond to the call by acting in a more or less automatic fashion. The path in the forest wants us to walk on it; the newly made bed wants us to lay down; the house of worship asks us to pray. In an instant, our bodies have attuned themselves to the mood of the situation in which they find themselves. This is how we suddenly find ourselves walking, laying down, and praying.

Since our bodies too are entrained, it is not surprising that our way of paying attention is reflected in our poise, gait, and general demeanor. In effect, our entrainment *is* our bodily poise, gait, and general demeanor. As a result, the state of our entrainment is often perfectly obvious to outsiders. “You are in a chipper/pesky/somber mood today,” someone might remark, and it is only once they tell us that we come to realize how we feel. Boredom too is revealed through bodily postures. When we are bored our head may suddenly become so heavy we must rest it in our hands; ‘I’m so bored,’ we say with a yawn as we flop ourselves down on a sofa. Yet in general, the body is not as easily bored as our minds. Our bodies can follow the same repetitive rhythm for hours. Our bodies, if left to themselves, would go on dancing until they were worn out.

Being and Time

These two forms of entrainment—the narrative and the embodied—function quite differently. Most obviously, paying attention to a narrative is to pay attention to the world at a remove. To follow a narrative is to experience the world vicariously. Here, the experiences and emotions are not our own but instead those of the protagonists of the story. This is a secondary form of entrainment, as it were, which relies on our ability to engage with a representation of the world as seen at a distance. When the body is entrained, by contrast, we experience the world directly. We ourselves are present in a certain situation, not just presented with a representation of it.

The two forms of entrainment result in two quite distinct phenomenological experiences. Notice, for example, what happens to time. A narrative has a time of its own. Reading the book we take time off from our ordinary lives and enter time as configured by the story. As a result, time may slow down, skip, turn back on itself, or go around in loops. But time is reconfigured in direct, embodied, and entrainment too. When our bodies are perfectly attuned to the situations in which they find themselves, we may lose our sense of time (Csíkszentmihályi 2008). Time is suspended, and we cannot tell if a minute has passed or perhaps an eternity. Likewise, when boredom strikes, our understanding of time is transformed. Time which used to be so light has suddenly become unbearably heavy. Time is like quicksand or like treacle. Once our feet are stuck in it, we cannot move. Or perhaps it is we who have become like quicksand or treacle. Once time has become stuck in us, it cannot move.

Notice also what happens to our sense of self. When we are fully entrained by a narrative, we appropriate the point of view of its protagonists. We identify with the characters and feel what they feel, want what they want, do what they do (De Graaf et al. 2012). We lose ourselves in the story, and we suddenly find ourselves as someone else. Embodied entrainment results in a similar loss of self. This, at least, is what rock climbers say, professional dancers, concert violinists, and yoga practitioners. As long as we are entrained by the activity, we may never find ourselves again. Somehow or another we have lost ourselves in the interaction between our bodies and the world. Come to think of it, this is not surprising. The body, as a body, has no sense of self, and when we become all body, the self is reduced to an unnecessary assumption.

Perhaps we need to spell out what this does *not* mean. The fact that the two forms of entrainment are distinct does not mean that minds can be separated from bodies. No Cartesian dualism is implied. And often enough the two forms of entrainment take place in synchrony with each other. Thus, a narrative attunement often requires a bodily attunement. For example: when we read a book or watch a play, we understand the plot not merely by means of our explicit interpretations but also by embodied means. The story may give us goosebumps or a queasy feeling in our stomachs. These, moreover, are not incidental reactions, but preconditions for our understanding of the plot (Thiele 2006, pp. 252–257; Rokotnitz 2017).

Similarly, our minds will often call upon our bodies. When we hear a piece of music, our minds may recognize it as a certain tune, but it is our bodies that get up, and stay, on the dance floor. Conversely, even fully embodied forms of entrainment require a form of proto-narrativity (Fisher 2010). Unless we are able to retain the memory of a previous part of a pattern, and form a premonition of a future part, the present part will fail to make sense. Always slightly ahead of itself, the body reaches out for the next thing that is coming up. This is the embodied sensation that all stories require. We can follow a story since our bodies know what it is like to move ahead.

Boredom 1: The Train Station

This is how Heidegger describes the scene:

> We are sitting, for example, in the tasteless station of some lonely minor railway. It is four hours until the next train arrives. The district is uninspiring. We do have a book in our rucksack, though—shall we read? No. Or think through a problem, some question? We are unable to. We read the timetables or study the table giving the various distances from this station to other places we are not otherwise acquainted with at all. We look at the clock—only a quarter of an hour has gone by. Then we go out onto the local road. We walk up and down, just to have something to do. But it is no use. Then we count the trees along the road, look at our watch again—exactly five minutes since we last looked at it. Fed up with walking back and forth, we sit down on a stone, draw all kinds of figures in the sand, and in so doing catch ourselves looking at our watch yet again—half an hour—and so on. (2001, p. 93)

A common complaint in the nineteenth century was that train journeys happened far too quickly. Whizzing past the lives of others at speeds of up to 40 km per hour, the passengers had no chance to engage with what they saw. Trains, conservative critics feared, encouraged their passengers to treat the lives of others as superficial, and quickly passing, amusements. Heidegger shared this critique of modernity and movement, but this is not his concern here. On the contrary, he is annoyed since he cannot get to where he is going fast enough.

But what exactly is the source of his annoyance? There are many ways to be in a train station after all which do not result in boredom. We might work there, for example, or treat it as a place to keep warm or as a venue for conducting illicit business. Or we might simply go there to watch trains go by. But Heidegger is on his way somewhere and this makes it into a completely different kind of train station for him. He was on a train, engaged in a steady forward movement; his body was entrained by the train, as it were. There is an explicit story here, of a departure and an anticipated arrival, but there is also a proto-story with which his body had engaged. His body was already ahead of itself and the mood in which he now finds himself is determined by this fact. The story has temporarily been suspended and time, as a result, has become unbearably heavy.

Faced with this situation, his body temporarily takes charge. Heidegger's body is trying to be helpful. Quite by itself, it is looking for *Gestalt*s which might engage him. Thus his eyes direct him first to a timetable on the wall, then to a clock; his legs start walking up and down the road outside of the train station; his hand picks up a stick and starts drawing patterns in the sand. Yet none of the *Gestalt*s which his body discovers in this way is engaging enough to catch his conscious attention. He is too annoyed to be entrained. He even rejects the book in his rucksack which would have provided an easy, conveniently narrated, escape. He is not interested; all he wants is for his journey to continue.

This is the beginning of Heidegger's account of boredom. Much as the situation annoys him, the experience is eye-opening. Heidegger has come up against nothing less than temporality itself. A train station experience is what all of our lives would be like if we were not entrained by all those patterns to which we normally pay attention. Train station experiences are exactly the kinds of experiences that we usually try our best to avoid. We are afraid of boredom since we are afraid of a life without entrainment; we are afraid of boredom since we are afraid of a life deprived of meaning. And yet, this kind of boredom is easily overcome. The suspension of entrainment is only temporary after all. As soon as our respective trains pull into our respective train stations, we all scramble to get on. Our stories continue and we are no longer bored. The trains take us away from all metaphysical queries.

Boredom 2: The Dinner Party

This is Heidegger's description:

> We have been invited out somewhere for the evening. We do not need to go along. Still, we have been tense all day, and we have time in the evening. So we go along. There we find the usual food and the usual table conversation, everything is not only very tasty, but tasteful as well. Afterward people sit together having a lively discussion, as they say, perhaps listening to music, having a chat, and things are witty and amusing. And already it is time to leave. The ladies assure us, not merely when leaving, but downstairs and outside too as we gather to leave, that it really was very nice, or that it was terribly charming. Indeed. There is nothing at all to be found that might have been boring about this evening, neither the conversation, nor the people, nor the rooms. Thus we come home quite satisfied. We cast a quick glance at the work we interrupted that evening, make a rough assessment of things and look ahead to the next day—and then it comes: I was bored after all this evening, on the occasion of this invitation. (2001, p. 109)

It is at first difficult to see how this could count as an example of boredom. On the contrary, the dinner party was not boring at all. It was a good night out and Heidegger enjoyed himself. And the reason he did, judging by his description, was more than anything that various social habits took charge of the situation. Everything was as expected and as it should be; the conversation flowed easily, each person adding their bits to the unfolding sequence; there was even music. Entrained in this way, Heidegger lost a sense of time and a sense of self. Time just flew and he forgot himself.

When he returned home, however, another set of entrenched habits kicked in. When he entered his study, he took a quick look at his desk. This movement of his body called up a story—the narrative which Heidegger tells himself about his life. This story informs him of the things that really matter to him and instructs him regarding how he should spend his time. This is the story which has "Martin Heidegger," the world-leading philosopher, as its main protagonist. It is in terms of this narrative that the dinner party was boring. It was boring since it was a waste of time, and it was a waste of time since the evening is impossible to fit into time as organized by his autobiography. In terms of that story, the evening out was nothing but a pointless digression. It was one of those darlings which movie directors are advised to leave on the floor of the cutting room.

Differently put, it is his autobiographical narrative that saves him. Much as the train that rescued him from the boring train station, the story he tells himself about 'Martin Heidegger' rescues him from the boring evening out. Or, to be more precise, the autobiographical narrative first determines that the evening was boring and then proceeds to rescue him from the boredom it has induced. But this also means that he experiences the boredom only at a remove. The boredom is not something that he actually feels. The boredom appears only in retrospect, once the story of his life has picked him up again and carried him away.

Boredom 3: Profound Boredom

When it comes to profound boredom, Heidegger provides no description of a scene. As he explains, there is no scene to describe. Profound boredom can overcome us anywhere and anytime—even when walking "through the streets of a large city on a Sunday afternoon" (Heidegger 2001, p. 135). What we are bored by here is nothing in particular, instead, it is life itself which becomes unbearable. "It makes everything of equally great or equally little worth… It takes us back to the point where all and everything appears indifferent to us" (Heidegger 2001, p. 137). In profound boredom, it is life itself which drags; life is the *Langeweile*, the "long while," which we cannot fill with any conceivable content. When confronting profound boredom, time loses its sense of direction and our identities begin to unravel.

What we are faced with here, differently put, is a state of total narrative collapse. All forms of narrative entrainment fail; there are no stories that can catch us, hold us, and carry us along. The stories are like broken tools that no longer can be used for their intended purposes. There is not even a biographical narrative and consequently no main protagonist and no sense of an individual self. This is why, according to Heidegger, we should talk about this condition as being boring "for one" rather than boring "for me" (Heidegger 2001, p. 141). In the absence of a narrative, time collapses too. Without a story, there is no way to separate the past from the present and the future. Time, in all its dimensions, folds into the present and ends up standing still. What we are left with is life reduced to bare-bone basics. It is as though the effects of all the drugs we have been taking for so long finally have worn off. What we have come up against, says Heidegger, is not this or that or the other thing, but instead Being itself.

This experience is unsettling, to say the least. One problem is that we have difficulties making sense of the encounter. The reason, simply put, is that Being has no *Gestalt.* Being is not an object and it does not look, sound, or smell like anything. The outrageous fact that we are alive is not itself an observable datum. As a result, Being is always going to be difficult to pay attention to. Instead, we are more likely to be overwhelmed by the encounter. When coming into the presence of Being, we become what Heidegger calls *gebannt,* "entranced"—a state of awe in which our minds freeze up, our knees go weak, and we lose our faculty of speech (2001, pp. 147–148). To be entranced is to be transfixed, rooted to the ground. Entrancement is thus the very opposite of entrainment. Being summons us, we could perhaps say, but we have no way of responding to its call.

Between Being and the Social

Heidegger's analysis here is similar to what he says about anxiety in *Being and time* (1962, pp. 228–235). Anxiety and profound boredom are both ways of liberating ourselves from the man-made meanings with which we normally surround ourselves. In both conditions, all attempts at narrative entrainment have failed, but embodied entrainment has failed too. In anxiety, we cannot focus on anything in the world around us; our attention-span reduced to zero, we flit from one thing to the other. And in boredom, as we saw, we are *gebannt,* transfixed. In neither condition are there any *Gestalt*s with the power to capture our attention, hold us and carry us along. We are pushed to the edge; we are staring into the abyss. Overcome with vertigo, we are sick to our stomachs.

The question is what happens next. According to Heidegger, we "flee" (Heidegger 1962, pp. 229–230). Once we realize that we are in the presence of Being, we start running in the opposite direction. And yet, given that Heidegger already has told us that profound boredom is an impersonal state and that we are rooted to the ground, we may wonder who it is who does the fleeing. The answer is that our bodies once again take charge. Much as in the previous cases of boredom, our bodies are trying to be helpful. It is as though when walking in a forest, we suddenly had come across a bear (James 1884, p. 190). At first, we are indeed transfixed by the encounter, but then—and without quite understanding how and why it happened—we suddenly find ourselves running. Our bodies react before our conscious minds are aware of what is going on. It is only once we already are running that we catch up with ourselves and only now that we suddenly become terrified.

This is at the same time, not just a random escape. Rather, our fleeing has a definite destination. More than anything, as Heidegger explains, we seek refuge in crowds. Given what we have experienced, the company of others is wonderfully comforting. Together with people who go about their ordinary lives in their ordinary fashion, we can put our encounter with Being out of our minds. In this way, a sense of normalcy is restored. Yet this re-engagement with the world will necessarily take place on terms which have been determined by other people (Heidegger 1962, pp. 163–168). We are eager to please and prepared to do just about anything to fit in. Hanging out with *das Man*—Mr. Everyman—we soon become *das Man* ourselves. This is a relief to be sure, but it is also our undoing. As perfectly socially determined, we are no longer the authors of our own lives.

The situation, in other words, is pretty bleak. On the one hand, there is our encounter with Being. And as Heidegger explains, this is always going to be an encounter with the inevitability our own deaths. Being is nothing if not being-towards-death (1962, pp. 279–311). On the other hand, we have the social, which it too presents us with a death of sorts, or at least with the end of the notion that we can live a life which is truly our own. It is between these two deaths that boredom has cleared a space—a tiny sliver of space between Being and the social—in which we still are fully alive. The only problem is that this is an unbearably uncomfortable location to be in and certainly no place where we can settle down and make a life for ourselves. Whenever we come too close to the bear, our bodies will start running.

The problem, in other words, is that we no longer can rely on our bodies to help us out. Our bodies react instinctively, and once our bodies have given upon us, we are surely lost. And yet, says Heidegger, our bodies can be trained to act in a different way than their instincts dictate. By means of a lot of hard work, we can develop new habits that impose themselves on our existing habits and keep them in check. This implies something akin to a physical workout program (Ringmar 2017). We need to steel ourselves, as it were; force our bodies to stay put and take a stand. We must learn to stand up straight no matter what happens, head raised and eyes cocked, like a guard in a watchtower or a lookout in the mast of a ship. In this way, our first, fleeing, nature can be replaced by a second nature which refuses to budge.

Provided that our exercise program is successful, we may find that the mood of the situation suddenly changes. Heidegger invokes a religious language here. He talks about a switch, a *kairos*, like Saint Paul's conversion on the way to Damascus (Svendsen 2005, p. 124). Nothing in the situation has actually changed to be sure, but in a blink of the eye, there is nevertheless a complete change of moods. Suddenly, everything feels entirely different. In the middle of this great calamity, Heidegger explains, we experience a "sober anxiety" which gives rise to an "unshakable joy" (1962, p. 358). This is a strange reaction to be sure. Like the serene smile of the Buddha, it conveys the impression of a sudden realization of a great truth. Yet just what we have realized is of course far from obvious. What is clear, though, is that our bodies once again are in charge of the situation. Even once our first nature has failed us, our bodies have found a way of rescuing us.

Re-engagement with the World

Experimental psychologists, we said, have discussed whether boredom can help us become more creative. Our phenomenological investigation gives us reasons to think that this indeed might be the case. By paying attention to something, we become followers of the *Gestalt* that unfolds before us; we are captured, held, and carried along by the pattern. Yet a person who is captured and held is not free and a person who is carried along is not even able to walk by herself. Attention makes us into subjects of whatever it is that entrains us and a state of subjectivity is unlikely to be conducive to creativity. This is where boredom can come to our assistance. Boredom allows us to ignore the *Gestalt*; boredom releases us from captivity and gives us a break from entrainment (Chylińska 2015). Suddenly we are free, and freedom is a precondition for creativity.

According to Friedrich Nietzsche and his many followers, it is in this new-found freedom that we can begin to construct a new and more authentic self (1924, p. 283). We can come up with our own *Gestalt*s, Nietzcheans believe, and once we have come up with them, we can proceed to be entrained by them. Although not everyone is capable of such feats of self-entrainment, this is an option that is open to an elite of uniquely creative individuals. These are the Supermen and Superwomen who can capture and hold themselves and carry themselves along. For Heidegger, however, there can be no such easy solution. As soon as we take refuge in crowds, he points out, we can claim no superiority over others, and we have no powers of self-entrainment. There is no freedom in society, as it were, and Heidegger's philosophy is no liberation theology. The best we can hope for is that when we eventually re-engage with society, we can do so on terms that preserve at least some of the serenity which we came to experience. Our bodies preserve the memory of our encounter with Being and this body-memory distances us from the world. Our bodies never quite allow us to forget the outrageous fact that we now are alive and that we one day will die. This is why we maintain a slightly rigid posture even as we are hanging out with *das Man*; we belong to society to be sure, but our bodies never allow us to be perfectly comfortable there.

In this way, a creativity of sorts might be possible after all. Life continuously places us in situations where we face challenges and are forced to make choices (Dewey 1890, pp. 417–419; Joas 1997, pp. 148–167; Ringmar 2016b, pp. 80–82). Although we all find ourselves the members of crowds, our particular place in the crowd is nevertheless our own. And the choices we make, and the actions we embark on, are our own too even if their content is fully socially determined. Between death and the social, we are temporarily free and each situation we encounter, every choice, has the potential to remind us of that fact. We start our life unsure of who we are and where we want to go, but once the choices accumulate over the course of a lifetime a certain path will be traced. We walk into our life, as it were. What we can say in the end is that we knew what we were doing; we were alive, we were awake, and we chose the kind of life which turned out to be our own.

References

Chylińska, M. (2015). *Is the bored mind an unconstrained mind? Third International Boredom Conference*. Warsaw, Poland: Universitas Varsoviensis.

Csíkszentmihályi, M. (2008). *Flow: The psychology of optimal experience*. New York, NY: Harper.

Davis, B. W. (2007). *Heidegger and the will: On the way to Gelassenheit*. Evanston, IL: Northwestern University Press.

De Graaf, A., Hoeken, H., Sanders, J., & Beentjes, J. W. J. (2012). Identification as a mechanism of narrative persuasion. *Communication Research, 39*(6), 802–823. https://doi.org/10.1177/0093650211408594.

Dewey, J. (1890). *Psychology*. New York, NY: Harper & Brothers.

Fisher, T. (2010). Heidegger and the narrativity debate. *Continental Philosophy Review, 43*(2), 241–265. https://doi.org/10.1007/s11007-010-9141-x.

Gasper, K., & Middlewood, B. L. (2014). Approaching novel thoughts: Understanding why elation and boredom promote associative thought more than distress and relaxation. *Journal of Experimental Social Psychology, 52*(May), 50–57. https://doi.org/10.1016/j.jesp.2013.12.007.

Haager, J. S., Kuhbandner, C., & Pekrun, R. (2018). To be bored or not to be bored: How task-related boredom influences creative performance. *The Journal of Creative Behavior, 52* (4), 297–304. https://doi.org/10.1002/jocb.154.

Heidegger, M. (1962). *Being and time*. New York, NY: Harper & Row.

Heidegger, M. (2001). *The fundamental concepts of metaphysics: World, finitude, solitude*. Bloomington, IN: Indiana University Press.

James, W. (1884). What is an emotion? *Mind, 9*(34), 188–205.

Joas, H. (1997). *The creativity of action*. Chicago, IL: University of Chicago Press.

Krueger, J. (2014). Affordances and the musically extended mind. *Theoretical and Philosophical Psychology, 4*(article 1003), 1–12. https://doi.org/10.3389/fpsyg.2013.01003.

Nietzsche, F. (1924). *The joyful wisdom ("La gaya scienza")*. New York, NY: MacMillan.

Ringmar, E. (2016a). Attention and the cause of modern boredom. In M. E. Gardiner & J. J. Haladyn (Eds.), *Boredom Studies: Postdisciplinary inquiries* (pp. 193–202). London, UK: Routledge.

Ringmar, E. (2016b). The problem of the modern self: Imitation, will power and the politics of character. *International Political Anthropology, 9*(1), 67–86. https://doi.org/10.1177/1368431017736995.

Ringmar, E. (2017). Heidegger on willpower and the mood of modernity. In A. Cerella & L. Odysseos (Eds.), *Heidegger and the global age* (pp. 1–34). Lanham, MD: Rowman & Littlefield.

Rokotnitz, N. (2017). Goosebumps, shivers, visualization, and embodied resonance in the reading experience: The God of small things. *Poetics Today, 38*(2), 273–293. https://doi.org/10.1215/03335372-3868603.

Svendsen, L. (2005). *A philosophy of boredom*. London, UK: Reaktion Books.

Thiele, L. P. (2006). *The heart of judgment: Practical wisdom, neuroscience, and narrative*. New York, NY: Cambridge University Press.

Erik Ringmar is a professor in the Department of Political Science and International Relations at Ibn Haldun University, Istanbul, Turkey. He has a Ph.D. from Yale University, and has previously worked at universities in Great Britain and China. He has written extensively on social theory and on European and world history. His interest in boredom began when thinking about the origins of the World War I. His next book (CUP, 2020) will deal with dance and international relations.

Chapter 8
Facing Boredom: Essential Indexicals and Narratives of the Self

Ricardo Gutiérrez Aguilar

> *To bring this out, consider the following story from William James, who insisted (rightly, if I am right) that consciousness is quite distinct from self-consciousness, [James] reproduces an instructive letter from a friend: "We were driving... in a wagonette the door flew open and X, alias "Baldy", fell out on the road. We pulled up at once, and then he said "Did anyone fall out?" or "Who fell out?"–I don't exactly remember the words. When told that Baldy fell out he said "Did Baldy fall out? Poor Baldy!""*
>
> (Anscombe 1981)

Introduction. Hitchin' a Ride

Morning sunshine. It is the perfect time for a trip through the canyons. All are in and the creaks of the jolly laughter mix with the springs of the carriage enlivening together the long road ahead. *X* leans maybe carefree on the door next to him, and accidentally happens to fall out from the wagonette he was sharing with friends. Unaware, life goes on—at the slow pace of the wagonette—without saying a word. There are two punctuation marks to the story in the form of a fall and of a stop, though. Each one prevents a narrative to continue. It is said James is prompt in stopping the carriage to assist, but no stop of the sort can prevent *Baldy* from tripping over his identity—'Who fell out? Did Baldy fall out?'—Not even James pulling up in time can avoid *Baldy* to reset himself in *ye olde* act of building his biography. It is Baldy who is unaware now that he is the one *being told—vividly by himself!*

Life within a story is taken in narrative pills. The correct frequency of the administration is not explained in any prescription. To lose the thread is the promise of failure. How much discontinuance are we narratively ready to gobble and save at

R. Gutiérrez Aguilar (✉)
Complutense University of Madrid, Madrid, Spain
e-mail: gutierrezaguilar.ricardo@gmail.com

J. Ros Velasco (ed.), *Boredom Is in Your Mind*,
https://doi.org/10.1007/978-3-030-26395-9_8

the same time the sense of the whole of our story? Each pill, an episode of the tale being told. Some more pleasant, other less: the falling, the stop. The falling out from the wagonette could be deemed of course one of the latter. *X (Baldy)* is an unexpected future episode of Baldy in *our* story, despite his own ignorance of this fundamental fact. A future episode hanging on the narrative cue of a body that sometimes is conscious and others is self-conscious that body operating as the gravity center of all possible accounts waiting to be told. A center of reference. In our succinct story, *Baldy* casts a backward glance to the immediate past. He is barely aware of it: the linear plot in which someone fell from the carriage in which he was riding is something he takes for granted. But *who fell*? *Who of the limited bodily references on the cart is to be the notch to the continuation of the story*? There is apparently proof upon which to decide the conundrum: two intended non-identical selves face each other, ironically the cognitive (tell-tale) one looking for the other one who is already present, but at the same time is found missing—the public self of *X* is missing. For now, *Baldy* is not Baldy and consciousness is not self-consciousness. Publicly though, what appears to be a concern on the reference allocation for *poor-X (Baldy)*—Where is Baldy? Is he doing alright?—is a thorny problem on the identity of the two of them for the rest of the attendees. Because they have two colliding narrations on identity to ascribe to the very same person—our version to the *who fell*? *It was really Baldy*?: *if* Anscombe and James would be right, *then awaken Baldy would be proof that consciousness is quite a distinct thing from self-consciousness*. Baldy and *Baldy* should get their stories straight. *Baldy*—the conscious one—for a moment is not Baldy to himself, that person befriended with James in *such-and-such* circumstances and coming from *such-and-such* background, a background—the past episodes—leading finally to a sunny day of travel on a wagonette. For one thing, *X (Baldy)* has been deprived of uttering the following statement: “I am who fell out. I'm Baldy.” That is, somebody fell out but there is no doubt I am *that* person. He can ask, he is in charge of other narratives, but *X* has been deprived of *a* narrative. *X* has been deprived of one simple and continuous administration of the episodes of the story on behalf of a sound treatment of the plot involved.

When we are dubious in stitching together this two-episode drama is when difficulties arise. It is the moment when we realize *for X there is doubt as there is certainty in him passing by the identification with the familiar nickname. He is not* “Baldy.” Consciousness is not a sufficient condition for *self*-consciousness (Anscombe 1981, p. 25). After the falling, we are awarded two narratives for the price of one *self*. Both arguments closing their events' arcs over themselves in an independent unity projected for sense and meaning. Anscombe informs us Russell called these narrative clusters *short-term selves*.[1] *Short-term narratives* for *short-term selves* then. For it is because there is no “guarantee [ever] that one got hold of

[1]The reference to Russell's suggestive idea in Anscombe is probably directed to the pairing concept of a possible *enlargement of the Self* in the process of acquisition of (mundane, philosophical) knowledge, an idea present in Russell (2001).

the right self" (Anscombe 1981, p. 25), of the right cue to resume the exercise to develop the well-known story.

Some stories are inextricably attached to items (others not). Here, we can take the word "*self*" as a designation for a class of them. Thus, in the process of tailoring the stories seamlessly around bodies, nicknames and utterances, if nothing is guaranteed, if we are uncertain of the right continuation of the story—of what makes it *the* story—, why bother? Why not begin with a totally brand new tale each time, why not make of the old jacket an original vest better suit for a lighter weather? Different, distinct criteria reign in both reference domains. Different available narrations too. Someone could say there are fluent discourses and narratives made for those *objects, proper names and selves*, highlighted episodes these to which a warrant to get good hold of the right narrative cue is more probable; and there are other tales of a more succinct nature relying on *whatever stands for X*, for "if "I" is a name it cannot be an empty name […] [In the light that] that hardly fits its grammar" (Anscombe 1981, pp. 28, 32).

"*I*" as *standing for a name*—in the place of a name—perfectly fits the grammar of the species, and it should not be an empty name then. Things are told *of* "I" and happen *to* "I". Functions like a character in the middle of a plot, of an articulated set of episodes—a grammar essentially. *Can something—a label—have the behavior of a name grammatically wise and have no concept behind beyond cultural assumptions to support its use*? Certainly, it can. But getting hold of the right reference attached to it becomes more problematic. These references are labeled "*quasi-names*." Because we do not need anything else as a requirement *to get hold of the* right "*I*"… For our case, *X* could eventually refer to himself as an "I" by all means and no one would need assistance in pointing out to the utterer. For the same reasons, *to be conscious would only imply the realization of being standing tall on a narrative episode*, while *being self-conscious would imply to be aware of the previous course of the stances held in the run to the entire set of episodes.*

Anyway, "I" is not a usual name at all. And the narrative you could fulfill with its sole help would be disappointing because in this case, it could match its glorious emptiness. *Quasi-names* are not exempted of stretching out in a grammar. Enlightening the distinction between *consciousness* and *self-consciousness* is for Anscombe the opportunity to join a pair of instruments for signposting in these grave storytelling exercises. If we attend to the devices proposed, they are nothing but *ergonomic-terms.* They are narratively *standing for* attributes and actions. To give a proper explanation of the categories of the phenomenon. Nothing more than a functional explanation. They are intended to match the use in which we wield them with preference over the instrument of *conception*—the semantic descriptive content—by means of which we usually orient ourselves in the identification and re-identification of the reference: in her opinion, we are prone in this latter sense to make good use of the linguistic objects that '*latch on to*' something—that *attach to* something—in order to ease the subsequent operations of allocating the reference in a later moment.

It is easier to tell the story with a narrative beacon. "Baldy, Baldy, sat on a wall; Baldy, Baldy, had a great fall; All the James's efforts and all the James's friends;

couldn't put Baldy together again." Baldy is the position around to which the diverse attributes tend to gather, he *himself* is the same who *was on a trip, who was on a wagonette, the one who had a great fall, the same who lost his consciousness,* and finally, *this Baldy was awakened and cared of*—all attributes that *latch on to* him. All these events are also *his* episodes. Properties, traits to/of him.

However—intervenes Anscombe—some terms are best understood as '*standing for*' something. That is, their use is better understood as landmarks for something else. In case they are considered representing they do not do that but for themselves, they do that as *indexes*. They are *in the place*—that's '*standing for*'—of something else. They simply highlight the location of the event that we are supposed to pay attention to. Anscombe insisted—rightly, if I am right—that *the mind, the self,* and the alleged *reference—if there is any—to "I" is not an object. And its sign, not really a name. It can give hold to terms that latch on to something—even if Baldy could not recognize himself as being* Baldy *the possibility is there present—but instead the would-be reference is an essential condition to any latching on of things, something worth the institution of a landmark.* It fits the grammar of a name but looks empty in its *conception*. The implications of the "I" thrive in its *standing for* among other competitive references and narratives. This *essential index* in its radical difference to the rest of them counts like one of the kind only in the sense it expels any other, marking an autonomy of its own—that is, the basic fitting of the grammar. Finally, if it thrives it does in measuring, counting (*temporal, spatial, contentwise*) distances with the *relative-to-it* references. The plot has a pace, the frequency of episodes makes it interesting—compelling, prone to call out our identification—or not. Measuring these references carefully in episodes, in pills. Not to close, not too soon:

> *Tædium, ennui, Langweile, boredom,* are words for which, probably, every language known to man has its equivalent. It comes about whenever, *from the relative emptiness of content* of a tract of time, we grow attentive to the passage of the time itself. Expecting, and being ready for, a new impression to succeed; when it fails to come, we get an empty time instead of it; and such experiences, ceaselessly renewed, make us most formidably aware of the extent of the mere time itself [...] Apprehension is vivid, retentiveness strong, and our recollections of that [early] times, like those of a time spent in rapid and interesting travel, are of something intricate, multitudinous, and long-drawn-out. But as each passing year converts some of this experience into automatic routine which we hardly note at all, the days and the weeks smooth themselves out in recollection to contentless units, and the years grow hollow and collapse. (James 1983, pp. 625–626)

Resuming Life. War, Peace, and the Narrative State of Nature

He or she who leaves me alone with myself—better said, who leaves my I *with my-I —gives me away.* Leaves me with the sole company of almost (a) nothing: *a quasi-nothing of which can be told only under the better circumstances a quasi-narrative.*

A *too personal* quasi-narrative. And no one wants to be the star in a tale like that. The duality of *I/my-I* and *nothing/a nothing* points in the direction to the note on the material reference—a property—of the *I* to bodily sustain the alluding *apprehension* and *retentiveness* in the passage from above.

Apprehension comes not from nowhere, *retentiveness* is not in anywhere. Also, there is an urge to *the-against-boredom grammar* of acquisition of contents. To James, the mysterious *X* of the previous anecdote is a *universal human condition* of the psyche. *A natural one* if asked. But 'condition' has a nuance so closely related to an illness as to give rise to a demand for some clarification on the health issues possibly summoned by this controversial label. It is a condition because it can be judged a liability. There is a narrative burden because there is necessity in avoiding danger. We are human beings and such a natural circumstance makes us—describes us—more than inclined, *afraid of tædium*, we are sensitive to the idea of the eventual illness. James displays his literary mastery in the depiction of the virtual human conditions to the inner-life of a *self*. The life of the *self* reduced to its minimum expression is but storytelling in preparation of a nothingness. And then, being alive is the *active* exercise of knitting units of significative moments. A self could trip over, fall ill and stop the knitting though. Autobiography held still or worse, fractured. A condition entails an ontological dependence. But the dependent condition and the attentive disposition to prevent that from happening are not necessarily related. Because it is *relative to us—each self—the possibility of completing the vivid narrative trip through episodes with adequate (of our interest) content, or fail and dwell in boredom and weariness—nothingness, to be almost nothing.*

For those not aware of it, there is here in the works—of course—*a proportion that equates content with identity, and every language known to mankind should have an equivalent.* After dully *standing for* something, the *I*—starving before—is eager, hungry for impressions. Hollow in its retentiveness triggers a tell-tale inertia. Attention, memory, is displayed in the form of helping attributes to the task. They are in fact tools oriented to the acquisition of sound materials to meaning, busy with widening the possibilities of the narrative arc of one *ego's* dominion. Gathering the core around of which the future episodes, events, happenings, even vicissitudes—like *falls from wagonettes*—will grow, the *I* learns a language. These 'early times' are certainly a monumental phase. They are devoted to the old-building activity. Idle hands are the devil's workshop, so time is expected to gulp down content by all means. It is already high time for *latching on to* something(s).

Having said that, there is nonsense to the situation as well. The necessary companion to the narrative success is narrative failure. It lies in wait for us. May we be prepared!: this proto-language seems to be able to develop a humble but effective defensive strategy in service for the *X*, it is a first defensive wall. The strategy goes like this. It parts from recognition. Enemy is welcome to this outer boundary of *self*, when there is the menace of *relative emptiness* and is immediately checked with the ascription of many *short-acts of nomination* in the absence of a better tale to tell: this is *tædium, ennui, Langweile, boredom.* Language defensive strategies aim precisely to prevent any diminishing in the ontological status of one*self*. They try to avoid the supreme *narrative humiliation* that of becoming almost (a) nothing to ourselves—in *boredom.*

For what we have seen, the doctor seems to recommend labor for this universal illness. It is only when the "I" has a chance to concoct its accounts that he or she avoids the charge against for emptiness. Starts a grammar, deploys a plot. With occasion of *the "I" fitting a grammar, of telling a story*, it plans an interesting travel. The narrative arc should have an extension then, and so does the *I*. No trip without itinerary and no self without experiences. From early times to later times, there is the chance at least of an intricate, multitudinous, long-drawn-out—in extension—and strong, vivid—in intension—density of episodes. *Like in Nature, like in life—Aristotle dixit— the I abhors a vacuum. A narrative vacuum in this case.* Despite it has no need at all of being labeled as a *pronoun, noun* or *name*, so perhaps "I" is not a name but rather another kind of expression indicating "singular reference" (Anscombe 1981, p. 27) even in that way identity grows pace to pace with meaning and sense. They are correlatives. For, attention is always enthusiast in using its proper grammar. It is always an avid foreseer in search for impressions—those are which grants vividness—and events—that is what grants a long-lasting identity—these being the collection—and then the matter for recollections—of the renewed narrative of happenings. Thus, the episodes to be told of and the faculties to be trained in grow within the same drill. The "I" swells. James, while talking about "*universal self conditions*," referring to the *Langweile, boredom…* is ready to elaborate the most suggestive description of a possible primal *narrative state of nature.*

The identity defends itself against boredom, firstly. It would count as the story of the origins of the primitive activity. It would count as the deduction of its minimal principles, too. The use here of the Hobbesian metaphor serves rhetorically to the analogy that makes our relationship with boredom an issue of defensive and preventive war. Because it is decidedly a state in confrontation with boredom. Paraphrasing at this point *Sir* Thomas Hobbes, *fear of nothingness, disposeth a self to anticipate, or to seek aid by the society of nouns*: *for there is no other way by which a self can secure his inner-life and liberty* (1998, p. 67).

> For *war, consisteth* not in battle only, or the act of fighting; but *in a tract of time*, wherein the will to contend by battle is sufficiently known: and therefore the notion of time, is to be considered in the nature of war; as it is in the nature of weather […] *In such condition* […] *the life of man* [can be], *solitary, poor, nasty, brutish, and short.* (1998, p. 84)

It is all about meaning in time. If there is a narration, there is a narrator and a will—*disposition, anticipation, seek*—to narrate. A will to contend by battle *renewed ceaselessly*. In our natural state, we tend *to grow attentive*, we have the *retentiveness—memory—strong and ready*, and the *apprehension* seeking for hold.

There is an expectation in this readiness for what is "*new*," a faculty apt for *latching on to* something else. Meaning, sense, like the exercise of keeping the track of time in good weather, depends on the on-going ascription of past, present, and future events to oneself (Hobbes 1998). *Seasons of the self.* It is the nude abstraction of the *self* in the exercise of its fundamental skills, though. *Who is really that* "*I*"? For, other of the possible descriptions with which James treated ourselves for this alleged *narrative state of nature* comes here in handy: "If we could say in English "it thinks" as we say "it rains" or "it blows," we should be stating the fact most simply and with the minimum assumption. As we cannot, we must simply say that *thought goes on*" (James 1983, pp. 224–225), and that for sure *hardly fits any grammar.*

'*New*' in these early times is a call in favor of narrative length. There is the need for episodes, of plot-thickness, and these episodes should be within an articulation —*the one a proper grammar concedes. Tædium, ennui, Langweile, boredom,* do not point to naked emptiness either. The phenomenon is just neutralized into the intimate story plot working as a limit. It is at this stage just the nominal representation of *inner-self*'s maybe solitary, poor, nasty, brutish, and still short virtual life. "If we should continue the game of "I am" formulations "beyond identity" we should have to change the tune. For now, the increment of identity [...] takes place, often with a pervading *sense of stagnation, boredom,*" *and personal impoverishment* (Erikson 1994, p. 138). Such a story would be more than brief, would be simply *hollow.* An adamant *stagnated automatic routine which we hardly note at all*: days and weeks smoothed and leveled to nothing.

There should be also the outstanding ability to be part of the story told while working it through from within as its very author. A second-guessed nature to the process of ascription, appropriation, and nude acquisition. It is under this reason that James carefully chooses to a more suitable expression: *boredom is only what marks the occasion presented by a* relative *emptiness of content.* Not an absolute one.

> [The state of labour we could call "*peace*" (Hobbes 1998, p. 84)] is an imitation of an action that is complete and whole *and that has some magnitude*, since it is possible for there to be a whole with no magnitude. And a whole is that which has a beginning, middle, and end [...] Also, since what is beautiful [and harmonious], both an animal and every organized thing made of any parts, *needs not only to have these arranged in an orderly way but also to start out with a magnitude that is not random* [...] for that reason neither could a very tiny animal become beautiful (for the contemplation of it runs together by coming about in a nearly imperceptible time) nor could one of huge magnitude (for the contemplation of it could not come about all at once, but the unity and wholeness are swept away). (Aristotle 2006, pp. 29–30)

***Weariness*, *Boredom*, and the Burden of Modern (epic) Narratives of the Self**

Aristotle offers quite the advice for those who got on board on the way to the *against-boredom narrative crusade*: tales, (auto)biographies, *memoires*, are organic entities looking for its due whole. Almost trivially—he says—a '*whole*' is something composed of a beginning, of a middle, and of an end. Content units which add up to a certain *magnitude*. For Aristotle, the suitable metaphor is "to catch the eye." All is hanging on the fortunate circumstance in which order and distinction close up onto themselves and can be comprehended at once. *Narrative peace* is primarily in this particular sense—and relative to subject's individuality and boredom—the constant state of labor in contemplation, meaning that the assumption and recognition of the produced symbolic representation (*imitation*) of the emplotment (1) *could come about all at once as a constituted and organized whole—the retentiveness labor*; and (2) in the same movement, *this contemplation—the attentive labor—runs together in an orderly way a complete set of parts—content salient units—coming about in a perceptible tract of time.*

Success—*peace*—in the process of narration seems to be dependant on the ability to construct an ongoing and growing meaning build out from the otherwise scattered events of a life and its actions. Bare chronology—a list of events one after another—is not the cure for the illness. It is assumed a rare formal trait to the set: it *should be coherent*, it *should be complete.* Narratives need of course a designated protagonist above everything. A center of gravity for the story around which it is constructed, but he or she could be still a self and not yet a *self.* One view in classical narratology lists all its strategies to cope with this requirement basically in a two-fold manner, one objective and one subjective: "sense," "meaning," appears as an explaining reasonable element—an *argument*, an *emplotment*—as soon a causal rationale or an analogous of it is utilized to put some order between the relatively chaotic configuration of events, and happenings.

The first candidate to the task of putting some order among events would be—of course—a *causal relation*, so each one of them can be told to lead to the other and be prepared by the previous (Gallie 1964; Danto 2007). The—let's call it—*narrative causal chain* eases the performative process of telling a story. Each episode has its cue leading to the next one *with necessity*. This sort of deterministic narrative could be deemed almost trivial. Gallie and Danto are well aware of this judgment. The literary connection between events—whether actions or facts—is guaranteed so long as it is considered a casual series. Even when it *has only in appearance the structure of a causal inference*: one event comes after the other and so on. There is no truth element to be sought in the line the otherwise disentangled events move behind to. We are who *put in* a *causal narrative*. The diverse units turn into a naturalized order, indeed.

It is not for nothing that from this fact it does not follow the criteria for making up the narration are not rational or justifiable: Danto (2007, p. 143) supports the idea that a linguistic instrument called *narrative sentence* is the most common structure every storyteller would be prone to use in describing their task. For our case, *narrative sentences*—serving to macro-narratives—would count as building what *self-consciousness* is. But to the *I*, there is no *ideal chronicle* to compare with and so there is no ideal standard to justify our literary works about it. A *narrative sentence*—like one of the very kind *historical judgments* are too—link together two separate events *in the tract of time*, past and present, binding preferably the latter to the former: a Newton's biography could perfectly begin with "The author of the *Principia Mathematica* was born in Woolsthorpe in 1643," *but* what if we were aware that only a baby child called Isaac Newton was noted on the Parrish Register? (Danto 2007, p. 158).

Of course, personal historical figures tend to be the *narrative focus*—indexical—of statements on the ascription of responsibilities in action. They are charismatic beacons, build their attributes around a meaning and give birth to a '*concept*' of his or her own this way. Caesar *was that man in the world who did such-and-such.* They have presented to us thanks to a mechanics—*automatic routine*—of macro-narratives, *master narratives* not so distant from the ones we as subjects—our *I*—develop. Are we also utilizing a '*concept for our self*'? *Does this have any meaning at all*?

> While people are of certain sorts as a result of their characters [...] It is not that they act in order that they might imitate states of character; rather they include states of character conjointly on account of the actions. *So the actions performed and the story are the end of the tragedy*, and the end is the greatest of all things. Also, without action a tragedy could not come to be, *but without states of character it could.* (Aristotle 2006, p. 28)

Aristotle's *reductio ad absurdum* on the relative importance of characters to the story—they are by all means disposable in favor of the plot—confronts us with a more determining question: *is it equally optional our own commitment to our story*? *Does the story collapse onto itself—weary, dull and boring—when it is*? We have introduced a second-guessed nature to the process of narrative ascription a few lines above. Pairing with the type of *ascription*$_1$—*regulative*, a guide to get hold of the right story—should be present an *ascription*$_2$—*constitutive*, a vivid, active engagement in the story. Now this second orientation within the story will open up for us a second complementary approach made out of a more performative strategy based on *self*-identification—*katharsis*, the *sublimation of our own proper motives*, a *narrative commitment*—and the meeting of the *expectations* the necessary elements need to be related to. The story is *lived* more than '*imitated.*' Nothing could appeal better to us in a personal way. *Meaning, sense, defense against boredom depends hugely on the conscious and committed ascription of past, present and future events to oneself*:

> I once followed a trail of sugar on a supermarket floor, pushing my cart down the aisle on one side of a tall counter and back the aisle on the other, seeking the shopper with the torn sack to tell him he was making a mess. With each trip around the counter, the trail became thicker. But I seemed unable to catch up. Finally it dawned on me. I was the shopper I was trying to catch [...] *I believed at the outset that the shopper with a torn sack was making a mess. And I was right. But I did not believe that I was making a mess* [...] My beliefs changed, didn't they, in that I came to have a new one, namely, that I am making a mess. But things are not so simple. The reason they are not is the importance of the word "I" in my expression of what I came to believe. *When we replace it with other designations of me, we no longer have an explanation of my behavior* [the behavior of *me*] and so, it seems, no longer an attribution of the same belief. *It seems to be an essential indexical* [*within* the belief]. (Perry 1993, p. 33)

James apparently followed just an intuition in order to establish the two very different moments in the process of learning that set of *I*-defensive strategies against boredom: *early times vs. late times*. While, for one thing those were the jolly early times in which awareness matched meaning and time itself—and *tædium*, *ennui*, *Langweile*, *boredom*...—was but a byproduct—not the aim of our attention—*late times* point to the exhaustion of the activity. There is a burden to the activity that sometimes is insurmountable. In aging narratives like *memoires,* we end up being so well-fed of contents all addition is tasted like the same. Smoothed bland units. That early time, on the contrary, was not really spent, for it ran unnoticed—it was not included in any important sense within the stories, for it would be absurd to *tell time* by then… thus, supporting the idea that personal evidence and escape from boredom are here the outcome of an exercise on Poetics. A flourished version of one*self* or the literary orientation of events, their hierarchy—nothing but a relation to power and force.

Modernity has made out of *master narratives* a necessity. This cultural era connects perfectly with the *early times*' spirit. Construction of subjectivity is devoted to the construction of *individuality*, the *privileged hold of the right me*. Because there is the possibility of error in getting hold of the right me as there is of getting hold of the wrong story. One piled up from the designations of a character. The second paragraph out of the second chapter and the first part of *Don Quixote* fits perfectly to support our argument:

> Thus our flaming adventurer jogged on, talking to himself, and saying: "Who doubts, but that, in future times, when the faithful history of my famous exploits shall come to light, the sage who writes them, when he gives a relation of this my first sally, so early in the morning, will do it in words like these: "Scarcely had the ruddy Phoebus spread the golden tresses of his beauteous hair over the face of the wide and spacious earth […] when the renowned Don Quixote de la Mancha, abandoning the lazy down, mounted his famous courser Rosinante, and began to travel through the ancient and noted field of Montiel"" (*and true it is, that was the very field*). (De Cervantes Saavedra 2008, pp. 26–27)[2]

The due whole, something composed of a beginning, of a middle and of an end gets the upper hand granting the privilege to *independence*—the constituted whole, the formal trait, the regulative standard—which is what determines *individuality. That knight traversing the ancient and famous field of Montiel, who did such-and-such* is the *master narrative* making the commitment to the story disposable in favor of the plot. The task is *renewed ceaselessly.* James has collected different species of boredom, *tædium, ennui,* refer precisely to this labor exhaustion. *Tædium*, from "*taedere*" points to fatigue, the state of annoyance and irritation linked to certain activity. In this case, a narrative fatigue. Thus, the story, the self, can be *too short, too long, too determined. Ennui* is the metaphysical disability. This being the institution of the fatigue as a trait of character. Immediately, we are offered by James a fair warning on the consequences—the collapse, the crumble of the edifice of the *self* because of material (episodical) exhaustion—when(ever) the activity surpasses its due extension. Short in events and characters, time is summoned and included in the *dramatis personae.* Anscombe, James, agree regarding the narrative pragmatics—of *the proper, suitable grammar*—of *communicative success* and

[2]*Don Quixote*'s quote is in great debt with Rafael Sánchez Ferlosio and his formidable essay "Carácter y destino" ["Character and fate"] (see Sánchez Ferlosio 2016). Prof. William Egginton (Johns Hopkins University) has been immersed in the deep narrative waters of Cervantes's mind and his modern invention of fiction (and subjectivity) (Egginton 2016).

failure. The many species of *tædium, ennui, Langweile, boredom* are names for the universal event of a *narrative failure*: *because there is no guarantee ever that one got hold in intricate, multitudinous, long-drawn-out units of any content.*

> A main concern I have with narratives in gerontology is that *the potential (and actual) presence of master cultural narratives is not discussed.* There are numerous master narratives of later life that can damage not only the identity of older adults, but also how older age is understood by others. For example, late life is often portrayed by the metaphor of the journey. The significance of the life-as-journey narrative is that importance is placed solely on the past, not the present or future. *This implies that from the standpoint of later life, everything worth doing has passed as a pilgrim-like progression through time, followed by a period of wisdom, reflection, and acceptance in older age. Related to this notion is loneliness* [*and boredom,* of course]. (De Medeiros 2016, p. 66)[3]

References

Anscombe, G. E. M. (1981). The first person. In *Anscombe collected philosophical papers, vol. II: Metaphysics and the philosophy of mind* (pp. 21–36). Oxford, UK: Blackwell.

Aristotle. (2006). *Poetics*. Newburyport, MA: Focus Publishing.

Danto, A. C. (2007). *Narration and knowledge: Including the integral text of analytical philosophy of history*. New York, NY: Columbia University Press.

De Cervantes Saavedra, M. (2008). *Don Quixote*. Oxford, UK: Oxford University Press.

De Medeiros, K. (2013). *Narrative gerontology in research and practice*. New York, NY: Springer.

De Medeiros, K. (2016). Narrative gerontology: Countering the master narratives of aging. *Narrative Works: Issues, Investigations and Interventions, 6*(1), 63–81.

Egginton, W. (2016). *The man who invented fiction: How Cervantes ushered in the modern world*. New York, NY/London, UK/Oxford, UK/New Delhi, India/Sydney, Australia: Bloomsbury.

Erikson, E. H. (1994). *Identity: Youth and crisis*. New York, NY/London, UK: W. W. Norton & Co.

Gallie, W. B. (1964). *Philosophy and the historical understanding*. Michigan, MI: Michigan University Press.

Greco, L. (2015). The self as narrative in Hume. *Journal of the History of Philosophy, 53*(4), 699–722. https://doi.org/10.1353/hph.2015.0086.

Hobbes, T. (1998). *Leviathan*. Oxford, UK: Oxford University Press.

James, W. (1983). *The principles of psychology*, vols. 1–2. Cambridge, MA: Harvard University Press.

Perry, J. (1993). *The problem of the essential indexical and other essays*. New York, NY/Oxford, UK: Oxford University Press.

[3]Lorenzo Greco finds a plausible solution to the 'unity' conundrum of *self* in Hume's portrayal of identity in books II and III of his *Treatise*. After the more epistemological set out in book I, it is in the parts devoted to *practical and moral action* where the *self* and the self are able to form a metaphysical and earthly collaboration. This collaboration is possible only within a narrative (Greco 2015). From this vantage moral standpoint parts the intuition of Prof. Galen Strawson should we carry necessarily the burden of a master moral narrative, that of a whole life? Could not that moral narrative be better the type for a *short-term moral self*? (2007). Prof. Alfonso Muñoz Corcuera presented me with this last reading and I am thankful for the more than suitable conceptual relation of his recommendation to the core problem of my present text.

Russell, B. (2001). The value of philosophy. *The problems of philosophy* (pp. 89–94). Oxford, UK: Oxford University Press.
Sánchez Ferlosio, R. (2016). Carácter y destino. In *Babel contra Babel. Asuntos internacionales. Sobre la guerra. Apuntes de polemología* (pp. 631–651). Barcelona: DeBolsillo.
Strawson, G. (2007). Episodic ethics. In D. D. Hutto (Ed.), *Narrative and understanding persons* (pp. 85–115). Cambridge, UK: Cambridge University Press.

Ricardo Gutiérrez Aguilar (MA in Philosophy, 2006; National Prize in Philosophy 2008; MA in Teachers Training, 2008) is an Assistant Professor and researcher in Philosophy at the Logic and Theoretical Philosophy Department (Complutense University of Madrid, UCM). He holds a Ph.D. (2014) with a European Mention awarded by UNED (Spain). He is Doktor der Philosophie by the *Technische Universität zu Berlin* (Germany) (2014) as well. Pre-doctoral fellow in the National Spanish Research Council (CSIC—Instituto de Filosofía) under the tutorship of Prof. Dr. Roberto R. Aramayo (2007–2010), and a *Marie Curie* Early Stage Researcher in *TU Berlin* (Project *ENGLOBE. Enlightenment and Global History–FP7-PEOPLE-238285*) (2010–2013). Dr. Gutiérrez has focused his research interests mainly in Analytical Philosophy of History and Philosophy of Mind. Narratives and values encrypted in them—or the absence thereof—throughout the course of ordered events and actions, and the subsequent critique of the historian's task with the help of ladden-institutional instruments, centered his developments in those fields. Among Dr. Gutiérrez's most recent publications can be counted his books *Virtud y sistema. Juicio moral y filosofía de la historia en Kant* [Virtue and system. Moral judgement and philosophy of history in Kant] (Alamanda, 2018), and *Deuda y legado en la filosofía de la historia de Schiller* [Debt and legacy in Schiller's philosophy of history] (Herder, 2018). Member of the Editorial Board of *Con-textos Kantianos. International Journal of Philosophy* (WoS, SCOPUS International Journal). Editor of the multidisciplinary volume *Empathy* (BRILL, 2019).

Chapter 9
Animal Boredom

Lars Svendsen

Goethe (1950) jokingly claimed that the capacity for being bored was the essential property that separates humans from nonhuman animals and that if monkeys could be bored, we would have to recognize them as fully human. Others have arrived at the same conclusion. For instance, Erich Fromm claims: "Man is the only animal that can be bored" (2002, p. 23). I also used to believe that this is the case. Contrary to what I claimed in *A philosophy of boredom* (2005), there is good reason to assume that boredom exists also outside of the human species. However, relatively little research has been done on animal boredom, and animals are virtually absent in boredom studies.[1]

A central problem in discussing animal boredom is related to the question as to how we can justify the ascription of various mental and emotional states to non-linguistic creatures. I here draw on my book *Understanding animals* (2019), arguing that such states are not hidden from view in some 'inner' realm, but are for the most part in plain view. This is especially clear in the case of such phenomena as fear, where the criteria for establishing that an animal experiences fear are quite straightforward. More complex emotions like grief, loneliness and boredom will have more complex criteria, and you need information about the context in which the emotional expression occurs. The criteria will further differ somewhat from species to species. Nevertheless, I will argue that we can plausibly argue that boredom occurs in many other species than humans and that this is especially clear in the case of mammals, birds, and at least some species of octopus. Using the term 'boredom' to describe the emotional state of these animals will invite charges of anthropomorphism, but I will argue that this is legitimate use of anthropomorphisms.

[1]One notable exception is Toohey (2011, Chap. 3). More work on animal boredom has been done within animal behavior studies, and especially the pioneering works of Françoise Wemelsfelder.

L. Svendsen (✉)
University of Bergen, Bergen, Norway
e-mail: Lars.svendsen@uib.no

J. Ros Velasco (ed.), *Boredom Is in Your Mind*,
https://doi.org/10.1007/978-3-030-26395-9_9

The acknowledgment of boredom as an emotion to be found also in nonhuman animals creates problems for theories of boredom that place the concept of meaning at the center of their account, and argue that boredom consists of a lack of meaning. My book, *A philosophy of boredom* (2005), is an example of such an approach. The main problem is that such meaning seems to presuppose language. I will claim that we have little reason to believe that any nonhuman animals have a capacity for proper language—and that includes even the most meticulously trained primates—and one is therefore forced to either provide an account of animal boredom that does not employ the concept of meaning or give an account of meaning that does not presuppose language. I choose the latter approach argument. When we analyze the concept of meaning, we find that the notion of caring is central. And it is no stretch to say that many nonhuman animals have a capacity for caring for various objects and activities, but what they care about will to a great extent vary from species to species. We can then define animal boredom in terms of being deprived of objects and activities for which they care.

Boredom as a Lack of Meaning

Defining boredom in terms of a lack of some sort of meaning is fairly commonplace in boredom studies. There are those who object to this, such as Toohey (2011). His main reason for doing so is that he believes that there is no such thing as 'existential boredom,' only 'simple' boredom. Contrary to Toohey, I believe that there is in fact good reason to explain boredom in terms of a lack meaning, one of them being that it can help us to differentiate between boredom and related phenomena, such as depression. Even though human boredom and depression are phenomena that can resemble each other, they can be distinguished empirically, and what sets them apart is *life meaning* (see Fahlman et al. 2009; Goldberg et al. 2011). Such a claim is based on the observation that changes in the experience of boredom can be predicted from changes in perceived life meaning, but one cannot make such predictions from perceived life meaning to the experience of depression. There is a fairly clear correlation between levels of perceived life meaning and boredom, then, but such a correlation tells us nothing about *how* they are related, if, for instance, low levels of perceived life meaning cause boredom or vice versa. I will not discuss this any further here and simply claim that the phenomenon of perceived life meaning is central to understanding human boredom.

There is no uncontroversial account of what we mean by 'meaning.' The sort of meaning we discuss in our present context differs from meaning as discussed by philosophical semantics. We are talking about an existential meaning, something related to the observation of some sort of *point* to our lives. It is tempting to reserve such meaning for the lives of creatures that possess a language because this meaning is tied to our conceptions of our past and future. I doubt that any other animals than humans have an understanding of their own past and future and of the fact that they are born and that their lives will end one day.

This account leaves us with the following problem with regard to animals: Meaning as described so far would seem to presuppose a capacity for language. If boredom presupposes a capacity for meaning, no nonlinguistic creature could experience boredom. Nevertheless, Françoise Wemelsfelder uses the term 'meaningful' when she is describing the lives of nonhuman animals: "To be able to create a meaningful life, the animal must be provided with materials that are biologically salient and enable it to fulfil its primary needs in an inventive, varying, and flexible way" (Wemelsfelder 2005, p. 87). Should animal existence be described in terms of 'meaningfulness'? Of course, it depends on how you understand 'meaningful.' 'Meaning' can refer to elements of language, but that is clearly not what is meant here. The term is also used in a different way, as referring to something important or worthwhile. Being 'meaningful' here simply means that something *matters* to someone that somebody *cares* about something. Such mattering and caring is hardly exclusive to human existence, and therefore, the use of the 'meaningful' appears to be warranted also when describing the lives of nonhuman animals. And such caring also seems to be central to the problem of boredom. Interestingly enough, this point is also contained in the premodern concept of boredom, *acedia*. The Latin word stems from the Greek *akedia*, a combination of a privative prefix and *kedos*, which literally means 'caring about something.' *Acedia* is, according to its etymology, about not caring, or perhaps not having anything to care about.

I have therefore made a full retreat from the claim I made with regard to animal boredom in *A philosophy of boredom*. Not only do I accept that there is such a thing as animal boredom, but I will also describe this form of boredom as in terms of a lack of meaning, and further that this meaning should be explained in terms of caring. The boredom of human and nonhuman animals will be different simply because human and nonhuman animals are different and care about different things. But it is nevertheless boredom.

Anthropomorphism and Anthropodenial

This approach will probably invite accusations of relying on *anthropomorphisms*. The term originates from the Greek words *anthropos* (human) and *morphe* (form), meaning to give something a human form or shape. In this context, it will refer to the projection of concepts from human psychology onto the mental lives of animals. Many philosophers and naturalists will systematically try to avoid using such expressions based on the idea that the animal, as part of the natural world, must be *explained* rather than *understood*.

In the nineteenth century, biology saw it otherwise, and Charles Darwin is an example of this, as he wrote a brilliant work entitled *The expression of the emotions in man and animals* (1872). However, George Romanes, who was Darwin's research assistant and designated heir to his project, got carried away in his use of anthropomorphisms with overly imaginative stories of animal behavior and mental life. Romanes's successor, C. Lloyd Morgan, warned against this practice and formulated what became known as 'Morgan's Canon:' We should never interpret behavior as a product of a higher mental ability if it can be interpreted as the product of a lower one (1894, p. 53). This means, for example, that if one and the same behavior can be interpreted as both a product of instinct and that the animal has reasoned, then one should give preference to the first, simpler explanation. The principle became widely accepted in twentieth-century biology, where it became increasingly less common to talk about an animal's emotions and mental life. It should be noted, however, that Morgan himself believed that there was sufficient evidence for ascribing emotions and advanced mental capabilities to a range of animals and that it was perfectly legitimate to describe their behavior as a product of having these capabilities. He argued that animal scientists should use terms and emotions from their own mental life and that they should consider the animals to be analogous to this.

Unfortunately, it became common to interpret Morgan's Canon in a far more restrictive way, and this led to what the zoologist and ethologist Frans de Waal has referred to as 'anthropodenial,' an untenable dismissal of all similarities between humans and nonhuman animals for no other reason than it is 'unscientific' (de Waal 1999). We should rather attribute higher characteristics to animals as long as it is the most *reasonable* explanation for the animal's behavior. We should be as open for animals to show us their emotions and intentions, as we are for people to do it, knowing that humans are different from other animals in several important respects. If you try to describe the behavior of nonhuman animals without any use of anthropomorphisms, you will be left with a collection of descriptions of movements with little meaning or inner context. The use of such 'human' terms creates context and therefore also meaning. It is the only possible way we can have any understanding of animals at all—by drawing from our own psychology, our own perceptions, and feelings. However, it is also crucial that one takes into account biological explanations when attempting to understand the animal. Then, we can prevent anthropomorphisms from running wild, attributing the animal with every possible human trait for which there is no sustainable basis for us claiming they have.

I can understand a dog by interpreting its behavior, and I have to view the dog as analogous with myself and consider how it would be for me to be in the situation the dog is now in. On the other hand, I have to take into account that the dog is, after all, a dog and not a person. We must then begin with the similarities between the animal's behavior and our own. If the behavior is similar, it is not unreasonable to assume that the mental state that underlies the behavior is also similar. As David Hume put it:

> Tis from the resemblance of the external actions of animals to those we ourselves perform, that we judge their internal likewise to resemble ours; and the same principle of reasoning, carry'd one step farther, will make us conclude that since our internal actions resemble each other, the causes from which they are deriv'd, must also be resembling. When any hypothesis, therefore, is advanc'd to explain a mental operation, which is common to men and beasts, we must apply the same hypothesis to both. (1984, p. 226)

The Mental States of Animals

On what grounds can we ascribe an emotion like boredom, or any other emotion, for that sake, to an animal? The following, famous remark by Wittgenstein, could lead us to believe that he argued that we can never understand any other animals than other humans: "If a lion could talk, we could not understand him" (1986, p. 223). One interpretation of this could be he wants to emphasize an abyss between the worlds of humans and animals, so deep that understanding would be impossible even if, for argument's sake, we assumed that an animal, for instance, could speak English. If that had been Wittgenstein's point, we would have to ask what the foundation for that distinction is, and when it emerged. Going backwards in our evolutionary history, we would have to as when we would have been entitled to claim unequivocally: 'If X could talk, we would not understand him?'

However, this is hardly the point that Wittgenstein was out to make with his famous remark. His point was that a lion and a human have such different forms of life that understanding would not follow immediately even if they—hypothetically —were to share a language. This problem also occurs in human communication, because also humans can have forms of life that differ significantly and they will suffer from communicative breakdowns. Just before his remark about the lion, Wittgenstein writes:

> We also say of some people that they are transparent to us. It is, however, important as regards this observation that one human being can be a complete enigma to another. We learn this when we come into a strange country with entirely strange traditions; and, what is more, even given a mastery of the country's language. We do not *understand* the people. (And not because of not knowing what they are saying to themselves). We cannot find our feet with them. (1986, p. 223)

You will have some understanding of these people, of course, especially of the activities we have in common with them, but there will be aspects of their form of life that we are unable to grasp. When Wittgenstein explains how people from different cultures are able to understand each other, he refers to "the common behaviour of mankind" (1986, § 206). There are also behaviors common to humans and animals that enable a form of communication. There are a number of activities we share with lions, and it is not impossible to understand these activities.

As I do not have the space to argue the point here, I will simply presuppose that no other animals than humans possess what we usually call 'language.' Having said that: Is it really so important whether we can refer to animal communication as 'language' or not? It is undeniably true that they communicate. Other species are clearly able to communicate feelings and intentions to each other and to us. This expressiveness is imposed upon us in a completely different way than other natural objects do, and it demands a response from us. Wittgenstein quotes Goethe's *Faust*: "In the beginning was the deed" (1993, p. 394). Language is, as Wittgenstein says, a refinement. In human actions, we find a regularity, and without such a regularity, understanding can never take place. He describes this regularity as "the common behaviour of mankind" (1986, § 206). However, there are not only common behaviors of mankind, but also behaviors we have in common with other animals. With a foundation like this, we can understand animals, even though they do not have a language.

Wittgenstein writes: “The human body is the best picture of the human soul” (1986, p. 178). This claim about the relationship between body and soul in humans can also be extended to animals: “If one sees the behaviour of a living thing, one sees its soul” (1986, § 357). Seeing a soul means seeing *somebody*, someone with a subjectivity or consciousness, and not a mere thing. You are seeing a subject, not a mere object. To see this soul is not about looking through a kind of shell. Seeing this body and its behavior *is* to see a soul, as the soul is manifest in the body. A person who does not *see* an animal’s consciousness, that it has feelings and intentions, suffers from what Wittgenstein calls ‘aspect-blindness.’ According to Wittgenstein, aspect-blindness is akin to being tone-deaf (1986). A tone-deaf person receives the same auditory stimuli as a person with a perfect pitch, but will not *hear* the same, and an aspect-blind person receives the same visual stimuli, but does not *see* the same as someone capable of seeing aspects. However, such a grasp of the mental state of the animal presupposes that what we are seeing has a sufficient resemblance to ourselves. For example, we can only say that an animal has pain, when it exhibits a behavior that resembles human pain behavior.

An animal’s intentions are often immediately understandable. As Wittgenstein writes: “What is the natural expression of an intention? – Look at a cat when it stalks a bird; or a beast when it wants to escape” (1986, § 647). We learn to understand the intentions of animals by dealing with them. For anyone who has grown up with animals, the accusation that there is something suspicious about attributing the intentions to animals, that one is falling prey to a fallacy due to the use of anthropomorphisms, is a rather odd. The critic seems to assume that one first learns to understand another’s intentions when dealing with humans, but then does something questionable by extending this to include animals. However, anyone who has grown up with both animals and humans has usually learned to understand the intentions of others—both animals and humans—by interacting with both animals and humans.

I know that a person who smiles and laughs warmly is happy because I learned what ‘happy’ means by referring to this sort of criteria. Pain, joy, and sadness usually have fairly simple criteria. More complex conditions, such as grief or loneliness, which go beyond mere sadness, will have more complex criteria. In all cases, the understanding of mental states will always require external criteria (1986, § 580). We can explain expressions that refer to mental states only by referring to observable signs. We *see* emotions. As a rule, I can *see* you are happy or sad. The ‘inner’ can also be hidden, such as when someone does their utmost to keep a straight face instead of expressing how funny they find something. However, it is not hidden because it is something ‘inner’—but rather because these people are deliberately showing a different face to the one that would be the normal expression of their inner condition.

The same considerations we make with regard to the ascription of mental states to humans can also be made about animals. However, the criteria become increasingly more uncertain the further we get from the situation in which we learned to detect them. For animals that have a very different form of life from ours, it would be much more difficult to decide what the criteria for joy or sadness are. The more we know about the animal—from species-defined traits of mannerisms and senses, to the individual traits of the specific animal—the more reliable these ascriptions of mental states are.

We cannot simply ask nonhuman animals about what they are thinking or feeling, and it is not always easy to interpret their body language. However, by interacting with animals, one can develop interpretative skills. For example, people used to interacting with dogs cannot have failed to notice that tail-wagging often, but not always, means that the dog is happy. Tail-wagging can have a number of different meanings, depending on whether it is slow or fast, pointed more to the right or left, and relative to the situation. Dog owners will most often learn to interpret their dog without thinking so carefully about it. However, those same people may regret using these interpretations when encountering a cat. Anyone viewing calm tail-wagging as an expression of friendliness or pleasure, rather than irritation, runs the imminent risk of getting their hands scratched. When a dog places its head in your lap, you can be certain that it is a sign of affection. Were an elephant to attempt the same, you would be advised to get away as quickly as possible, because it is trying to kill you, by crushing you with its forehead. We frequently misunderstand animals, just like animals misunderstand each other, as the joyful, play bark of one dog can be interpreted as an aggressive bark by another dog. Humans also frequently misunderstand each other. However, all misunderstanding is possible only on the basis of a far larger area of understanding.

In one sense, the expression of emotions and intentions is often more reliable in animals than in humans. As a human, I often have the capacity to choose to express an emotion or intention. Not always, of course, because I can, for instance, be so overwhelmed by pain or grief that the thought of attempting to suppress it has not even occurred to me. And when one is in extraordinarily great pain, it obliterates everything, both language and the sense of self, such that nothing but the pain itself remains in consciousness. But on many occasions, we have a capacity for choosing what to express. Animals do not seem to have such a capacity to the same extent, even though they can, for instance, hide that they are wounded in order to protect themselves from predators. A well-documented example of an animal hiding its intentions and emotions is the chimpanzee Santino at Furuvik Park in Sweden (Osvath 2009). Like so many other chimpanzees in captivity, Santino had a strong dislike for zoo visitors. Captive chimpanzees often throw objects, such as excrement, at them. Early in the day, before visitors arrived, Santino would gather stones in piles. When the visitors arrived later, he bombarded them. When Santino displayed aggression, and the guides began ushering the visitors away from him, and out of his throwing range, his response was to pretend to be a peaceful chimpanzee and approach the visitors in a friendly manner, only to explode with rage and bombard them with stones as soon as they were within range. In this sense, a capacity for hiding one's true intentions and emotions is not unique to humans, but humans seem to have a far more developed capacity for this. This is also why I would not describe my dog as 'honest' for the simple reason that she cannot be dishonest—she cannot lie to me. The concepts of honesty and dishonesty do not apply to her life. My dog cannot choose whether or not to reveal her intention to try to capture a hare or a pigeon. If she has such intentions, it is immediately manifest in her behavior. Likewise, I can choose to express my boredom or suppress that expression, for instance, if it occurs in a context in which it would be inappropriate to express boredom. My dog cannot choose this. In this sense, we cannot say that the expressions humans make of their inner state are in principle more reliable than the expressions of animals. In both human and nonhuman animals, the conscious states of others can be interpreted only by means of outer signs, and that includes linguistic acts, and there is no essential difference between the access we have to mental states of other humans and the access we have to nonhuman animals.

If we discard the idea of consciousness as something hidden, something that can only be revealed by a language that breaks through the barrier separating the internal from the external, and instead recognize that the internal is *visible* in what is external, there is no principle difficulty in ascribing different states of consciousness to animals. This does not mean there will not be interpretation problems in practice, because we do not always know how to understand a behavior, but the problem is not that the internal is 'hidden.' If we take a Wittgensteinian approach, the subjective experience of animals—and other humans, for that sake—is not hidden, but can to some extent be observed.

All emotions will have a private character in the sense that I cannot experience your emotions as you do. It is conceivable that what you describe as an experience of joy differs from my experience. However, emotions are not just private. They are also expressed, and in that sense, they are public, available for external observation. Of course, you cannot know exactly what it is like for a mink to live in a small cage, but you can get some idea because there is sufficient overlap between you and the mink. Similarly, you can never know exactly what it is like for your dog to feel boredom, but again, there is sufficient overlap between your life and your dog's to give you an idea. My dog's boredom will differ from mine, simply because she is a dog and I am human. Nevertheless, I believe that the sort of experience she and I have when being deprived of the activities we care about—even though we care about different activities—is sufficiently similar to warrant the use of the term 'boredom' to describe both of our emotional states. I also cannot know exactly what boredom feels like for another human being, for that matter, and people will describe boredom in slightly different ways.

Criteria for Animal Boredom

What sort of behavior can give us reason to believe that an animal is bored? To some extent, these will resemble human behavior when afflicted by boredom. Humans deal with boredom by resorting certain acts, such as repeatedly shifting one's position in a chair, yawning, various pastimes, and so on. In animals, we will typically find repetitive acts, such as going back and forth in a cage in an agitated, almost compulsive style. I once saw a polar bear in a zoo, and it did nothing except repeating the same pattern of movement, going in a small circle diving under water, going back on land, diving under over and over, in a way that seemed to express no joy at all, but rather came across as a pure pastime, as way of coping with not being able to act 'normally.' With insufficient relevant options for agency, animals turn to actions that seem to have very little purpose and that also seem to give them little real satisfaction.

Other criteria for animal boredom is redirected behavior, such a gnawing on a cage, on its own leg or on other animals. It is well documented that boredom in humans is correlated with a stronger tendency to self-harm, and aggression toward others, and we find the same correlation in animals (Wemelsfelder 2005). As for the chimpanzee, Santino, that we discussed earlier, Toohey (2011) suggests that his aggressive behavior toward visitors at the zoo was in fact caused by boredom, and this might be the case.

We might also find the opposite behavior, hardly any movement at all and general apathy. As for this last category: Could we not just as well claim that the animal suffers from depression? I believe that we could, as I see no possibility of making a general distinction between these two mental states based on observable behavior in the animal. However, with the context of the behavior, you would have a better basis for claiming that we are dealing with one emotion rather another.

In order to ascribe a specific emotional state, such as boredom, to an animal, you will need information about the context in which the emotion occurs. This also holds for human emotions. If you see a child crying, you cannot determine whether it is crying from fear or pain unless you know something about the context in which the child cries. Or take the behavior of Flint, a chimpanzee described by Goodall (1990). He one day climbed up a tree, hardly moved, was apathetic and did not eat. Was Flint ill? Was he bored? Or depressed? His behavior was certainly abnormal. When you learn about the context of the behavior, the most plausible explanation is that he was paralyzed by grief. The behavior occurred after the death of his mother. Flint was born when his mother, Flo, was in her forties, which is late, and she was more nurturing toward Flint than she had been with his older siblings. They were inseparable—until she died. Flint then climbed up a tree, into the nest he and his mother had shared, and refused to eat. He stayed there until he died a month later. You would not be able to determine his emotional state if you had just been given a quick glimpse of him. You need context.

This also holds for the ascription of boredom to animals. As we have seen both apathy, stereotypical behavior and redirected behavior are criteria for boredom, but they could also indicate other emotional states. In order to argue plausibly that an animal is bored, you will have to take a look at its living conditions, if it is possible for the animal to what it usually cares about doing. A monotonous environment that causes boredom in the animal can explain monotonous behavior. This hypothesis can find support in observations of reduced monotony in behavior when the animal is provided with an environment that allows for greater variety in its agency.

The Good Life

Why should we concern ourselves with the question as to whether nonhuman animals are capable of experiencing boredom? The most essential concern is probably ethical that we take animal welfare seriously and believe that animals should be able to have good lives.

Following Aristotle, we can say that the good life for a creature is a life in accordance with the *nature* of that creature. I will refrain from discussing how 'nature' should be understood, if an essentialist or nonessentialist account is most plausible and so on. The central point is simply that what *living well* means will differ depending on what sort of creature we are talking about. It will differ from species to species, as the good life from me differs from the good life of my dog. It will also to some extent also differ from individual to individual, at least among more complex or developed creatures, such that the good life for me is not identical to the good life for my neighbor, just like the good life for my dog is not necessarily identical to the good life for my neighbor's dog, as a Whippet has a greater need for running than a Bulldog. However, there will be a fairly large overlap in the natures and needs among the members of a given species that it will suffice for our purposes. My Whippet and my neighbor's Bulldog are sufficiently similar to warrant talking about their needs for living a good life as *canine* needs. Similarly, my neighbor and I are, in spite of having fairly different personalities, sufficiently similar to have our needs described as *human* needs.

A good life for an animal is a life in which it is capable of doing what it cares for doing. A bird will have need for flying and a dog for socializing. They may not perish if these needs are not met, but an animal will have an impoverished existence without them. Boredom is one possible effect of having to live under impoverished conditions. Different animals will be bored under different conditions, depending on their nature. Can all animals be bored? That seems highly unlikely. There is little, if any, reason to think that a tick is bored while it is waiting to pick up the smell of lactic acid, detect a temperature of approximately 37 degrees Celsius, and feel that a portion of skin is not covered by too much hair. I also doubt that oysters can be bored, and the same goes for lobsters and insects. I assume that all mammals have the capacity for boredom, based on their behavior and the neurological conditions they have for consciousness. I am also inclined to include birds and at least some species of octopus. However, I will not enter into any further discussion here of where we should draw the line within the animal kingdom.

It seems clear that animals do not engage in activities only as a means to an end, but also because they find certain activities enjoyable in themselves. They enjoy playing. Everybody who has ever had a cat or a dog can confirm that. But it is also a case for other species. For instance, smaller octopuses have been observed carrying two coconut shells which they use for protection by curling up inside them, but they sometimes also use these shells for entertainment when they curl up inside two coconut shells at the top of a hill and roll down, and then carry the coconut shells back to the top, and roll down again. This is almost identical to what we humans do when sledding. Why do octopuses do it? Probably because it is fun. One view on the concept of play is that it is just a preparation for the serious life that young individuals will have to deal with when they get older. Play then serves another purpose, outside of the playful activity itself. The problem with an explanation like this is that it does not capture a crucial aspect of play: It is fun. There is play that is a preparation for later tasks, but there is also play that is just play. We say that play is *autotelic*, meaning that it is its own purpose. It is this sort of play that octopuses seem to indulge in, just like countless other species. When an animal that enjoys playing is deprived of possibilities for playing, for instance, because it is placed in a cage that does not allow playing, it is deprived of something central to its existence, and such deprivation can cause boredom.

I would say that the polar bear I described earlier acted abnormally under abnormal conditions. It differs from normal behavior; i.e., the sort of environment polar bears have adapted to through their evolutionary history. I am not arguing that a species such as polar bears can live a good, fulfilling life only in such a 'normal' environment. On the contrary, I believe that an animal can thrive also in a highly artificial environment. However, the normal environment will show us the normal behavior of the species, which is the sort of behavior that should be facilitated also in an artificial environment or at least serve as a normative standard one can aim for. The important distinction is not between a natural and an artificial environment, as an animal can live in a highly engaging, artificial environment or in a natural environment that is so barren that the animal is bored. Animals can lead good lives in captivity as long as their living conditions are sufficiently and relevantly fashioned for the activities for which the animal cares. Unfortunately, this is not the case for most animals that live in captivity. They are deprived of the possibility of doing what they typically care for doing. And, as I have pointed out, what they care for will differ from species to species and to some extent also from individual to individual. One activity that most animals care for is searching for food, and it would probably be a good idea to let confined animals search for food or solve a task to get their food.

Using a term from von Uexküll (1980), we can argue that the animal needs an environment with a sufficient number of 'carriers of significance.' Different species will have different carriers if significance in their worlds, to a great extent, defined by what organs the animals use for perception and action, which in turn determine the function of the object for the animal. Primitive organisms will live in a world with just a few carriers of significance, whereas the surroundings of cats and dogs will have a fairly large number of them. An object without function does not really exist in the animal's world, and the very same object can have widely different meanings in the worlds of different animals. Much of what has an obvious function for us humans, like a fork or a clock, will be meaningless to a dog. If a clock is ticking loudly, a dog might notice it, but most likely the ticking will simply blend in with the background noise of the dog's surroundings. To a dog, a pen is not a writing tool, but perhaps a stick you can chew on. It is astonishing how much of a dog's world that actually falls into the 'something to chew on' category. This is also why different species will have a preference for different toys.

For social animals, such as dogs, others with whom to socialize are clearly crucial carriers of significance. A world in which they cannot socialize is an impoverished world for them. For other animals, such as many felines, but certainly not lions, this is not the case, except for mating and caring for offspring. Consequently, the typical dog will be more susceptible not only to loneliness, but also to boredom, in the absence of others with whom to socialize than the typical cat. That being said, my two Burmese cats were as social as any dog I have ever known, and some dogs are not very social. Smells are certainly more important to dogs than to cats, and staying in an environment with little variety in smells will promote boredom in dogs, whereas cats have a greater preference than dogs for being able to move vertically.

I have had animals, cats, and dogs, my entire life, and it is not as if I had never seen them have the sort of behavior that I now describe as expressing boredom. However, I refused to use the term 'boredom' when describing animal experience, unwilling to go any further than to say that animals may be understimulated, but not bored. I did so because I had other ideas of boredom and animals that were not compatible. Such an unwillingness to ascribe a certain experience to an organism, even if it clearly expresses having that experience, is hardly unique. This is not the case only in our relation to animals, but also sometimes to other humans. Until the 1980s, it was common to perform surgery on human infants without anesthesia. One reason for this was the increased risk when anesthetizing infants, but it was also argued that the infant's ability to experience pain was so small—or nonexistent—that it was unnecessary to take such a risk. Today, it is widely agreed that infants have a well-developed ability to feel pain, and therefore, anesthesia is also normally given during procedures presumed to be painful. How could the doctors make such a mistake? The infants, after all, showed behavior indicating they were in pain. The doctors were able to see it, but they interpreted the behavior as though it was not a genuine expression of pain awareness, because of other beliefs they had about infants. Similarly, I now recognize that I have on many occasions observed animals being bored, but I earlier refused to recognize it as boredom. One might say that I suffered from a theoretically induced aspect-blindness.

Just like a creature who has the capacity to feel love for another creature will have a capacity for feeling lonely, a creature who has the capacity to care for something will also have a capacity for being bored. In both cases, the negative state is characterized by a privation, a lack of attachment, and a lack of meaning. Animals that have a capacity for meaningful lives should be able to live meaningful lives, to the extent that we are able to provide them with the conditions for such lives.

References

Darwin, C. (1872). *The expression of emotions in man and animals*. London, UK: John Murray.

de Waal, F. B. M. (1999). Anthropomorphism and anthropodenial: Consistency in our thinking about humans and other animals. *Philosophical Topics, 27*(1), 255–280. https://doi.org/10.5840/philtopics199927122.

Fahlman, S. A., Mercer, K. B., Gaskovski, P., Eastwood, A. E., & Eastwood, J. D. (2009). Does a lack of life meaning cause boredom? Results from psychometric, longitudinal, and experimental analyses. *Journal of Social and Clinical Psychology, 28*(3), 307–340. https://doi.org/10.1521/jscp.2009.28.3.307.

Fromm, E. (2002). *The sane society*. London, UK/New York, NY: Routledge.

Goethe, J.W.v. (1950). *West-östlicher Divan, Epen. Maximen und Reflexionen, Goethes poetische Werke*, Vol. 2. Stuttgart: Cotta'sche Buchhandlung.

Goldberg, Y. K., Eastwood, J. D., LaGuardia, J., & Danckert, J. (2011). Boredom: An emotional experience distinct from apathy, anhedonia, or depression. *Journal of Social and Clinical Psychology, 30*(6), 647–666. https://doi.org/10.1521/jscp.2011.30.6.647.

Goodall, J. (1990). *Through a window: My thirty years with the chimpanzees of Gombe*. Boston, MA: Houghton Mifflin.

Hume, D. (1984). *A treatise of human nature*. London, UK: Penguin.

Lloyd Morgan, C. (1894). *An introduction to comparative psychology*. London, UK: W. Scott.

Osvath, M. (2009). Spontaneous planning for future stone throwing by a male chimpanzee. *Current Biology, 19*(5), R190–R191. https://doi.org/10.1016/j.cub.2009.01.010.

Svendsen, L. (2005). *A philosophy of boredom*. London, UK: Reaktion Books.

Svendsen, L. (2019). *Understanding animals*. London, UK: Reaktion Books.

Toohey, P. (2011). *Boredom. A lively history*. New Haven, CT: Yale University Press.

von Uexküll, J. (1980). *Kompositionslehre der Natur: Biologie als undogmatische Naturwissenschaft*. Frankfurt a.M./Berlin/Wien: Propyläen Verlag.

Wemelsfelder, F. (2005). Animal boredom: Understanding the tedium of confined lives. In F. D. McMillan (Ed.), *Mental health and well-being in animals* (pp. 77–91). Oxford, UK: Blackwell. https://doi.org/10.1002/9780470384947.ch6.

Wittgenstein, L. (1986). *Philosophical investigations*. Oxford, UK.: Basil Blackwell.

Wittgenstein, L. (1993). *Philosophical occasions 1912–1951*. Indianapolis, IN/Cambridge, MA: Hackett Publishing Co.

Lars Svendsen (born on September 16, 1970) is a Norwegian philosopher. He is Professor in the Department of Philosophy at the University of Bergen, Norway. He is the author of 12 books and has been translated to 27 languages. Seven of his books are available in English: *A philosophy of boredom* (Reaktion Books, 2005), *Fashion: A philosophy* (Reaktion Books, 2006), *A philosophy of fear* (Reaktion Books, 2008), *A philosophy of evil* (Dalkey Archive Press, 2010), *A philosophy of freedom* (Reaktion Books, 2014), *A philosophy of loneliness* (Reaktion Books, 2017) and *Understanding animals* (Reaktion Books, 2019). He is currently working on a book on loneliness. In *A philosophy of boredom*, he investigates one of the central preoccupations of our age as it probes the nature of boredom, how it originated, how and why it afflicts us, and why we cannot seem to overcome it by any act of will.

Chapter 10
The Helix Center Roundtable on Boredom (New York, April 2018)

Josefa Ros Velasco

The Helix Center Roundtable on Boredom

On April 21, 2018, took place, at the New York Psychoanalytic Society and Institute, a *Roundtable on boredom* organized by The Helix Center, whose mission is to draw together leaders from distinct spheres of knowledge in the arts, humanities, sciences, and technology for interdisciplinary roundtables. Its Director, Dr. Edward Nersessian, invited some specialists on boredom, including John Eastwood, Jacqueline Gottlieb, Gerald Hurowitz, Mark Polizzotti, and myself, to promote brainstorming on boredom. Such an encounter consisted of two parts. In the first one, we were free to discuss on boredom, show our concernings, and drive the conversation naturally toward any direction during an hour. In the second one, the audience had the opportunity to ask questions to participants and also to present their own ideas and concerns. This roundtable was, as usually, broadcasted, recorded, and uploaded to the Web site of The Helix Center (http://www.helixcenter.org/videos/#/oAK_olUjP5Y).

To work up an appetite thinking and discussing the topic of boredom, a short text was previously disseminated to the invitees and the attendees. This was as follows:

> Schopenhauer described boredom as a tame longing without any particular object, Dostoevsky as a bestial and indefinable affliction, and poet Joseph Brodsky as time's invasion of your world system. Unsurprisingly, not many can describe boredom even though most have felt it, and it is one of the central preoccupations of the age. The most current definition comes from John Eastwood in Toronto: Drawing from research across many areas of psychological science and neuroscience, Eastwood and colleagues define boredom as an aversive state of wanting but being unable to engage in satisfying activity, which arises from failures in one of the brain's attention networks. Interestingly, people who investigate boredom, find it thus: Boredom is a blast! To a curious and creative

J. Ros Velasco (✉)
Harvard University, Cambridge, USA
e-mail: josros@ucm.es

J. Ros Velasco (ed.), *Boredom Is in Your Mind*,
https://doi.org/10.1007/978-3-030-26395-9_10

> scholar, nothing is ever too trivial. And, Peter Toohey finds a perverse kind of glee in his subject. Curiously, the subject seems to invigorate those who study it. We hope that this roundtable will, in bringing together scholars from literature, psychiatry, neurology, cultural history, and the law who have thought deeply about the subject, continue the exploration of the meaning and characteristics of boredom, and in so doing give the audience a chance to enlarge their own ideas.

This special contribution consists of a transcription-summary of the main ideas presented during this meeting. It occupies the last place in the volume *Boredom is in your mind* since it brings together the ideas discussed in the rest of the chapters. In this sense, not only does it serve as a sample of our living dialogue and the methodology we want to pursue, but also as an overview and, even most important, as a benchmark to determine future research lines we need to explore. Moreover, this is perhaps one of the best examples of how we should conduct our research on boredom from a multidisciplinary approach from now on.

Invitees to the Roundtable on Boredom

Let's start by introducing the participants. The reader is now familiarized with both, Dr. Eastwood and I myself, as well as with our ideas. From its part, Dr. Edward Nersessian, the organizer of the encounter, is Clinical Professor of Psychiatry at Weill Cornell Medical College, Training and Supervising Psychoanalyst at the New York Psychoanalytic Institute, Distinguished Life Member of the American Psychiatric Association, and Corresponding Member of Société Psychanalytique de Paris. He is co-founder and first co-editor of the journal *Neuropsychoanalysis*, co-editor of the textbook of psychoanalysis *Controversies in contemporary psychoanalysis* (International Universities Press, 1997). He has published papers on a variety of psychoanalytic subjects and his current interest is reassessing the fundamental tenets of the psychoanalytic theory. Co-founder of the Philoctetes Center, he is the founder and current Director of the Helix Center for Interdisciplinary Studies.

Jacqueline Gottlieb is Professor of Neuroscience in the Kavli Institute for Brain Science and the Mortimer B. Zuckerman Institute for Mind Brain and Behavior at Columbia University. She completed her education at the Massachusetts Institute of Technology, Yale University and the National Institute of Health, and she joined the Columbia Faculty in 2001. Dr. Gottlieb is an internationally renowned expert on the neural mechanisms of attention and decision making, and the recipient of numerous awards, including the McKnight Scholarship, Klingenstein Fellowship, and Human Frontiers research grants. Her work pioneers the study of active information sampling and curiosity, which she investigates using behavioral, computational, and neurophysiological methods. A central goal of her research is to understand cognition as an adaptive process, whereby the brain dynamically allocates its resources to best serve the demands of a decision situation.

Gerald Hurowitz is Assistant Professor of Clinical Psychiatry and Faculty for the past 30 years at Columbia University College of Physicians and Surgeons. He has a full-time clinical practice in psychopharmacology and neuropsychiatry in New York City. Dr. Hurowitz is a founder and Chief Medical Officer at M3 Information, an information technology company that focuses on mental health integration into primary care. He has co-authored the chapter "Psychopharmacology and electroconvulsive therapy" in *The American psychiatric press synopsis of psychiatry* (APA, 1996), and is the author of several articles in the fields of psychopharmacology and neuropsychiatry. He has presented in a wide range of venues, including at the annual meeting of the American Psychiatric Association, at Columbia's Comprehensive Review of Current Neuro-psychiatry, at the New York State Psychiatric Institute's Arden House Conference, and at Open Minds. He has co-directed since 1992 the course in Clinical Neuropsychiatry for Columbia's fourth-year Psychiatry residents and ran a weekly clinical psychopharmacology conference on Columbia's inpatient teaching unit for much of the 1990s and 2000s. Dr. Hurowitz received a Master's Degree in Philosophy from NYU, an MD from Jefferson Medical College, and a Bachelor of Arts (Physics and Philosophy) from Yale University in 1979. He attended the NYU/Bellevue residency in psychiatry in New York City, where he served as Chief Resident in 1984–1985.

Finally, Mark Polizzotti has translated more than fifty books from the French, including works by Gustave Flaubert, Patrick Modiano, Marguerite Duras, André Breton, and Raymond Roussel. A Chevalier de l'Ordre des Arts et des Lettres and the recipient of a 2016 American Academy of Arts and Letters Award for Literature, he is the author of eleven books, including *Revolution of the mind: The life of André Breton* (Farrar, Straus and Giroux, 1995), which was a finalist for the PEN/Martha Albrand Award for Best Nonfiction; *Luis Buñuel's Los Olvidados* (British Film Institute, 2006); *Bob Dylan: Highway 61 revisited* (Bloomsbury, 2006); and *Sympathy for the traitor: A translation manifesto* (MIT Press, 2018). His essays and reviews have appeared in *The New York Times, The New Republic, The Wall Street Journal, The Nation, Parnassus, Partisan Review, Bookforum*, and elsewhere. He directs the publications program at The Metropolitan Museum of Art in New York.

Transcription of the Roundtable on Boredom

Introduction: The Bane and Boon of Boredom by Mark Polizzotti

I would rather you hate me than be indifferent to me. Schopenhauer wrote that 'the two enemies of human happiness are pain and boredom'—and of the two, the more fearsome is clearly boredom. We rot our brain cells with drugs or Twitter to avoid it. We willingly endanger life and limb to get away from it. Here today, I would much rather you throw tomatoes at me than yawn. So, if you must walk out, please do it from anger or disgust, not from lack of interest.

What is it about boredom that so frightens and discomforts us? Tolstoy defined it as 'the desire for desires,' which speaks of a yearning, but one that can never be satisfied because it is a failure of yearning itself. The fact is that boredom is hard to concentrate on. We get restless. We are literally 'driven to distraction.' The desperation we feel when we are forced to endure it for long periods can be positively claustrophobic.

And, yet, somewhat paradoxically, boredom maintains a real hold on our imaginations. You find unexpected references to it everywhere. Robert Musil, in his novel *Three women*, writes of a group of prospectors: 'What caused them more suffering than food poisoning was melancholy and boredom'—which seems to buttress my conviction that we would much rather endure physical pain than tedium.

Others have taken a more prescriptive approach to boredom, offering recipes on how not to be a bore. Voltaire's formulation was: 'The secret of being a bore is to tell everything'—a sentiment echoed by American humorist Bert Leston Taylor, in a well-known quip: 'A bore is a man who, when you ask him how he is, tells you.' Still others have tried to combat boredom proactively, if not always considerately. The surrealist leader André Breton, having cruelly humiliated one of his closest friends in public, explained afterward to his nonplussed companions: 'It's only natural, when I'm bored, to provoke an argument, even a nasty one, to avoid losing stamina.'

Now, you have before you five people who are going to spend the next two hours trying to engage your interest in the negation of interest, which might seem like the very definition of a fool's errand. But fear not! Because, for every sage who has despaired of boredom, others have zeroed in on its redeeming qualities. The American educator Jon Kabat-Zinn, reflecting his work on mindfulness, points out that 'when you pay attention to boredom it gets unbelievably interesting.' Similarly, John Ashbery wrote in his poem "The short answer":

> Why make things more difficult
> than they already are? Because if it is boring
> in a different way, that will be interesting too.

Indeed, the potential of boredom to spur creativity is well-known to any artist. 'The life of the creative man,' said Susan Sontag, 'is led, directed and controlled by boredom. Avoiding boredom is one of our most important purposes.' Robert M. Pirsig, the author of *Zen and the art of motorcycle maintenance*, put it even more bluntly when he said that 'boredom always precedes a period of great creativity.'

Are they protesting too much, putting a happy mask over their agonized faces? Perhaps, but many are those who have written not only out of boredom, in both senses of *out of*, but have even made boredom their pet subject. Alberto Moravia's most celebrated novel is titled *Boredom*, though it is actually about a young man's —but a *bored* young man's—dangerous infatuation. The decadent writer Joris-Karl Huysmans made a career of displaying in book after book his lack of interest in society and all its works. If you search under *boredom* in the book listings on

Amazon, it will return more than a hundred pages of results, suggesting that the literature of boredom is practically an industry unto itself.

The mention of literature quickly steers us toward boredom's highfalutin French cousin *ennui*, as well as to its German relative *Weltschmerz*. Even though the terms are nearly synonymous, each carries a particular resonance and stands apart from plain-Jane boredom in its connotations of romantic world-weariness, of being not only bored but extravagantly, even exotically, bored. From Kierkegaard to Sartre, *ennui* has got something that mere boredom hasn't got: cachet. So much so, in fact, that a company making protective sports gear chose it as their brand name. Here is the pitch on their Web site: 'Urban sports are extremely fun, don't ruin the experience with the wrong gear, choose ENNUI.'

While *ennui* and *Weltschmerz* give off a paradoxical whiff of excitement and intensity, plain, old boredom is just boring. It is *ennui* stripped of its glamour. It's what we all know when we're at home. It is the tedium of the familiar.

Still, I will posit that that very familiarity of the same-old-same-old can also be a comfort, and I'll end my remarks with one last quote. This was said not by a famous pundit but by the woman in a couple I know, who, for years, have been maintaining a bicoastal relationship. Once, when the three of us were dining together, they were lamenting the difficulties of never quite seeing each other for long enough. And, after thinking it over, she came out with one of the most romantic sentences I have ever heard: 'It's not that I want you here all the time,' she told her partner. 'I just want the luxury of being bored with you.'

Brainstorming on Boredom

Gerald Hurowitz [GH]: I am really struck, as a psychiatrist, with the very mundane nature of boredom and how something just in front of us—it is in front of everybody, a little bit like sleep every night—is still so mysterious. A recent review of two books on Jewish humor by Cathleen Schine in the *New York Review of Books* quotes the poet Billy Collins to say: 'Humor is the dog that leaves the room when you call its name.' It is well-known and it is an old saw that if you have a clinical or critical discussion around humor, it won't be funny. Humor and mirth, and other positive affects or feelings and emotional states, become less humorous the more you talk about them. Mirth's evil twin sibling, boredom, perhaps has a negative valence but it seems the more we speak of it, the less boring it is. I wonder about mirth as being, more literally, the other side of boredom.

John Eastwood [JE]: One of the things that I would like to say is that if you give boredom at least a second thought, it is beguiling and enticing. This is both a blessing and a curse for boredom scholars because it is so open to a variety of definitions and interpretations, and there are so many different ways of studying it. It is almost like a Rorschach that can capture all of our thoughts; and it indeed does seem to provide an organizing framework for a lot of preoccupation and concern that people have today. So, on the one hand, it is just plain fun as a scholar because you can roll around in this unconstrained, limitless landscape. But if we want to really collaborate with one another, if we want to be able to make some progress, we should create a *lingua franca* with which we all can work. We need to find some way to work together to develop some precision around terms and the uses of our words, because the term 'boredom' is so elastic that, as a scientist, it is really difficult to wrestle with it. When one person uses the term they might mean something very different than another. Multidisciplinary and multi-method approaches are absolutely the way to go, but it would be wise for us to find ways to corral and constrain our thinking so we can communicate across disciplines and work with each other.

Josefa Ros Velasco [JRV]: Nowadays, concerning boredom, we have to admit we have more questions than solutions. We all recognize that we have to speak of boredom. I am wondering about the affirmation that boredom leads to disasters. Boredom leads to disasters as a result of being bored and not being able to get rid of our boredom. This might happen in two different situations: (1) When subjects are unable to give a response to their boredom due to psychological or psychiatrical conditions—e.g., concerning attention deficit; and (2) when the context is so closed and restrictive that does not offer opportunities to respond to boredom, I mean, there are possibilities, but all of them are well-known and are unable to put boredom aside. In this sense, boredom leads to disasters, to deviant behaviors, when either people are not able to fix boredom because of their mental problems or when the context does not offer enough and new possibilities for being engaged. Pathological boredom and its pathological consequences are the results of one of these two circumstances.

Mark Polizzotti [MP]: May be we should differentiate between boredom and the feeling of discomfort we feel. We call the latter boredom, but it is not quite the same thing. When I am on my own, I can feel tired, dispirited, lacking in energy, but I do not feel bored in the sense of being desperately anxious to get out of whatever state I'm in. Where I do get bored, sometimes, it is when I am in a place I can't leave. The classic example for me is being stuck in a meeting at work. Sometimes these meetings are fascinating, but sometimes they get really painful, and such situations do cause that sense of claustrophobia. My 'astral self' gets up from the table and runs out of the room, but my physical self, because of the expectations of the job, is still sitting there, just waiting for this to end. The former director of the Louvre once talked about one of his predecessors who used to go to zillions of meetings. At a certain point, he would simply stand up and say: 'Okay, I am going to the movies now.' The other curators sitting around the table were completely nonplussed, because this man actually dared to do what they probably wanted to do themselves. It eventually cost him his job, but it did not matter—he didn't want to be bored anymore.

JRV: This is the second type of boredom Heidegger talked about, when you are in a situation in which you are not forced, strictly speaking, to be, but you should be, you decided to go there voluntarily, nobody is forcing you, but you know in advance you are going to be bored.

MP: The fact is that there *are* pressures and constraints. You are not forced physically at gunpoint, it is not like being in jail, but the dictates of my job require me to be in that room, to pay attention, to care what the people around me are talking about. I cannot just walk out, as much as I would sometimes love to.

Jacqueline Gottlieb [JG]: I have a question about the other kind of boredom that happens when you are alone by yourself. Some people do not get bored in that situation, but there are other people who do get bored. What do you think is the difference for you to get bored when you are by yourself? What is the role of boredom in mental illness, in psychopathology?

JE: There are many different factors—cultural, social, environmental, psychological—that can cause boredom. To move forward, we need a clear definition of what is the state of boredom. I define boredom as the uncomfortable feeling of being mentally unengaged. When bored our mental capacity is not utilized and this causes an inherently uncomfortable feeling; we have been evolutionarily designed to experience being mentally unengaged as aversive. We would not be here today having this conversation if we were happy to be mentally unengaged. Thus, boredom is this uncomfortable feeling of being mentally unengaged.

You can compare it to physical pain. The discomfort of boredom is analogous to that of physical pain. They both keep us safe. It is a good thing that we have the capacity for boredom. That does not mean that we should cultivate boredom, as we do not cultivate pain even though it is a good thing. Nor do I think we should become preoccupied with trying to avoid pain or boredom at any cost. That would not be advantageous. Similarly, like pain, boredom can become chronic and problematic. Similarly, like pain, boredom is the signal: How we respond to it is what is really critical. Boredom is just a message that tells us we are in a non-optimal state when we are cognitively unengaged, and gives us that impetus to do something about it. We can all respond in very different ways and this is the point that boredom can become problematic. It is all about our response to it.

I am not a fan of the idea of pathologizing boredom. I do not think we should consider it an illness or a problem. This chronic form does co-occur with what we call mental disorders, but boredom itself as not a pathological state; rather one that we need to handle carefully in many different contexts.

GH: Could you expand that idea a little bit and make it more intuitive for people who are listening to your excellent analogy to pain? When you say that people need pain since it does serve a function, most of us are thinking of something like a stubbed toe. But there are those individuals who do not have pain fibers and, consequently, any sense of pain. Also, pain can happen in microdoses. People in hospital who are forced to be in the same position can start to develop pain and it becomes worse and worse. Pain can also happen in these sort of microdoses and have an effect in spurring us to whatever hopefully we will do next.

To be a little bit argumentative with your [JE] wish to define boredom, there is an idea that goes back to the beginning of the Enlightenment, that if only we could have a language, a 'scientific language,' all our problems would be solved. Whereas the protean nature of boredom is actually a very interesting issue, because it has many sides and aspects, and fits in so many places, we can also bear in mind that boredom is an ambiguous term and it does serve in different context slightly differently. We do not want to cut off an idea about boredom by reducing it too much.

JE: Fair enough. I remember actually once attending a conference where this poet was talking about T. S. Eliot and how any definition of H2O needed to include a little duckweed. I am quite comfortable with that idea but I think now the problem is that we have too many duckweeds and not enough precision. But, certainly, we need to stay open and use these precise ideas that cut across contexts to find those common patterns.

Edward Nersessian [EN]: I have been in that position that is confused with boredom sometimes, but I have never described it as boredom to myself. I described it as restless, irritation, impatience, annoyance… When I am bored is more like that kind of passive state of not knowing what to do or how to engage.

MP: The French translation of boredom is *ennui. Ennui* comes from Old French, which means annoyance, and that comes from Latin, which means hatred. So, etymologically, there is an annoyance-hatred aspect of boredom.

GH: There is also the cultural quality of boredom. One may at times choose to use the term boredom when others label what you are experiencing as 'boredom.' Yet, there may be something in common between those two states of not knowing what one wants to do and wishing to have a wish. In both cases, there is the underutilization of one's cognitive capacity. The fact of knowing one can do more or that one is constrained to act creates a sense of boredom.

JG: There is a point in the use of the active voice to say 'I am annoyed, I am irritated.' They are all active words where the ornaments to talk of boredom are passive. I think boredom is a passive state.

GH: People have some sense that they are not acting as much as they might and yet they have an impulse to do so. There is an active impulse and then there is the feeling of not knowing what to do.

EN: In French, *ennui* has a passive quality. When you say '*je m'ennuie*,' you mean: 'That annoys me, I am just passively feeling something uncomfortable.'

JG: This goes back to a concept that comes up in many contexts: the Optimum Stimulation Level [OSL]. Your brain is a big dynamical system of neurons interacting, and there is presumably some optimal rate of interaction. I imagine boredom being a state that is 'understimulated' or 'overstimulated' with regard to that optimal one. But it is not really determined by any single external circumstance. If some people are in the same boring meeting, it may be experienced as irritating by somebody and fascinating by others; or even by yourself on a different day!

GH: What we might use as a stimulus for boredom is almost an oxymoron.

JG: It is never property only of the external environment. What does that external environment do to you? What kind of memories does it evoke? What kind of mental life does it stimulate? If during that boring meeting something comes that triggered your memory, then you could distract yourself. What is the memory not to be bored anymore? There is some happy medium: If things are too simple or too complicated they can both be boring.

JRV: Understimulated and overstimulated. Boredom comes from both states just because the flow is broken, as Csíkszentmihályi stated.

JE: There is not an a priori right answer concerning where we should put the definitional boundaries of boredom. We have to decide what is useful. Boredom has a long history. Culture, situations, and time have shifted where that boundary has been put. I would think about it as an emotion that needs to be distinguished from frustration, on the one hand, and apathy, on the other hand. Boredom fits somewhere in between those two. It is important not to conflate boredom with apathy. Boredom involves the desire for desires. There is this restless longing and desire, but an inability to articulate what is longed for. Boredom is not at all a passive state: There is a sense of urgency and the desire for action. Psychoanalytic writers talked about the desire being too threatening and therefore repressed, but that desire for action remained without any target for discharging the energy. So, boredom is not apathetic. On the other hand, frustration has a goal out on the horizon. Something is thwarting your progress toward it; something is standing between you and the desired state. That is frustration. In boredom, you do not have that future desired activity in mind so you cannot be frustrated.

In terms of over- or under-stimulation I would, again, go back to the idea that if we attend a lecture on some topic that we know nothing about, it is like we cannot get a foothold in and so we are not cognitively able to engage with what is happening. If the lecture is on something we know too well and the material being presented is below our capacity, it does not engage us either. Both cases, those over- and under-challenging, have a final common pathway of being cognitively unengaged.

Finally, when I say that there is the underlying, sub-personal cognitive mechanism, I do not wish to say that this is all there is; there is a phenomenological, subjective part on top of that underlying mechanism which is very important. And that is where all of the affective components come in.

JRV: On a slightly different note, we are talking about one kind of boredom all the time. We should talk of *boredoms*, perhaps. We are talking about the boredom that suffers an individual, but we are not taking into account the boredom of which a whole society can complain: the societal boredom. There is a difference between that endogenous or exogenous boredom, but individual, in which you can do something and get rid of boredom, and the profound and complex boredom that literature and philosophy were talking about in the past centuries. This is also different from the differentiation between simple and complex boredom that was first established by the French poet Paul Valèry a century ago and then repeated by Siegfried Kracauer. This kind of boredom may be both endogenous and exogenous. But societal boredom it is only exogenous. It is this kind of boredom people suffer when they all are hesitated with their cultural, social, and economic structures. Perhaps, apart from trying to define boredom, we should have started talking about *boredoms*.

MP: When you [JRV] talk about societies and societal boredom, is that really boredom in the sense we are understanding it, or is it more metaphorical? Societal boredom sounds to me like frustration. You [JRV] are talking of people in a society who feel something is not working, whether it is an economic structure, a political situation, their ability to affect it… That is not really boredom, that is frustration. We are not bored with the current administration, we are frustrated with it.

GH: Enculturation in a particular society may fail to introduce ideas or activities so individuals may go on to cultivate interests and goals. If such goals are not cultivated by people as they are coming up through school, they may later say they do not know what they want to do with themselves. Maybe they need to be helped with discovering some interest they were not aware they had. Frustration implies there are things preventing people from expressing themselves. I think that is a more philosophical, sociological description to explain that the causes of boredom are social issues and to ask: 'Why are you treating it like a psychological problem when it is, in fact, a societal problem?' In this case, I think you [JRV] want to say with 'boredom' that people do not know what to do with themselves and they may also be frustrated. It is not just one or the other.

JE: When we judge something to be boring we are doing social work. We are dismissing and denigrating. I would definitely agree in that regard. But you can think about a child in a classroom who is struggling with maths and says 'This is boring.' What is happening right there? Well, maybe this child lacks the capacity to be successful in this context and saying the class is boring is a way to save face. Is it an aloof kind of stepping back? We use boredom to judge people as well. It is interesting that when people say: 'Well, I am never bored because I have got too much work to do… it is just those rich guys over there that get bored,' it is a way of rejecting the other. Social work is happening around boredom in a way that is interesting and quite different than other kinds of emotions. And so I think your [JRV] point is well-taken in that regard. There are many different potential factors that can cause boredom. But if we are thinking about it as an emotional state, we should think of it in terms of individuals with lots of different causes and responses. There is certainly variety that needs to be explored and understood.

EN: Many years ago we were talking in one of the earliest meetings like that Karl Pribram said: 'Many of these words we use,' we were talking about creativity imagination zone, 'these are just words. That is because we do not really know what they are about and we give them a name.' Do you think boredom falls into that category? For example, when we say 'fear' as an emotion it seems to be a lot more specific, and now you can talk about fear circuits and so on. But boredom seems like different people feel and describe it. Do we actually have an emotion that is specific and can be called boredom?

JE: Boredom could be like fear if we work together and come up with a definition. The person in the street will use the term very broadly and loosely. The way people use the term 'fear' is not the same as the way a neuroscientist would use the term. Neuroscientists work with distinctions between fear and anxiety, and all kind of nuances that the others would not make. We should start by listening to the person in the street to develop a grounded definition of our concepts and to make sure they are culturally relevant, and we should look at theories too. We need to then do a little pruning and come up with a scientifically viable definition so that we can work with it as we can work with fear.

JG: In neuroscience, we are not studying a lot of interesting higher-level concepts like curiosity. But it is not that they cannot be studied, it is just we did not get to them yet. Fear seemed impossible to study at the biological level long ago.

JRV: That is why just some disciplines are studying boredom: because it is so difficult to define at certain levels. For example, palaeoanthropologists would say: 'What are we going to say about boredom?'

JG: It is the same dark side of mental life. Even when we study feeding behavior in neuroscience we do not say we study hunger. Hunger is a motivation for feeding, so boredom is the motivation for engaging in mental life. I started thinking about what motivates us to engage with something, to be curious. In neurosciences, we think of mental activity as a cost in an economic framework. Attention mental capacity is limited so we have to decide how to engage it. We engage our mental life in order to obtain some benefit, optimally or rationally, at the minimum effort. That opens the question of why are we curious? Why are people reading books for no apparent benefit when you could just go to sleep to conserve energy?

JE: That is a great question. You could summarize that maybe through the Cognitive-Miser Model of Cognition [CMMC]. The idea is that we want to reduce our expenditure of resources. I do not see a conflict there because the CMMC is about the exertion of effort and there are ways to be cognitively engaged that do not necessarily require a lot of cognitive effort. Reverie, daydream, mind-wandering… these all are ways of being engaged mentally that do not involve cognitive effort. However, curiosity sometimes requires the exertion of an effort and therefore it might be counter to the CMMC. I do not have a solution to that paradox when it comes to curiosity, but I feel confident that we can say that being mentally unengaged is inherently aversive without being in conflict with the CMMC. I think the CMMC is too simplistic since it has its bases in this very narrow cognitive science that does not apply more broadly when we look at human life.

MP: Maybe one pathway into it is to broaden our definition of 'payback.' I've taken on jobs that have cost me enormous amounts of time and effort for very little monetary gain, simply because I just wanted to do them. The payback in those cases is my satisfaction in putting in the effort and doing what I consider a good job. If we talk about why people engage in altruistic events, or why they do things that do not seem to earn them any particular return, perhaps the return is, in fact, the feeling of having engaged in some sort of altruistic effort.

GH: That does involve the effects of dopamine transmission through the brain. I am also interested in the Default Mode Network [DMN] to note, in keeping with our talk about boredom, that it is not a passive state. The DMN is how our brain seems to be functioning, the network of connections between parts of our brain, when we are idle. And while we say the brain is 'idling,' it is not a very passive thing. It is actually an active state that needs to be sustained in some fashion. We have to carefully imagine where boredom fits in that paradigm.

JE: One of the most exciting things is looking for the neural and the physiological signatures of boredom. You [GH] have already mentioned the DMN, which is active when you are at rest or when you are engaged in internal thought, and then there is a Central Executive Network [CEN] that is working when you are engaged with tasks in the world. Certainly, when you are bored the DMN is more active than when you are engaged in some activity. Importantly, there was a study by James Danckert, at the University of Waterloo, where he compared someone in a bored state versus a resting state. There is a difference. The insular cortex is another part of the brain that has been thought, amongst other things, to be involved in helping you toggle back and forth between the DMN and the CEN. It is also responsible for tagging salience in our environment. The DMN is quite centrally involved in boredom, but it is not equivalent to boredom. There are some very important distinctions.

JRV: In fact, there are very different external signs that you are switching from one state to another, like yawning.

GH: Yawning is involved in this toggling act. Yawning can actually facilitate someone switches out of the DMN.

JG: Thinking about curiosity, again, the DMN is engaged in resting state and it is involved in all kinds of mind wandering. When people do not do anything, they do stuff. Usually, you are planning or singing songs or reciting stuff. That is associated with a DMN, but that is a resting state which is not boring. If you can engage your DMN together with your memories and somehow engage the reward system, then you are happy, in a good mental state. But, there must be some other state where you are resting and you cannot engage that whole network, and then you are not happy.

JE: You are in between the two. You cannot get into one mode and activate one neural network fully or the other. Mind wandering is a consequence of boredom in situations where you are constrained and you cannot leave. You might say mind wandering is a way to try and engage cognitive resources and therefore eliminate bored. When you are able to do that, then you just see the DMN working. But when you are being told you have to pay attention to something in the external world, and you do not really want to, you are sort of stuck between daydreaming and paying attention to the external world and doing neither effectively.

GH: When you become interested in what your mind is doing, thinking when it is wandering, that becomes salient. What is that exactly? People who are creative are certainly riffing off these mind wandering events and then paying attention to them.

JE: Immordino-Yang, a psychologist, talked about the need to develop the capacity for Constructive Internal Reflection [CIR]. She was referring to that mind wandering state when you are riffing off ideas and creativity is happening. What happens with boredom is that we often go to the external world for salvation, for relief, and that short-circuits the capacity to develop CIR as a skill or as an ability and, at the same time, a resource. We are in a culture right now where our attention is being yanked around by the caller from all these exogenous demands: 'Look here,' 'Do this.' For example, Times Square is overwhelming and your attention is just drawn everywhere. What happens is that the capacity for CIR—and endogenous control of attention—can atrophy. Boredom can push us to seek out external stimulation as a short-term solution to our problems. But, in the long-term, it may actually end up really making the situation worse.

MP: In the Times Square model, you start moving in one direction and immediately another one is calling you. There is no attention really paid to anything in particular. The question is, do you get bored in Times Square?

Attendees' Comments and Questions

A_1: Concerning the word you used first, 'unengaged,' the grammatical word is 'disengaged.' Disengaged carries an ethical aspect to us. In other words, it is keyed to taking some kind of action and actions have ethical aspects. Could you [JE] comment on that?

JE: 'Engaged' is a description of my relationship with something else: 'I am engaged with this or I am not engaged with this.' It is action-oriented and it contains ethical implications when I choose to engage with or whether I commit myself to something or not. 'Unengaged' is a description of my cognitive resources that are not being utilized. The way to utilize them would be to become engaged. I think it is important to define boredom in a context-free way, because if you try to define it in a way that is linked to disengagement, then you will need the context to define the state. But if you define the state as this unengaged one, then it is a definition that transcends the context.

A_2: I would like to emphasize the importance of time when we speak of boredom. This preoccupation with time goes about how to avoid boredom, goes far beyond the Enlightenment. There is a beautiful story about the Palazzo Schifanoia, in Ferrara. The Duke of Ferrara, built in the fourteenth century a new palace he called Palazzo Schifanoia. Schifanoia in Italian is *schivare la noia*, which is to avoid the boredom. He commissioned two painters of the Renaissance to paint a fresco on the walls of a room which was called Il salone dei Mesi, The room of the Months, because these two painters, Francesco del Cossa and Cosmè Tura, painted the months of the year. It is about time that they painted. The preoccupation of boredom led them to the artistical creation of representing the time. And the time is important because it maybe could link us to *melancholia* to engage mentally through things. For example, our patients very often are not able to engage because they are not able or have not a capacity for catharsis, and that is also about boredom.

JRV: The relationship between time and boredom is everywhere. We have just to pay attention to the German word *Langeweile* and its opposite *Kurzweil.*

A_2: The subjective impression that the time is not passing.

JRV: Sometimes, what makes us feel bad about being bored is the experience of not being spending our time in doing anything valuable.

A_2: As a translator of Gustave Flaubert [MP], could you say some words on *Madame Bovary*? If we speak about boredom we have to talk of *Madame Bovary*.

MP: The simplest thing to say is that she is a good case study of the self-destructive behavior that one can indulge if one is bored.

A_2: In French psychiatry, the term 'bovarisme' means a very particular kind of boredom, that boredom within satisfaction.

MP: It is the sense that there is this 'ideal' out there that can be attained and that, in fact, does not really exist. I would be curious at some point to know if the scientists and the philosophers think of the relationship between boredom and depression. Boredom and depression may be two sides of the same coin.

JRV: By the way, Emma Bovary was not depressed, she was frustrated!

GH: In this regard, there is a nice correspondence between the way time is perceived by people and the levels of dopamine they have. The most representative case is that of someone with much reduced dopamine, of folks suffering from Parkinson's disease, who move in slow motion: their time is much slower and their time sense is changed as well. Depression, of course, affects several diverse neurotransmitters in the brain. But, again, depression does often reduce dopamine transmission. Some people, especially elderly patients, when they become depressed, can actually appear somewhat 'parkinsonian' because their dopamine levels have dropped sufficiently for that to be manifest.

JE: Time is part of the definition of the phenomenological feeling of the slow passage of the time in boredom. We have already heard about the relationship between dopamine and time passing. We also know that cognitively, when you are not engaged there is a sense of time passing slowly as well. We know that boredom prone people do not judge the passage of time well. In our studies, when we try to manipulate and make people bored we rig the passage of the time as one of our variables to try induce boredom. There is time but there are things happening in that time too, and so you can think about boredom as a sort of 'everything is happening at that moment and nothing is about to happen.' Think about that as the difference between art versus propaganda. In propaganda, what you see is what you get, there is nothing more whereas art draws you in. There is that sense of walking through the garden and, as you turn a corner, a new vista presents itself a new possibility. In boredom, that possibility of *more* stops.

A_3: What is the effect of mindfulness and meditation on boredom? Are curious people less bored? Could be, in fact, an antidote to boredom? This is my pedestrian definition: Perhaps boredom is just the nanosecond before we are reached for our phones.

JG: *Nanoboredom.*

JE: On the issue about mindfulness, people that are high in trait mindfulness or people who regularly practice mindfulness meditation, when put in a vigilance task or a sustained attention task experience less boredom, discomfort, and agitation. Indeed, mindfulness prevents or protects one from boredom and there are some open questions about precisely why. One idea is that mindfulness actually results in the strengthening of attentional capacity so that you then can attend more effectively. But there is also the idea that mindfulness may make you less emotionally reactive to the state of being under-aroused. We just have one study that we have not published yet where we are looking at this and so far the data seems to be more consistent with the idea that mindfulness has its beneficial effects via that emotional reactivity pathway, not through an increasing attention capacity.

JG: Concerning curiosity, more curious people are less bored. It all goes back to this idea of being able to generate questions. It is the willingness to engage and answer your own questions. In a sense, it goes back to the same thing as being able to generate mental activity, which is then very satisfying and rewarding. I think that fuels human civilization. If we did not have curiosity, we would still be back in the caves. It is exactly the antithesis. I think of boredom as the failure in some way to trigger that mental activity.

GH: If you feel more comfortable managing this state of being idle-minded and you can master it, that might be a way also to master being able to focus your attention when you want to be able to focus it, without getting anxious about it. Moreover, we want to be able to cultivate curiosity in people. Art, science, and literature are our most common ways to do that. There is proof that it works.

JG: Emotional reactivity actually affects memory: The way you remember an item or an event depends on the circumstances. If you are motivated by rewards, you will encode more incidental information. There is a richer context that is being stored. On the contrary, motivation by punishment, which presumably induces anxiety, narrows the focus.

A_4: I used to live in a neighborhood in which there are a lot of children of working parents. I have observed they say 'I am bored' when one activity is over. They say that whoever is around and that is their responsibility you to find how it should be resolved. What happens in that kind of situation when you are not allowed to be bored or it quickly has to be resolved whereas another time children were left supposedly to their own, finding their own answers to these things?

JE: There is one metaphor from Georg Simmel, a sociologist who many years ago talked about the relationship between technology and boredom and how they collude with one another. Simmel's idea was that using technology is like falling into a fast-moving river where you can forget how to swim: The river carries you along and you do not even need to know how to swim anymore, you are automatically carried downstream. I would use that metaphor to communicate the idea that if your time is structured exogenously, i.e., if your attention is directed exogenously, the capacity to endogenously direct your attention may atrophy. Metaphorically, it is like a skill that atrophies. When we are bored, we have a hard time directing our attention—our attention is very much stimulus bound—and it takes some development for us to be able to disengage from that and to engage in internal reflection. This is a skill that needs to be taught and developed. The excessive use of technology may short-circuit opportunities to develop that skill.

MP: We do not live in a society that fosters a sense of self-reliance or promotes the beneficial effects of being bored—that is, using your own devices, your creative capacity, to mentally come out of that state. People are constantly being distracted. I try to read when I'm in the subway, but my concentration is often broken by announcements that seem to have no purpose other than to make noise. When I lived in Boston, the subway authority tried an experiment consisting of blasting music on the platform, so that people would not be left alone with their thoughts while waiting for the train to come. Personally, I want to be left alone with my thoughts, I want a little bit of quiet.

A_4: That is like going into a doctor's office where they are playing some kind of musical thread.

JE: This also slides into the ethical issue: Who controls the focus of our attention? And who controls what is in the focus of our attention?

A_5: In the clinical situation, how people use their own boredom and their understanding of their patients' boredom? Is boredom related to some pathological interior state? If you are very healthy and always curious, you do not get bored unless somebody else annoys you.

GH: There is this toggling back and forth between our minds being empty and then taking action. One of the mechanisms that may stymie that would be if the person has an act in mind, usually unconsciously but not always, and cannot do it, as in Hamlet. It could also lead to depression because of the resulting failure to attain goals. Where is the action? Why is the action not taking place?

A_6: You started by saying that boredom was the desire for desires, but there is also this rejection of the offered options. For example, for a child who is bored we offer going out and swing, or stay in and play with the cars; things that were engaging yesterday and will be engaging again tomorrow, but for some reason are failing to capture that attention at this particular time. The physical pain of a hot stove will always be the same—i.e., always gives you the signal that is something you should avoid—whereas this attentional pain of boredom can vary, that is to say, a day in which you are not interested in the things that have been interesting and will be interesting again is giving you this boredom signal, this attentional pain that does not happen every single time.

JE: When the signal does happen, it is pushing you to find engagement either with what you were doing (that may have engaged you in the past) or something else. Boredom is this desire for an actionable desire. When you are bored there is a rejection of the present moment. It is like saying 'I won't have this; I won't commit to this; I won't engage with this.' The degree of obstinacy can vary. Is it driven by an oppositional stance or by a situation I do not have the capacity to connect with it? We can talk of boredom as the desire for a desire but there is an inverse side of that as well that is very much part of the phenomenology.

MP: There could be some feeling of frustration, in the sense that something interested me yesterday, but today I can't get interested in it anymore.

JG: Just because you have that toy there today, it does not mean it is going to engage me in the same way. There is a very complex filter going on that determinates my response to that toy. If the stimuli are really strong, like a hot stove or if somebody hits you on the head, you can engage with that, but that is a very small fraction of the information we have.

JRV: Boredom is definitively a rejection of the possibilities. Sometimes boredom is just the consequence of your rejection of the possibilities the environment is offering to you, because the offer is well-known, i.e., you can previously expect what these possibilities are. If you know them in advance there is no novelty in these possibilities in the environment.

JG: We can see the prospect of any new pattern. We are constantly looking for patterns in the brain and if you do not see it coming it is just not engaging you.

GH: The range of choices can become hackneyed.

A_7: Is boredom a state with which we are not comfortable? Is boredom a state of being uncomfortable with ourselves? Is it okay to be bored? Should it be encouraged among especially children? Can one allow their own experience to choose what they want to do and be in until that comes to be bored?

JE: Kierkegaard talked about boredom throwing you back into yourself. When we cannot have that engagement with the world—that intentional stance towards the world—something falls apart and we are left with nothing but ourselves. That is a very aversive state. We should not be fostering the state of boredom; we should be encouraging the development of the capacity to be quiet, understimulated, the capacity for that constructive internal reflection we spoke about earlier. That is not the same as being bored: that is being quiet and with yourself. That is what needs to be fostered.

MP: The idea that it might not be okay to be bored increases that sense of anxiety that goes hand-in-hand with boredom. Of course, it is okay to be bored; everyone is bored at some point.

JRV: It is not a matter of promoting boredom but to simply let it happen.

MP: People get worried about boredom but there are very good things that could come out of it.

GH: The existential challenge of just *being* is such a wonderful possibility… We do not teach that very well to people. 'This is very exciting for me to create myself in some way.' It is wonderful to get people really engaged at that level.

MP: This is a society in which the possibility of just *being* without distraction is becoming harder and harder.

JG: You live in this society and you manage to enjoy being by yourself without distraction. To what extent do you think individual differences have something to do in this regard? There are people able to always occupy themselves thinking about something, inquiring, no matter how many cell phones they have. But other people are unable. How would we structure an environment that encourages the other situation?

JE: There are a lot of individual differences in the propensity to be bored. That is a whole topic: What are the psychological characteristics that predispose someone to feel bored? In the psychology literature, there is actually more work that has been done on that than on the state of boredom. But now the field is circling back and realizing that the way we had defined and measured trait boredom was quite problematic. Anyway, there are some findings with regard to the question in a clinical setting. Alexithymia, the lack of capacity for labeling feelings and reflecting on emotions, is highly correlated with boredom proneness, and this is just one example. If we have problems labeling our emotional states we are more likely to then struggle with boredom.

GH: This is because the insula, in the cortex, is closer to the speech center of the brain.

A_8: Mirth as the opposite of boredom makes me think, as a millennial, about memes. Memes have become the vector of a lot of millennial humor in the Generation Z. If mirth is the opposite of boredom, it is a cure for boredom. How do you think about that statement of 'meme culture is the millennials attempt at curing boredom?' Do you think they are just distracting us from the reality that boredom exists and it is going to exist always?

GH: Mirth is not the opposite of boredom strictly speaking. The playfulness of the mind is what allows people to find beauty, it is another version of curiosity. Memes are about what is funny and what might engage you and encompass a feeling of mirth. They are just exciting and sensational, but not very helpful to stave off boredom. It is just like getting a shot of cocaine. But if it engages you to think in a funny way or in a playful way, I think it is a wonderful remedy to boredom.

JE: Creating clever memes is a better antidote than observing them.

A_9: Playfulness has to do with infant and child development and what we have learned about the importance of parent-infant play or caregiver-infant play from very early in terms of regulating both emotional and attentional states. These shared interpersonal experiences are important in expanding the capacity for both attention and curiosity. When my patient says 'I am bored' it has to do with what was the interpersonal joining and the shared experience of both curiosity and affection.

JE: There is a study that we need to do there: if there is sort of generational boredom.

Dr. Josefa Ros Velasco is Associate and Teaching Assistant in the Department of Romance Languages and Literatures at Harvard University and Real Colegio Complutense at Harvard Postdoctoral Fellow. She is conducting multidisciplinary research on the evolution of the understanding of boredom as a mental pathology. As part of this approach, she is examining how the comprehension of boredom in terms of mental disease has gradually formed historically by paying attention to philosophical, theological, and literary narratives. Dr. Ros Velasco holds a Ph. D. in Philosophy with International Mention at the Excellent Program of Doctorate in Philosophy at the Complutense University of Madrid (UCM, Spain), funded by the Spanish Ministry of Culture and Education. Her Dissertation was entitled *Boredom as a selective pressure in Hans Blumenberg*, with which she got the Extraordinary Doctorate Award (2016–2017), MA in Contemporary Thinking, and MA in Teachers Training. She was visiting researcher at the *Internationales Zentrum für Kultur- und Technikforschung* at Stuttgart Universität (IZKT, Germany) as a DAAD (Deutscher Akademischer Austauschdienst) scholar, and at the Deutsches Literatur-Archiv Marbach (DLA, Germany) as a DLA fellow. She is a member of the Research Groups *Saavedra Fajardo Library for Hispanic Political Thought* at the UCM; *History and Video Games* at the University of Murcia; and *History and Philosophy of Emotions* at CCHS-CSIC. She is the editor and the author of academic papers such as "Hans Blumenverg's philosophical anthropology of boredom" (Karl Alber, 2019), "Boredom: humanising or dehumanising treatment" (Vernon, 2018); or "Boredom: A comprehensive study of the state of affairs" (*Thémata*, 2017). She is currently working on her next books: *La enfermedad del aburrimiento. El camino de la medicalización y sus alternativas* (2020), *The culture of boredom* (Brill, 2019), and *The faces of depression in literature* (Peter Lang, 2019).

Glossary

Acedia This term comes from a combination of the negative prefix *a-* and the Greek noun *kēdos*, meaning care or concern. Initially, it referred to the deadly sin of sloth in the Middle Ages. Today, it tends to be used more generally to simply imply a lack of interest and also sometimes as a synonymous of laziness and boredom.

Alexithymia It is a personality construct characterized by the subclinical inability to identify and describe emotions in the self. The core characteristics of alexithymia are marked dysfunction in emotional awareness, social attachment, and interpersonal relating. Furthermore, people with alexithymia have difficulty in distinguishing and appreciating the emotions of others, which is thought to lead to unemphatic and ineffective emotional responding.

Anhedonia People who experience anhedonia have lost interest in activities they used to enjoy and have a decreased ability to feel pleasure. It is a core symptom of major depressive disorder, but it can also be a symptom of other mental health disorders. Some people who experience anhedonia do not have a mental disorder.

Anxiety According to the APA, anxiety is an emotion characterized by feelings of tension, worried thoughts, and physical changes like increased blood pressure.

Attention-deficit hyperactivity disorder (ADHD) Attention-deficit hyperactivity disorder (ADHD) is a brain disorder marked by an ongoing pattern of inattention and/or hyperactivity–impulsivity that interferes with functioning or development.

Benzedrine sulfate Benzedrine was the first pharmaceutical drug that contained amphetamine, marketed in 1933 as a decongestant in the USA. Benzedrine sulfate was introduced later to treat a variety of medical conditions including narcolepsy, obesity, low libido, low blood pressure, and chronic pain, among others.

J. Ros Velasco (ed.), *Boredom Is in Your Mind*,
https://doi.org/10.1007/978-3-030-26395-9

Boredom proneness Tendency of individuals to feel bored taking into account a wide range of cognitive and personality variables. It is measured by the Boredom Proneness Scale (BPS), developed by psychologists Norman D. Sundberg and Richard F. Farmer. The propensity to become bored is closely related to the propensity to become depressed. People with boredom proneness personality suffer from a lack of impulse.

Boredom Proneness Scale (BPS) The BPS was created in 1986 to assess boredom and determine the cause for periods of boredom and the steps to get rid off it. Some subscales include external stimulation, perception of time, constraints, affective responses, and focusing endurance. The test includes a 28 true–false questions.

Bovarism A conception of oneself as other than one that goes to the extent that one's general behavior is conditioned or dominated by the conception; dominated by an idealized, glamorized, glorified, or otherwise unreal conception of oneself that it results in dramatic personal conflict, in markedly unusual behavior (as in paranoia), or in great achievement.

Central Executive Network (CEN) The CEN is a frontoparietal network that is crucial to working memory and cognitive control of thought, emotion, and behavior. Abnormal activation in the central executive network has been related to psychosis and schizophrenia.

Chronic boredom A pathology of chronic boredom is a disorder consisting of a lack of dopamine neurotransmitters or a continuous low level of dopamine. The solution involves the stimulation of such a chemical component through amphetamine, ephedrine, and caffeine.

Cognitive-Miser Model of Cognition (CMMC) In psychology, the human mind is considered to be a cognitive miser due to the tendency of people to think and solve problems in simpler and less effortful ways rather than in more sophisticated and more effortful ways, regardless of intelligence.

Constructive Internal Reflection This is the process in which the reflection is undertaken in a structured and layered manner creating space and opportunity for individuals to assess, explore, and evaluate themselves, develop new skills, new attitudes, and new ways of thinking through reconceptualizing knowledge and renewing their identity and values.

Candy Crush Candy Crush Saga is a free-to-play match-three puzzle video game for Facebook.

Catechol-O-methyltransferase (COMT) is one of several enzymes that degrade catecholamines—monoamine neurotransmitters organically compounded by catechol and a side-chain amine, such as dopamine, epinephrine, and norepinephrine—and various drugs and substances having a catechol structure.

Dasein is a German word that means 'being there' and is translated into English as 'existence.' It is a fundamental concept of Martin Heidegger's existential philosophy. Heidegger uses the term *Dasein* to refer to the experience of being that is unique to human beings.

Default Mode Network In neuroscience, the default mode network (DMN), also default network, or default state network, is a large-scale brain network of interacting brain regions. It is most commonly shown to be active when a person is not focused on the outside world and the brain is at wakeful rest, such as during daydreaming and mind-wandering.

Demon of noontide Also known as Noonday Demon and *Mittagsdämon*, this expression comes from the Ancient Greek *μεσημβρινὸν δαίμονά* and appears for the first time in Salmo 91: 5–6. Defined especially by the Medieval theologists Evagrius Ponticus and John Cassian, it refers to the sixth hour of the day when the monks fall prey to *acedia*.

Depression is a mood disorder that causes a persistent feeling of sadness and loss of interest. Also called major depressive disorder or clinical depression, it affects how people feel, think, and behave and can lead to a variety of emotional and physical problems. People usually have trouble doing normal day-to-day activities and sometimes feel as if life is not worth living.

Dopamine It is a neurotransmitter that helps control the brain's reward and pleasure centers. Dopamine also helps regulate movement and emotional responses, and it enables us not only to see rewards, but to take action to move toward them. Dopamine deficiency results in Parkinson's disease, and people with low dopamine activity may be more prone to addiction.

Dopamine Active Transporter 1 (DAT1) The dopamine transporter gene (DAT1/SLC6A3) is a membrane-spanning protein that mediates the reuptake of dopamine from the synapse. It has been associated with bipolar disorder and ADHD.

Endogenous attention Goal-driven attention is referred to as top-down or endogenous attention, whereas stimulus-driven attention is referred to as bottom-up or exogenous attention, being driven by external events in the environment.

Endogenous boredom Boredom generated from within the individual. It is defined from its opposite, the exogenous boredom or reactive boredom, that boredom in reaction to what was going on in the environment.

Ennui Usually defined as a feeling of utter weariness and discontent resulting from satiety or lack of interest, this French term is very often translated as boredom. It is used in Philosophy and Psychology sometimes with regard to depression or chronic boredom, that is to say, as a permanent state instead of a situational, circumstantial state.

Ephedrine Hydrochloride Ephedrine is a stimulant drug often used to prevent low blood pressure during spinal anesthesia. It is also used for asthma, narcolepsy, depression, obesity, heart failure, urinary incontinence, rhinitis, and in nasal congestion.

Eros and Thanatos Freud identifies two drives that both coincide and conflict within the individual and among individuals. Eros is the drive of life, love, creativity, and sexuality, self-satisfaction, and species preservation. Thanatos, or deadly pulse, is the drive of aggression, sadism, destruction, violence, and death.

Facebook Inc. is an American online social media and social networking service company, founded by Mark Zuckerberg, where users can post comments, share photographs and post links to news or other interesting content on the Web, chat live, and watch short-form video.

Feedback loop Feedback is defined as the information gained about a reaction to a product, which will allow the modification of the product. Feedback loops are therefore the process whereby a change to the system results in an alarm which will trigger a certain result. This result will either increase the change to the system or reduce it to bring the system back to normal.

Flow Theory This theory was developed by Mihály Csíkszentmihályi to explain that feeling of complete and energized focus in an activity, with a high level of enjoyment and engagement. When there is not a high correlation between the challenge and the ability to meet that challenge, the flow is broken. Maintaining the dynamic balance between abilities and challenge is key to avoid boredom.

fMRI Functional magnetic resonance imaging or functional MRI measures brain activity by detecting changes associated with blood flow. This is a technique based on the fact that cerebral blood flow and neuronal activation are coupled, that is to say, when an area of the brain is in use, blood flow to that region also increases.

Goldilocks zone The Goldilocks Zone refers to the habitable zone around a star where the temperature is just right—not too hot and not too cold—for liquid water to exist on a planet.

Instagram Also known as IG or Insta, this is a photograph and video-sharing social networking service owned by Facebook, Inc. The app allows users to upload photographs and videos to the service, which can be edited with filters and organized with tags and location information. Users can "like" photographs and follow other users.

Meaning and Attentional Components (MAC) Model The MAC model of Boredom and Cognitive Engagement is an approach by Westgate and Wilson that suggests that boredom acts as an online affective indicator of unsuccessful attentional engagement in a valued goal-congruent activity. Boredom tells us whether our current activity (internal or external) is something we are able to focus on and want to be engaged in. Boredom thus has both attentional and meaning components. The experience of boredom motivates people to take steps toward restoring successful engagement in a meaningful activity.

Methylxanthines Methylated xanthines (methylxanthines), which include caffeine, aminophylline, IBMX, paraxanthine, pentoxifylline, theobromine, and theophylline, affect not only the airways but stimulate heart rate, force of contraction, and cardiac arrhythmias at high concentrations.

Mindfulness This is the psychological process of bringing one's attention to experiences occurring in the present moment, which can be developed through the practice of meditation and other training.

Netflix Inc. is an American media service provider headquartered in California. The company's primary business is its subscription-based streaming OTT service which offers online streaming of a library of films and television programs, including those produced in-house.

Optimum Stimulation Level (OSL) The OSL is a property that characterizes an individual in terms of their general response to environmental stimuli. Every organism prefers a certain level of stimulation, which may be termed optimum stimulation. When the environmental stimulation is below optimum, an individual will attempt to increase stimulation; when it is above optimum, they will strive to reduce it.

Protein Kinase CGMP-Dependent 1 (PRKG1) The PRKG1 proteins play a central role in regulating cardiovascular and neuronal functions in addition to relaxing smooth muscle tone, preventing platelet aggregation, and modulating cell growth. This gene is most strongly expressed in all types of smooth muscle, platelets, cerebellar Purkinje cells, hippocampal neurons, and the lateral amygdala.

Psychodynamic Theory In psychology, psychodynamic theory is a view that explains personality in terms of conscious and unconscious forces, such as unconscious desires and beliefs. Psychodynamic theories commonly hold that childhood experiences shape personality. Such theories are associated with psychoanalysis, a type of therapy that attempts to reveal unconscious thoughts and desires. Not all psychologists accept psychodynamic theories, and critics claim the theories lack supporting scientific data.

Psychological homeostasis In psychological terms, this is a kind of balance referred to as homeostasis, which is most easily defined as a psychological and physiological state of stability. The concept of homeostasis is not limited to psychology, but can actually be applied widely to any person or thing that demonstrates a stable equilibrium.

Reticular Activating System (RAS) The reticular activating system (RAS) is a network of neurons located in the brain stem that project anteriorly to the hypothalamus to mediate behavior, as well as both posteriorly to the thalamus and directly to the cortex for activation of awake, desynchronized cortical EEG patterns.

Sensation Seeking Scale (SSS) This is a scale developed in its fifth version by Zuckerman. It consists of 40 forced-choice questions designed to assess individual differences in the optimal level of stimulation. One of its subscales is the Boredom Susceptibility Scale (BS).

Shamrock A shamrock is a young sprig used as a symbol in Ireland. Saint Patrick, Ireland's patron saint, is said to have used it as a metaphor for the Christian Holy Trinity.

Single Nucleotide Polymorphism (SNP) Single nucleotide polymorphisms, frequently called SNPs (pronounced 'snips'), are the most common type of genetic variation among people. Each SNP represents a difference in a single DNA building block, called a nucleotide. For example, an SNP may replace the nucleotide cytosine (C) with the nucleotide thymine (T) in a certain stretch of DNA.

STEM Within the framework of education, STEM is a curriculum based on the idea of educating students in four specific disciplines: science, technology, engineering, and mathematics. The curriculum should be designed based on an interdisciplinary and applied approach. Rather than teach the four disciplines as separate and discrete subjects, STEM integrates them into a cohesive learning paradigm based on real-world applications.

Subjective perception of boredom Boredom may appear as a pathology in individuals who perceive stimuli unidirectionally, as meaningless, because of a distorted subjective perception. The patients are bored because they cannot confer sense to the stimuli.

The Darkroom Problem In 2012, Karl Friston, Christopher Ethornton, and Andy Eclark (University College London, University of Sussex, and University of Edinburgh, respectively) described the so-called darkroom problem to provide a new focus on the debate on free-energy minimization. According to this proposal, if agents operate on the basis of reducing surprise, they should proceed directly to the last stimulating environment and stay there. They should take up a position in the nearest "darkroom" and never move again.

The Self-Authoring Mind Developmental psychologist Robert Kegan distinguishes three main stages of human development: the socialized, the self-authoring, and the self-transforming mind. Since the socialized mind is able to live in a stable relationship with others in a community, the self-authoring mind can take a step back from one's surroundings and upbringing and regard them critically. One forms one's owns judgments based on the evidence that is provided. As a result, one is 'self-authoring' an identity that is independent of one's environment. From its part, the self-transforming mind is able to look at multiple value systems simultaneously and evaluate which one is suitable for this occasion.

Twitter Inc. is an American online news and social networking service on which users post and interact with no longer than 280 characters messages known as 'tweets.' Registered users can post, like, and retweet tweets, but unregistered users can only read them.

Weltschmerz From the German, literally world-pain, world weariness, is a term coined by the German author Jean Paul and denotes the kind of feeling experienced by someone who believes that physical reality can never satisfy the demands of the mind. It is a mood of weariness or sadness about life arising from the acute awareness or oversensitivity.

Index

J. Ros Velasco (ed.), *Boredom Is in Your Mind*,
https://doi.org/10.1007/978-3-030-26395-9

The manufacturer's authorised representative in the EU is Springer Nature Customer Service Centre GmbH, Europaplatz 3, 69115 Heidelberg, Germany. If you have any concerns regarding our products, please contact ProductSafety@springernature.com

Printed and bound by CPI Group (UK) Ltd, Croydon, CR0 4YY
28/11/2025
02007692-0006